UNEVEN ODDS

UNEVEN ODDS

Social Mobility in Contemporary India

DIVYA VAID

OXFORD
UNIVERSITY PRESS

OXFORD
UNIVERSITY PRESS

Oxford University Press is a department of the University of Oxford.
It furthers the University's objective of excellence in research, scholarship,
and education by publishing worldwide. Oxford is a registered trademark of
Oxford University Press in the UK and in certain other countries.

Published in India by
Oxford University Press
2/11 Ground Floor, Ansari Road, Daryaganj, New Delhi 110 002, India

© Oxford University Press 2018

The moral rights of the author have been asserted.

First Edition published in 2018

ISBN-13 (print edition): 978-0-19-948014-2
ISBN-10 (print edition): 0-19-948014-1

ISBN-13 (eBook): 978-0-19-909364-9
ISBN-10 (eBook): 0-19-909364-4

Typeset in Trump Mediaeval LT Std 9.5/13
by The Graphics Solution, New Delhi 110 092
Printed in India by Replika Press Pvt. Ltd

Figures, Tables, and Boxes

Figures

Tables

Boxes

Acknowledgements

This book began as my doctoral work at Nuffield College, Oxford, United Kingdom, and has seen many additions along the way. There are a number of people to whom I owe a debt of gratitude for help and support over the period this book has taken to reach its fruition.

I am grateful to Anthony Heath not only for his guidance as my supervisor and his patience in reading numerous drafts of the chapters but also for his encouragement and advice since I finished my doctorate. My time at Oxford was enriched by the faculty at Nuffield College and in the Department of Sociology. I am grateful to many others who have commented on various drafts of my research over the years: Lucy Carpenter who provided much needed support as my College supervisor at Nuffield; David Grusky, Alistair McMillan, Colin Mills, and Barbara Harriss-White who in their role as my examiners over the course of the doctoral degree commented in detail on my thesis; Richard Breen and David Firth for help with the statistics especially Unidiff modelling; Louis-Andre Vallet and John Goldthorpe who read and commented on a conference paper arising from my thesis.

At Yale, USA, where I did my postdoctoral research, I was fortunate to have Richard Breen as my postdoctoral mentor. I thank him for his guidance. I also thank other colleagues at Yale who at various times read and commented on papers: Karl Ulrich Mayer, Hannah Brueckner, Scott Boorman, Stefanie Gundert, Juho Harkonen, and Elizabeth Roberto.

In New Delhi, at the Centre for the Study of Developing Societies (CSDS), my gratitude is due to the larger Lokniti family, especially to Sanjay Kumar, Suhas Palshikar, Yogendra Yadav, Sandeep Shastri, Rajeshwari Deshpande, and Sanjeer Alam for their academic support. I also thank the data unit at CSDS for providing access to their datasets and technical support over the years. As a visiting associate fellow at CSDS I received valuable advice from colleagues at the Centre, for which I am grateful. Friends at CSDS made the research experience more enjoyable: Ankur Datta, Devika Bordia, Hemachandran Karah, Venugopal Maddipati, and Ananya Vajpeyi; and at Lokniti: Rahul Verma, Banasmita Bora, and Shreyas Sardesai.

I thank my colleagues at Jawaharlal Nehru University, New Delhi, for providing a supportive environment conducive to research: A. Bimol Akoijam, Maitrayee Chaudhuri, Tanweer Fazal, Vivek Kumar, Ratheesh Kumar, Nilika Mehrotra, Harish Naraindas, Tiplut Nongbri, Avijit Pathak, L. Lam Khan Piang, Edward Rodrigues, Renuka Singh, Gurram Srinivas, V. Sujatha, Amit Kumar Sharma, and Susan Visvanathan. I am especially grateful to Surinder S. Jodhka for his advice and encouragement throughout the writing process. I thank Jyoti Bala for assistance with the secondary data tables.

The academic journey is often a lonely one. Friends along the way make this journey less cumbersome: Maria Sobolewska, Jamie Sargeant, Laurence Lessard-Phillips, Sonia Exley, Carmel Hannan, Tehmina Shaukat Khan, Oisin Tansey, and Vikki Boliver helped immensely by reading chapters from my thesis, helping with graphs, and in generally discussing a wide variety of topics and innumerable statistical models. Along with Pamela Ngwenya and Sarah Byrne they were also patient listeners over the many cups of tea when I whinged about 'the dissertation monster'. I thank my friends from the network on development and social inequality with whom I have discussed many aspects of my work: Vishwas Satgar, Naxhelli Ruiz, Iliana Yaschine, Marina Moguillansky, and Rodrigo Rodrigues-Silveira. Over the years many others have contributed to my research experience: Pradeep Chhibber, Nandini Sundar, Ravinder Kaur, Jules Naudet, Roland Lardinois, John Harriss, Patrick Heller, and Roger Jeffery's advice is gratefully acknowledged.

At Oxford University Press, New Delhi, I thank the editorial team for their patience and help. I thank the two anonymous reviewers of this manuscript for their critical and insightful comments.

I gratefully acknowledge the financial support I received as a student for my dissertation from the Nuffield Funded Studentship, the Overseas Research Students Award and the Frere Exhibition, Oxford. I am also grateful for the UPE-II grant from Jawaharlal Nehru University (Project ID 57) for support during the writing of this book.

The enthusiastic support of my family is deeply acknowledged. My grandparents have been the strongest supporters of whatever we have set out to do. My parents Alka and Yogi Vaid have been pillars of sanity during the toughest of times. They have helped immensely both during and after my doctoral work by editing chapters, helping with the bibliography, and generally being the most effective morale boosters. My brother Ambar has been a special co-traveller and his sense of the ridiculous has lightened many a serious moment. I thank Aabha Datt, Shobha Banerjee, Shil Banerjee, Shafiqua Vaid, and Krishna Datta for providing strong familial support and embracing my eccentricities. My husband Ankur Datta has been a critical reader of my work; his patience and ready sense of humour during the uphill moments has made everything, including the writing of this book, more enjoyable. This book is for Antara who has been a part of the last leg of this journey and with whom the next stage of our life begins.

Certain sections of this book have been produced in earlier versions using older data and permission to reproduce sections are gratefully acknowledged.

I thank *Asian Survey* (University of California Press) for permission to use the following article: Vaid, Divya. 2012. 'The Caste-Class Association: An Empirical Analysis,' *Asian Survey*, Vol. 52 (2): 395–422.

I also thank Taylor and Francis Ltd. (www.tandfonline.com) for permission to use some work derived in part from an article published in *Contemporary South Asia* on 23 August 2016, available at http://tandfonline.com/10.1080/09584935.2016.1208637 : 'Patterns of Social Mobility and the Role of Education in India', *Contemporary South Asia* 24(3): 285–312.

Abbreviations

CmSF	Common Social Fluidity
CnSF	Constant Social Fluidity
CSDS	Centre for the Study of Developing Societies
GDP	Gross Domestic Product
IMF	International Monetary Fund
LFPR	Labour Force Participation Rate
MGNREGA	Mahatma Gandhi National Rural Employment Guarantee Act
NES	National Election Study
NFHS	National Family and Health Survey
NSS	National Sample Survey
OBC	Other Backward Classes
RNM	Routine Non-Manual
SAP	Structural Adjustment Policies
SC	Scheduled Castes
ST	Scheduled Tribes
WPR	Worker Population Ratio

1

Introduction

Approaching Social Mobility

In 2014, the World Bank published a report stating that between 2004–5 and 2009–10, 15 per cent of the Indian population had 'moved above the poverty line', achieving levels of social mobility 'comparable' to the United States. The report emphasized that urbanization has contributed to improving life in an area often marked by inequality:

> Increasingly, jobs are beating class and caste routes to prosperity. While they still do matter, factors like where you were born and your parents occupation matter less and less in modern India. In fact, upward mobility has been stronger, relative to the population, among the lowest castes, known as 'untouchables'. Where children would usually take up the jobs of their parents, occupational mobility of the younger generation has increased to greater levels than the general population. (Metzger 2015)

While the tone is upbeat and positive, a glance at other reports causes us to pause a bit. India is listed at 131 out of 188 on the Human Development Index. While poverty levels may have gone down, it is impossible to avoid news stories of child malnutrition and health inequalities widespread in various parts of India. Leaving news reports aside, one could simply look at a university campus. Education, we are told, will pull people out of poverty and enable us to achieve a better and fulfilling life. Yet, any conversation with students enrolled in a university suggests a more complicated picture. While students in the same grade may be involved in the pursuit of the same kind of knowledge, they will have come to the classroom with different life experiences and opportunities refracted by experiences of caste, religion, how they speak, and where they are from. After completing their studies, it remains to be seen whether they will all have similar experiences in the labour market or will be able to build equally fulfilling lives. How many will be able to achieve one of the most pressing concerns of everyday life in India: the pursuit of upward social mobility?

Social mobility, or the movement between socio-economic positions or strata, is an indicator of the opportunities available in a society and has held a central place in the sociological analysis of industrialized countries of the West since Sorokin's seminal work in the 1920s, particularly with regard to the study of stratification systems, their forms, and processes (Goldthorpe 2005; Grusky 2001). However, the research on India thus far has been scattered. The lack of systematic, national research in this area implies that we do not, at present, have a sense of exactly how much mobility there is in India, and whether there have been changes over time and across demographics.

Much of our understanding of social mobility, inequality, and social change in Indian society in the fields of sociology or social anthropology draws on qualitative research methods (for example, see Benei [2010]) and is specific to a particular region or group of people. Sociologists and social anthropologists have examined the experiences of mobility in certain regions and among specific castes (see Osella and Osella [2000] on Izhavas of Kerala; Fuller and Narasimhan's [2014] work on Tamil Brahmins in Chennai; Ram's [1988] work on social mobility among Dalits). Anthropologists have also engaged with issues of anxieties (Dickey 2012) associated with social mobility or lack of it. Rather than the individual, the collective aspect of mobility has been stressed (see Naudet [2008] for community expectations and anxieties around upward mobility). More critically, a significant part of existing research has focused on mobility within the caste system (Silverberg 1968 among others) while only a handful of studies have observed social class or occupational mobility (Kumar, Heath, and Heath 2002a and b). While not focusing on class mobility per se, there has been much interest in the rise of the 'middle class' (Fernandes 2000, 2006); and recent scholarship has looked exclusively at mobility with regard to specific professions or locations and provides an interesting perspective on change or lack thereof where social positions are concerned (for example, Krishna [2014] on opportunities of access to engineering jobs; Béteille [1993] looks at the role of the family where reproduction of inequalities in the service class is concerned; see Krishna [2013] on mobility in Bangalore slums).

While this rich literature is significant for understanding experiences of mobility, few studies provide a national picture of mobility, and of the studies that do exist, few have looked at the experience of women[1] along with the barriers to mobility faced by various social groups. Vaid and Heath's paper (2010) is one exception and provides a comparative base for some of the analysis in this book allowing for a *longue duree* view.

The study of mobility is significant as social mobility provides avenues for the redistribution of social and economic opportunities and rewards. Conversely, the lack of mobility can lead to the reproduction of inequalities over generations. The implications of the lack of mobility, or indeed the unevenness of mobility opportunities, on persisting social inequalities are, hence, manifold, especially for a developing country such as India. With the move to economic liberalization, there has been an expectation of increased social mobility opportunities along with a resultant decrease in 'non-meritocratic' inheritance of occupations or class positions. However, enough research indicates that while economic growth may have occurred in India, it has largely been jobless growth. Also, despite economic growth, there are persisting caste and gender inequalities and sharp regional differences.

Further, social mobility is seldom a linear process and neither does it play out in similar ways across countries or in regions within a country. The history, economy, social context, and other

---

[1] Jain (1969), for example, claims to include both women and men, but does not separate the mobility experiences of the two genders, and refers to his respondents throughout in the masculine gender.

specificities lead to varied patterns and experiences of mobility around the world and even among countries fairly similarly placed in terms of economic growth. India, thus, provides an important case study for testing some of the theories of social mobility that have risen out of research on more industrialized countries. The lack of any comprehensive research in this field, especially involving women, has influenced the use of a unique theoretical framework in the present study involving the interplay of caste, class, gender, and locality. The exclusion of women from social stratification and mobility research (Acker 1990, 1998; Crompton and Mann 1986) has been a cause for concern. This book looks specifically at women's mobility experiences alongside those of men allowing for a more comprehensive picture of mobility and inequality.

This book provides the first overview of patterns and trends of social mobility (interchangeably referred to as class mobility) in India for women and men using national level datasets (discussed in Appendix A)—that is, it will review the changing relation between social origins and destinations over the past six decades in Indian society. The book highlights in particular the inequality of opportunity, that is, the barriers to mobility faced by different groups. This is particularly important in light of the Indian government's preferential policies aimed at alleviating the historical inequalities suffered by certain groups. In this respect, the association between caste and class is analysed, especially the role that caste plays in mediating the effects of class reproduction. Finally, the role of education as a driver of social mobility is investigated. Given the diversity within India, this book compares the rural and urban patterns of mobility.

Are certain groups disadvantaged from the opportunity of being upwardly mobile? Are the outcomes of mobility differentially patterned for different castes, by gender, or locality? Has liberalization led to the expected distancing of caste from class and the equalizing of social mobility opportunities? What are the processes or drivers of mobility? Has education been a successful avenue for increased upward social mobility? This book, drawing on national level datasets and quantitative methods, addresses some of these questions and approaches individual social mobility[2] through interactions between social class, caste, and gender while adopting a rural–urban perspective capturing changes over time and the implications of social mobility on a national scale. As mentioned by Vaid and Heath (2010), sociological research in India broadly, and research on social mobility in particular, has had a limited engagement with quantitative data and techniques. Since our aim is to provide a national picture of mobility, we use and expand on advanced quantitative techniques needed for such a study.

Theoretically, this book engages with the liberal theories of industrialism and modernization (Treiman 1970) that predict a distancing of origin from destination characteristics, that is, the weakening of the link between parental characteristics and the characteristics of the children leading to increased mobility over time as societies industrialze. Under this theory (as discussed by Vaid and Heath 2010), we expect to see a decline in the significance of ascription and an increase in the role of achievement where access to opportunities or social mobility is concerned. However, in contrast to this theory of change is the idea of the 'constant flux' (Erikson and Goldthorpe 1992). This posits that there is a similarity both in terms of *within* and *across* country trends of relative social mobility over time rather than a consistent increase. Further, in the Indian context *Sanskritization* and reference group theories and their impact on social change have often been evoked in the discussions of caste and mobility (Srinivas 1966, 1996a and 1996b; see also contributions in Gupta 1991). This book will draw on these theories and weave together the contradictory patterns of social change with the persisting stability in over time patterns.

[2] Bardhan (1986) provides one possible explanation for why the family as the unit of analysis is insufficient in India, especially in the rural areas and why the individual approach to the study of mobility assumes importance. She comes to this conclusion based on her study that shows that women are often primary earners in rural areas and play a 'direct and indirect' role in household and village economy. Also, it is often customary for a woman 'to work in order to support herself and her children' (p. 94); and thus, ignoring women's chances of mobility might provide us with an incomplete picture of the openness of Indian society.

Social Mobility: A Conceptual Clarification

A review of past studies on social mobility in India (some of which are discussed in the subsequent sections of this chapter) highlights the discrepancy in the definition of the term 'mobility' itself. Mobility has been construed by some to have a much broader meaning than social class mobility; while others have a narrow definition, restricting it to mobility within the caste system.

According to Marshall (1998), *social mobility* is the 'movement—usually of individuals but sometimes of whole groups—between different positions within the system of social stratification in any society' (p. 422). Thus defined, if we see India as being stratified on the basis of both caste and class in addition to numerous other forms of stratification, such as income and wealth, social mobility in India could mean much more than class mobility.[3] In economics, there is a rich literature on 'economic' mobility—which aims to 'analyse dynamic behaviour underlying aggregate shifts in economic structure' (Swaminathan 1989: 1). It has been seen by some to mean the 'gain or loss of economic status, measured either by control of productive assets or by household income' (Cain 1978: 427). Thus, economic mobility has more generally been studied by analysing either income or wealth mobility. One aim of income mobility studies is to help in identifying individuals in the top or the bottom of the income structure over different time points—which then helps in the analysis of different aspects of poverty and inequality (for example, by helping to identify households that are chronically poor versus those that are going through a transition period) over time.[4] This persisting inequality in income, if any, can also be used as an indicator of the welfare of individuals over the course of structural change (Swaminathan 1989). In the West, Cohen (1986) uses theories of occupational/class mobility, but uses income rather than social class as a measure to study mobility. In contrast, rather than using income as a basis for the

---

[3] Geographical mobility—movement from one place to another—is not within the present definition of social mobility. Migration may influence opportunity structures, and may be both the cause and consequence of social mobility, but is a matter for further enquiry (see Vaid 2014a).

[4] Gaiha (1988) provides a study of income mobility for rural India.

study of economic mobility, many economists use wealth, the use of which according to Swaminathan (1989: 7) is a more likely way to represent a 'permanent change in economic status'. In an economic mobility study wealth is often conceptualized and operationalized through *asset* ownership (for example, the ownership of land, machinery) as well as by the *credit status* of the household (for example, its financial assets) (Swaminathan 1989; for Cain 1981) economic mobility was measured by studying changes in land possession).

As can be seen, mobility studies are motivated by different research perspectives. In the current book which uses a sociological perspective, the direction of research is that of mobility in terms of class since people's class position is more closely linked to a host of life chances that a study of their income or wealth might fail to capture (discussed later in this chapter). In addition, using income or wealth as an indicator of class is problematic for practical reasons, as not only is their measurement difficult (particularly income measures, especially on a national scale), but given the present focus on individual rather than family-level mobility, it is problematic.

With this in view, this book studies intergenerational[5] class mobility sociologically, that is, mobility between classes, with classes categorized on the basis of occupations sharing similar market and work situations.[6] While this book does not directly address caste mobility, caste as a factor that helps or hinders class mobility is significant. For instance, we enquire whether belonging to a higher caste cushions one from downward class mobility and conversely, whether being from a lower caste prevents one from achieving upward mobility.[7]

---

[5] We restrict ourselves to individual intergenerational mobility, the question of *intra*-generational mobility (that is, movement through the career or life course of an individual) is important, but is not our focus, nor is there information in the current data to conduct such a study.

[6] This conceptualization of class, as well as the choice of a class structure or categorical schema is discussed in Chapter 3.

[7] Mobility in terms of status or prestige more generally is also out of the scope of this research. Further, no subjective measure of class is

The decision to study mobility between classes rather than castes was taken primarily on the ground that the study of class mobility by itself is valuable for India (discussed later). This was also a pragmatic decision as data needed to fulfil the requirement of a national caste mobility study is not available. Detailed work on caste mobility, especially where caste-occupations are concerned, would require more than just information on groups of castes. We would need detailed information on each individual's *jati* or sub-caste affiliation and their hereditary and current occupation; such information is not available.

In terms of the sociological perspective in the West, generally, literature on social mobility can be viewed in terms of 'two divergent research programmes which have set the terms of discussion of this subject since 1945' (Marshall 1998: 423).[8] The first approach is essentially the status attainment approach, followed mostly in the United States. This approach views 'mobility in the context of a social hierarchy, within which individuals can be ranked according to income, educational attainment, or socio-economic prestige' (Marshall 1998: 423). The Blau and Duncan model (1967) is viewed as one of the primary models of status attainment. 'In this model father's occupation, father's education, and subject's education and first job are considered to be important antecedent variables which influence the current occupational attainment of the subjects' (Sharda 1977: 11). The major research question in the status attainment approach asks what determines an individual's occupational attainment. These models of status attainment highlight the importance of both the achieved and the ascribed characteristics of an individual.

---

used in this book; while it is an interesting aspect of class identity, this subjective class analysis is not central to the present study.

[8] Ganzeboom, Treiman, and Ultee (1991) divide the history of intergenerational stratification research into three generations. The first according to them used 'simple statistical techniques, and in which occupational mobility figured as only one issue among many. The second generation of such research was dominated by path models of status attainment and the final model is characterised by occupational mobility analysis using log-linear modelling' (Ganzeboom, Treiman, and Ultee 1991: 278; see also Goldthorpe 2005).

The second social mobility approach sets the study of mobility within the class structure. This (neo-Weberian) view has been most forcefully propounded by John Goldthorpe and his colleagues at Nuffield College at Oxford University and used in studies of mobility in Europe. Goldthorpe's initial class schema within which mobility was studied aggregated individuals on the basis of their 'market' and 'work' situations. According to Marshall, 'the class analysis tradition starts from a rather different assumption that individuals are born into distinct social classes, membership of which has clear consequences for life chances, values, norms, lifestyles and patterns of association' (1998: 424). Furthermore, this social mobility approach differs from the status attainment approach in its major research question, that is, what determines the relative and absolute rates of mobility in society?[9]

These two research programmes diverge primarily on the basis of the key research questions posed, the different statistical modelling strategies followed, and also critically on their emphasis on what comprises class. The first research tradition of status attainment usually uses a hierarchical scale of occupations ranked by prestige or social standing (broadly conceived). In contrast, the second tradition of class mobility studies the movement of individuals between classes (which, analysed in one way, are agglomerates of different occupations) which would yield differing life chances to their holder.

In Chapter 3 we discuss debates surrounding class in general, particularly with reference to these two social mobility approaches. At this point it would suffice to say that in this book, mobility in India is studied within the framework of the class structural, rather than the status attainment, approach.

Given this framework of the social class mobility approach, we now provide an outline of what is expected under the class mobility approach in the context of economic development or 'modernization'.

---

[9] For India, for example, Sharda (1977) followed the status attainment approach for the study of rural India, and the class mobility approach was employed by Kumar, Heath, and Heath (2002a); McMillan (2005); and Vaid and Heath (2010) for their national-level studies. See Mukherji (2012) for an alternative orientation for mobility research for India.

Becoming Modern: The Modernization Thesis

One of the most important contexts for understanding social
mobility has been the thesis of modernization (also called the
liberal theory of industrialism, see Kerr, Dunlop, Harbison and
Myers 1960; Parsons 1960). Rapid growth of the Indian economy
and its concomitant effects on the social and economic landscape
has underlined the need to comprehensively analyse the effects of
industrialization and economic liberalization or 'modernization'
especially with regard to opportunities of social mobility. Since this
was discussed by Vaid and Heath (2010) in detail, in this section we
draw on their discussion and provide a context for our study.

The modernization thesis, though much critiqued, has been one
of the key theories to explain trends and patterns of social mobility in Western Industrial Societies (Erikson and Goldthorpe 2001:
344). Erikson and Goldthorpe highlight 'three distinctive features
of industrial societies in comparison to pre-industrial ones' (Vaid
and Heath 2010: 132):

1. 'Industrial societies are characterized by high absolute mobility rates, and a distinctive *pattern* of mobility, with more
   upward rather than downward mobility' (Vaid and Heath
   2010: 132).
2. There is 'declining inequality of opportunity as measured by
   relative rates of mobility' (Vaid and Heath 2010: 132), 'in the
   sense that individuals of differing social origins compete on
   more equal terms to attain (or avoid) particular destinations'
   (Erikson and Goldthorpe 2001: 344).
3. And finally, absolute and relative rates of mobility 'tend to
   increase over time' (Erikson and Goldthorpe 2001: 344).[10]

With reference to the first feature, high rates of absolute mobility are caused by structural changes associated with increasing

[10] In this book we are not concerned with the predictions and
expectations of the modernization thesis with regard to similarity or
convergence in rates of mobility and fluidity across countries. For more
on this see Featherman, Jones, and Hauser (1975); Erikson and Goldthorpe
(1992); and Grusky and Hauser (1984), among others.

industrialization. According to Treiman (1970) the influence of industrialization on social stratification leads to various structural changes. These changes comprise a decline in people engaged in agriculture, a shift from manual to non-manual occupations accompanied by a decline in the production of goods and an increase in the production of services, a rise in new occupations due to increasing employment of technology which leads to an increase in 'clerical and managerial positions to manage' the spread of these 'complex production systems'. Hence 'these structural changes lead to industrial societies becoming 'increasingly "middle class"'' (Erikson and Goldthorpe 2001: 344; Vaid and Heath 2010: 133). In Chapters 3, 4, and 5 these aspects of structural change are analysed with regard to India, especially to see the pattern of changes.

Modernization theorists (Ganzeboom, Luijkx, and Treiman 1989; Kerr, Dunlop, Harbison and Myers 1960; Treiman 1970) also underline some of the *processual effects* of industrialization (Erikson and Goldthorpe 2001: 344) which relate to the second feature of industrialization mentioned above. Particularly, that 'with an increase in economic development over time, ascription (inherited characteristics such as caste, gender, or class origins) will no longer be the main determining factor with regard to gaining access to advantaged class destinations' (Vaid and Heath 2010: 133). Achievement instead will be more critical. This would lead to a weakening between class origins and class destinations as 'merit'-based criteria like educational qualifications gain in salience. Chapter 6 explores this dimension.

Moving on to the third feature of the modernization thesis, the weakening of the origin-destination link would lead to an increase in openness in fluidity patterns over time, that is, we would expect to see a rise in relative rates of mobility (expanded in Chapter 4).

As discussed by Vaid and Heath (2010: 134), while Ganzeboom, Luijkx, and Treiman (1989), in their study of 149 countries (including Indian data from the 1970s), have found support for this hypothesis, researchers like Erikson and Goldthorpe do not support the modernization hypothesis, especially as they found limited change in fluidity patterns over time (1987, 1992; see also Featherman, Jones, and Hauser 1975; Breen 1997 and 2004; see Goldthorpe 1992). Heath and Payne (2000) who draw on British Election Study surveys from 1964–97 see some change, especially increased fluidity for men. Nevertheless the results they unearthed are uncertain and are not supported by Goldthorpe and Mills (2004; see especially p. 207, footnote 12).

With regard to India, the modernization theory has three particular implications for our research. Firstly, with respect to men and women's own class mobility we might, if modernization were to hold, expect to find an increase in both absolute mobility and fluidity in India over time. Secondly, modernization may also have an important role to play with regard to caste. Particularly, it has been predicted by theorists that economic development and the outcome of modernization would lead to a decline in the influence of ascribed characteristics such as caste on occupational destinations, while the association between caste and class is expected to change. Thirdly, the impact of education is expected to increase where occupational attainment is concerned—that is, educational attainment becomes more critical for social mobility.

The first of the implications of modernization concerning patterns of class mobility will be studied in Chapter 4; the second concerning its impact on caste and class mobility will be studied in Chapter 5; and, the third regarding education is explored in Chapter 6. Before analysing these aspects, in Chapter 2 using Census and other national survey data, we map the changes that have taken place in the Indian occupational structure.

The OED Triad

Figure 1.1 provides a possible visual representation of social mobility and factors affecting mobility in the context of the previous discussion. In this figure, 'O' signifies class origins, 'D' signifies class destinations, 'E' implies highest educational attainment, and 'C' signifies caste. The stronger the association between O and D (referred to as the OD association), the *less* the social mobility we would expect, as a strong OD link implies stronger inheritance. Put another way, if we observe a strong OD association then we can conclude that destinations (or respondent's class) are heavily influenced by origins (or parental class). While the obverse is true if the OD association is weak; that is, destinations are less influenced by origins.

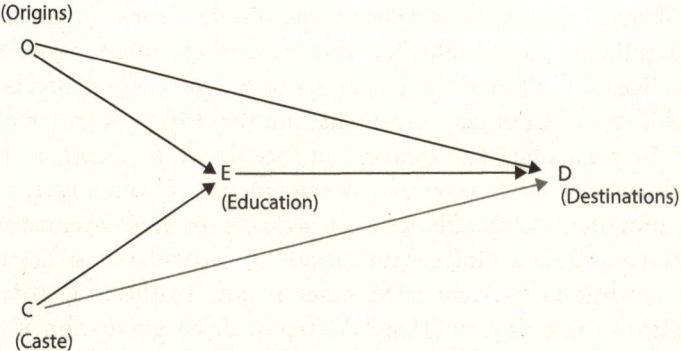

Figure 1.1 A Visual Representation of the OED Triad (and its Extension) for the Indian Case

Source: Vaid (2016: 286).

Note: O = father's (or mother's) class; D = respondent's own class; E = education; C = caste; interaction effects are not included in this figure (see also footnote 12).

The OD association (social mobility) can be studied both in absolute and in relative terms. On one hand, when we talk of absolute mobility we imply the 'raw' numbers of people/groups moving up/down or staying stable in a particular position. Absolute mobility is the mobility that occurs as a function of structural changes in the economy. For example, a movement of an economy away from agriculture towards industry, which would lead to an increase of jobs in the industrial sector, would push people out from agriculture and into industry, and lead to mobility in society. On the other hand, relative mobility patterns imply mobility net of any structural change (Breen 2004; Erikson and Goldthorpe 1992). This implies that relative rates of mobility are not affected by a contraction or expansion in any one particular class, and provide a preferred measure of openness and comparison across place and time. In this regard, for example, one can compare the relative chances of a woman or a man from working class origins of making it to the salariat as compared to those from intermediate or salariat origins.[11]

[11] See Heath and Payne (2000) for a discussion of absolute and relative rates of mobility. Vaid and Heath (2010) provide a discussion on India.

Though the study of relative and absolute rates of mobility is significant for establishing and comparing mobility patterns, this does not allow for any analysis of the 'processual effects' of mobility. Or, in other words, what are the drivers of this mobility. In particular, as discussed previously, it is theorized that with an increase in economic development over time, ascription (or inherited characteristics such as caste or class origins) will weaken as a factor influencing access to particular class destinations; while, 'achievement' becomes a more significant factor (see Treiman 1970; Vaid and Heath 2010 provide an application of this liberal thesis of industrialism with regard to mobility patterns in the Indian context). With criteria like educational qualifications gaining in importance we expect to see a strengthening of the link between education and class-destinations (the ED link) and a subsequent weakening of the link between class-origins and class-destinations (OD link). This implies that an increase in the importance of education would lead to a reduction in the role of family characteristics for gaining access to certain occupations or social class destinations. This in turn would lead to increased social mobility. Whether we see any indication of these processes in India is a question that this book explores while taking forward the initial research by Vaid and Heath (2010). This question is also significant in the context of reservation in educational institutions, and debates on whether education has indeed been a mediator for upward social mobility for people from *all* communities.

This, however, is not the complete story, as access to education itself is influenced by origins (Breen and Vaid 2008; Desai and Kulkarni 2008), with certain groups able to maintain their 'edge' by securing elite education for their members (hence, the OE line which mediates the effect of education on class destination). This relation, depicted in Figure 1.1, is often referred to as the OED triad (see also Shavit and Blossfeld 1993).[12]

While this model is used widely across countries, the Indian case calls for a more nuanced view, especially due to the role

---

[12] For models tracing the OED association see Ganzeboom, De Graff, and Treiman (1992); Breen (2004); Blau, Duncan, and Tyree (1967) provide a discussion of the elements of social mobility in their classic 'status attainment model'.

played by caste. Thus, a caste dimension is added to the original OED triad. We see that the CD association maps the link between caste and class destination (similar to the OD association mentioned earlier), while the CE association posits the impact of caste on educational attainment.

However, this is still missing a crucial relationship which is the link or interaction between caste and class origins (OC association). This, in turn, allows us to analyse whether an interaction between caste and class may in turn be impacting the amount and patterns of social mobility. So, for instance, could it be that certain castes within a particular class are more upwardly mobile? Or in other words, are the benefits of mobility accruing only to a few?[13] Through various empirical analysis this book attempts a comparative study of mobility as indicated by Figure 1.1.

The Significance of Mobility for India

As is clear from the discussion this far, the study of class mobility in India assumes importance for a number of reasons. Firstly, not only is there a gap where the study of patterns of class mobility in India is concerned, the analysis of India as a case study is in itself fascinating. Highly developed, technologically advanced cities coexist with some less developed, and rural areas. India, thus, presents an unusual case in terms of this developed—developing dichotomy (with its large 'modern' and 'traditional' sectors (Vaid and Heath 2010)), a study of which can throw light on differing mobility experiences within the same broader national framework.

Secondly, in the past three decades, particularly since the early 1990s, India has experienced rapid industrial and economic growth as part of the liberalization of the economy (particularly in the

[13] In addition to these main relationships, there are certain interaction effects that allow us to complete the model. These interaction effects particularly explore how layers *within* caste and *within* class may be influencing any patterns of social mobility. For example: two individuals who are identical in terms of class origins (let's say they are both from business class families), may not have the same chance of gaining access to higher education—as all else being equal their caste may determine whether they get into, and graduate, college or not.

service sector, see Acharya, Cassen, and McNay 2004). Moreover, the agricultural sector too has become more mechanised particularly since the 'green revolution' period of the 1970s (Parthasarathy and Nirmala 1999). These technological, industrial changes have also led to the creation of new jobs unconnected with any caste. This diversification and expansion may in turn lead to some changes in the class structure, particularly the contraction in absolute terms of the agrarian class and the expansion of the service class.[14] However, while economic growth has occurred, it has not concomitantly led to an increase in employment per se. Furthermore, as mechanization has been shown to lead to a marginalization of the female workforce in India,[15] these changes would in turn impact the mobility patterns of women and men differently.

Thirdly, the existence of the caste system makes India distinct. Certain jatis have been historically associated with particular occupations. But, given rapid industrialization and the resultant urbanization and rural–urban migration, it is believed by many researchers that the association between traditional jatis or caste positions and occupations will begin to melt.[16] Moreover, since India's independence in 1947, various preferential policies to safeguard the interests of disadvantaged castes and alleviate their position with regard to the sharp historical social inequalities have been implemented. This book questions whether these castes have indeed been able to take advantage of upward mobility chances or whether the association between caste and class persists. This book also questions whether class, rather than caste or community, could be a determining characteristic to define the 'backwardness' of these communities. Not much national research has been conducted with regard to these issues except, for example, by

[14] According to Kumar, Heath, and Heath (2002a: 2984) 'With its high proportion of farmers and agriculturalists, India looks like a developing country; but with its salariat outstripping the manual working class in size India looks like a highly developed western country'.

[15] See the section 'Gender: Women's Mobility' in Chapter 2 for a discussion.

[16] See Gist (1954); Marnane (1967); also Phillips (1978) succinctly lays down these changes in India; for more on this aspect refer to Chapter 2 and the section titled 'Caste'.

McMillan (2005) and Kumar, Heath, and Heath (2002a and b), and hence, this book contributes to this research area.

Fourthly, the persisting large gender inequalities, for example as manifested through the high male-to-female sex ratio and labour market segregation (see Kynch and Sen [1983] for more on this; Agnihotri 2000), set India apart. In a country with such wide gender inequalities, a strong cultural boy preference, and a persisting patriarchal system of inheritance despite legal and constitutional provisions, we might expect the patterns of class mobility for women to be somewhat different from those in Western and developing countries where gender inequalities though present may not be so extreme. Thus, a study of mobility which might throw more light on this issue seems crucial.

Finally, in addition to the above reasons, analysing the mobility of Indian women along with men is of interest due also to the changing economic and social environment. The opening up of the Indian economy and recent technological growth has led to, or in some cases has occurred concurrently with, an increase in the participation of women in higher education, as well as changing patterns of their participation in the labour market and their entry into a broader range of occupations (Liddle and Joshi 1986). What impact, if any, has this had on their mobility chances?

This research is critical since no previous study has systematically analysed what influence modernization, with regard to its effect on caste, gender, and economic participation, may have on patterns of mobility, especially in terms of inequality of opportunity in Indian society for both women and men.

Before discussing the main research questions posed by this book and the methods employed, we survey some of the existing research on mobility in India. We discuss the choice of a class structural approach and the separation of the two concepts of caste and class for a more fruitful analysis of mobility, a distinction not often made in the Indian literature.

'Class Mobility' Studies in India

The study of mobility in terms of class and not in terms of income or wealth is common within sociology. This is because not only is there usually no good data available on income or wealth transmission, but also because class is closely linked to a host of life chances[17] that income and wealth may not be. For example, in the West it has been seen that class (rather than income) is associated with a wide range of outcomes—for example, education, mortality, political behaviour, and so on.[18] In India, too, class was shown to be associated with inequalities in educational transitions for both girls and boys (Vaid 2004). The persisting class inequality in education showed that not all these inequalities could be reduced to caste, and that class had a stronger role to play.

Moreover, Sheth (1999: 2509), through an analysis of a study of the Indian national electorate, shows that class was associated with certain political and cultural variables. He concludes that there are

> statistically highly significant differences in political attitudes and preferences, between members of the middle class and the rest of the population. More importantly, on certain crucial political ... and cultural variables ..., the difference between the lower caste and upper-caste members of the middle class was found to be much less than that between members of the middle class and their caste compatriots not belonging to the middle class.

This seems to indicate that to look only through a caste lens may provide an important but restricted view of the importance that class might have in people's lives. What is needed is a study of class mobility that studies the *interaction* between class and caste to be able to provide a more comprehensive picture.

Kumar, Heath, and Heath (2002a) too, in their study of the social mobility of men in India document these persisting class inequalities, which they see as distinct from those arising from membership in a particular 'community'.[19] Most importantly, they conclude

---

[17] 'Life chances can be understood ... as the chances that individuals have of gaining access to scarce and valued outcomes' (Breen 2005: 32). In the Weberian sense life chances refer to a broad range of outcomes—which include but are in no means restricted to mortality rates (Breen 2005: 32).

[18] See Breen and Rottman (1995: 76) for why class is a key concept in sociological imagination.

[19] *Community* for them is a six category variable including religion and caste; this variable was used previously by one of the authors in an

through their analysis that the 'relationship between community and class destination seems to be rather weaker than that between class origins and class destinations .... That is, class origins cannot be reduced to community, nor vice versa ... even among people from the same caste or community, class origins still make a very substantial difference to their class destinations' (pp. 2986–7).

This leads us to maintain a clear distinction between class and caste in this book. For a discussion of why this distinction is significant, we now briefly summarize the broader debates on class and status (Béteille 1996b; Chan and Goldthorpe 2002; Weber 1958, 1978). For Max Weber (1958 reproduced in Grusky 2001: 136):[20]

> In contrast to the purely economically determined 'class situation' we wish to designate as 'status situation' every typical component of the life fate of men that is determined by a specific, positive or negative, social estimation of honour ... status honour need not necessarily be linked with a 'class situation'.

Thus, for Weber, status groups in contrast to class groups were separated on the basis of the lifestyle they followed and the honour and prestige they held in a community.[21]

Theorists like Prandy (Stewart, Prandy, and Blackburn 1980; Prandy 1998b) however reject outrightly the distinction between class and status and 'claim its empirical irrelevance' (Chan and Goldthorpe [2002] criticize their view). According to them (Prandy 1998b: 361; Stewart, Prandy, and Blackburn 1980: 28) the distinction between the two concepts of class and status has been 'based on a false division between the social and the economic'. They go on to stress the need for an 'integrated conceptualisation of

---

electoral research study (Heath and Yadav 1999). The influence of caste and community is discussed in Chapter 5 in this book.

[20] For Weber caste was an extreme form of status. In a closed 'caste' according to him, 'status distinctions are guaranteed not merely by conventions and laws, but also by rituals' (Weber [1958] reproduced in Grusky [2001: 137]).

[21] For Weber's discussion on status or *Stand* as well as characteristics of a status group, see Weber (1978).

stratification, which allows both for the resources associated with work and employment that typically figure in class schemas and for those associated with social interaction and evaluation that inform ideas of status. The two are simply aspects of a unified social reality' (Prandy 1998b: 361; Stewart, Prandy, and Blackburn 1980).

Prandy's view that the distinction between status and class can be rejected is debatable. Especially in the Indian context it would be theoretically quite meaningful to look at these two concepts, in terms for instance of class and caste, as conceptually separate and yet empirically connected parts of a whole. This is because the way that class and caste would shape certain outcomes, or life chances, is expected to be different from each other. As Saunders (1990: 5) argues and we quote at length:

> Rather than motives, the central contrast between class and status is the nature of the mechanisms through which class and status shape inequalities of the material and symbolic conditions (of) people's lives. Class affects material wellbeing directly through the kinds of economic assets people bring to market exchanges. Status affects material well-being indirectly, through the ways that categories of social honour underwrite various coercive mechanisms that, in Weber's ([1924] 1978: 935) words, 'go hand in hand with the monopolisation of ideal and material goods or opportunities'.

In India caste and class have often been taken to be quite closely associated,[22] but given that they both might shape people's life chances in distinct ways and through distinct mechanisms, as well as due to the changes that are believed to be occurring in the caste system, the two can no longer be directly equated. According to Jayaram (1996: 82) the 'conjugation of caste and class status is no more a sociological axiom'. This change has

---

[22] Nowhere has this association been more apparent than in the debates surrounding affirmative action or reservation policies in the country (discussed in Chapter 2).

See Sharma (1984) for a critique of the conceptual differences between caste and class in India.

been brought about due to various factors such as the erosion of the traditional patron-client relations among other things and has 'profoundly altered the economic bearing of the caste system' (Jayaram 1996: 82).

In light of these changes, not only in agriculture but in non-agricultural employment as well, we maintain that the two—class and caste—should be separated for a fruitful study and interactions between the two should be analysed.[23] Béteille (1996b: 513) too thinks this distinction between class and status is an important one when he states that even though, 'sociologists differ on how the distinction should be made, just as they differ on what they mean by status and by class. Nevertheless, they would agree upon the need to maintain as consistently as possible some kind of distinction between the two'.

We revisit this discussion on class and status in Chapter 3 where we discuss the major debates on class and our conceptualization of class. We now briefly look at the main studies on mobility in India.

Social Mobility—The Indian Literature[24]

As mentioned in the introduction to this chapter, since Sorokin began the social mobility debate in the 1920s (Sorokin 1928) it has developed into an important aspect of sociological analysis in the West (Westergaard 1990).[25] However, this has not been the case in India. The past five decades have seen intermittent work on social mobility in India, and a major part of this work has been limited

---

[23] For example, if one wishes to observe caste on its own as a factor that helps or hinders class mobility, the merging of class and caste might then not be fruitful at all.

[24] This review of the literature looks briefly at social mobility studies broadly defined, that is, it deals with more than just class mobility. In India, few studies ever separately study class mobility, and most tend to conflate class and status as will be seen in this review.

[25] See Payne (1989) for a review of three generations of social mobility research in Britain.

to mobility within the caste system or on economic mobility. Relatively little attention has been paid to social class mobility and the studies that have had class as their focus have seldom looked at the mobility of women.

In this section we briefly discuss the main elements of the research studies that have touched on social mobility of Indian men to provide a background for our research. We begin by mentioning studies on mobility in the caste system. In addition to mobility of one caste from a lower position in the caste hierarchy to a higher position, some caste mobility studies have also looked at occupational mobility *within* the caste system. Towards the end of this section we discuss the few studies on social mobility not restricted to mobility within the caste structure.

One of the primary books on social mobility within the caste system (referred to as 'caste mobility') is edited by Silverberg (1968). This book includes contributions by various sociologists and anthropologists as part of a symposium on social mobility in India. Most noticeably the articles by Damle (1968: 95–102), and by Marriott (1968: 103–14) using Robert Merton's (1957) 'reference group theory' employ this concept to the analysis of 'how one caste establishes a reference group (a higher jati within the broader caste group) and models itself' on it for upward mobility (Vaid 2014: 396).

Sivaram (1990) provides a 'summary of mobility studies in different parts of the country and delves into occupational mobility *within* the caste system' (Vaid 2014: 397). The author lists a number of studies covering caste and occupational mobility that have been conducted in India and abroad. But a listing of studies provides no background on the robustness of findings of those studies, nor does it tell one about the techniques used, data interpreted, and results obtained. This lack of rigour in empirical research seems to pervade social mobility studies in India.

The 1960s and 1970s saw a spurt in class mobility (loosely defined) studies in India, but this petered out in the 1980s, with a resurgence in ethnographic studies in the last decade (mentioned earlier). 'Most studies on mobility focused on a state or a small region within a state' (Vaid 2014: 397). Out of the list of studies reviewed a few, Kumar, Heath, and Heath (2002a and b); Nijhawan

(1969); and McMillan (2005); Vaid and Heath (2010)[26] all using National Election Study (NES) data look at the national picture.[27]

As mentioned by Vaid (2014: 397) in view of the 'Indian government's policies to redress the inequalities suffered by the backward castes and tribes, Kumar, Heath, and Heath set out to study whether these political and social movements have made India a more mobile society in the past five decades'. In their first paper (2002a) they lay out the determinants of mobility of men; and in the second one (2002b) they trace the mobility trends over time. In brief, as discussed by Vaid, using the 1971 and the 1996, *male only* NES data they conclude that 'there has been no systematic additional weakening of links between father's and son's class positions, or between caste and class' (2002a: 2987). They show in their paper that certain castes are 'associated with particular class destinations'. For example, the 'upper castes show a relatively high propensity to be in the salariat, 20 per cent of upper castes being in the salariat compared with the overall figure of 10 per cent in this class'. 'Similar results are obtained for business as well ' (Vaid 2014: 397–8). But, as Vaid (2014: 398) states, they also show that 'class inequalities seem to be more persistent than caste inequalities' as discussed in an earlier section of this chapter (on *Class Mobility Studies in India*).

Nijhawan (1969) also used the NES male only data but for the NES of 1967. Looking at absolute rates of mobility, and not at the relative mobility chances of the respondents, he concluded that 'sons inheriting non-agricultural occupations' found it easier to move out of their father's class than their counterparts in agricultural occupations. For example, 'the out-mobility of sons of white-collar fathers, of professionals, and of businessmen was higher than those of skilled and unskilled workers' (p. 1556). And in agriculture, he found that the out-mobility was higher for sons of agricultural labourers as compared to the sons of owner or tenant cultivators (p. 1553). In the case of in-mobility, the 'in-mobility

---

[26] McMillan's work focuses on the social mobility of the Scheduled Castes (SCs)and Scheduled Tribes (STs).

[27] A discussion on the class schemas employed by the studies mentioned here is included in Chapter 3.

into professional and other white-collar occupations was relatively more than into other classes', and the 'in-mobility into business was the least' (p. 1556). Irrespective of their origins, sons more often moved into non-agricultural occupations than into agricultural ones. His final conclusion was that equal opportunities are not available to sons of all origins. The 'professions, business and white collar occupations, considered separately, offered far greater opportunities of admission to the sons of the other two classes than to the sons of the rest of the classes' (p. 1556).

More recent work using NES data by McMillan (2005: 133–49) and others expands this research. As discussed by Vaid (2014: 398), while studying the 'various aspects of the development of SCs and STs in light of reservations, particularly electoral', McMillan 'analyses the social mobility patterns of these scheduled groups, and especially compares these patterns with those of the 'other' group' (including the Other Backward Classes (OBCs) and other minority groups like the Muslims). McMillan used both the 1971 and 1996 NES surveys (combining women and men). While studying absolute mobility patterns using the 1996 data he concludes that the 'growth in the number of skilled and professional occupations has given the Scheduled Castes some opportunity for upward mobility' (McMillan 2005: 147). But in terms of mobility relative to the non-scheduled castes, the picture shows otherwise: as the SCs and STs 'have not been able to compete with the non-SCs/STs successfully, and their relative disadvantage has got worse' (p. 149). In Chapter 5 of this book we deal in more detail with the class mobility of the various caste/communities, including the SCs, STs, and OBCs. Vaid and Heath (2010) provide perhaps the only analysis of women and men's patterns together using the 2004 NES data. Since the data used in this book is the most recent round of the NES, Vaid and Heath's study (2010) provides a key comparison to the analysis here.

Other studies, looking only at one region, have come up with similar results to national studies. Ramu and Weibe (1973) used both surveys and participant observation to conduct their mobility study in the Kolar Gold Mines (in Mysore, now Mysuru, Karnataka). Studying both caste and class, they concluded that there has been 'educational mobility' for all classes, though differences remain, in as much as higher castes are still able to maintain their *pre-dominance* in terms of access to education. Vaid (2014: 398) discusses that this 'association between castes and their traditionally defined occupations is still quite high, Brahmins predominate at the executive and professional positions', that is, higher white-collar levels, but there has not been much movement for the Kshatriya castes.[28]

Jorapur (1971) in his occupational mobility study of Dharwar (also in Mysore, Karnataka) restricts his study to households with both father and son currently working and concludes that inheritance of father's occupations was highest among sons of unskilled manual workers, and lowest among the professions. Using the index of association[29] he shows that there is higher association between father and son's occupations among lower status categories. Better education, he concludes, leads to sons of higher status categories retaining their status, and sons from lower status backgrounds moving up.

Mehra, Sharma, and Dak (1985) studying social mobility trends in two districts in rural Haryana in the context of rural development, conclude that development of a region promotes 'simultaneous changes in the structural components of society, as manifested in declining occupational inheritance, diversification of occupational structure, increased urban-ward movement, change in the composition of population and disassociation of caste and occupational structure' (p. 85).

Another city specific study by Sovani and Pradhan (1955) studying Pune city (in Maharashtra) looks at data on over 4,500 families and the occupation of the head of household, as well as the head's father and grandfather, and concludes that there is more mobility in the younger generation than there was between the father and the grandfather. This they believe could be due to urbanization, which could be leading to movement away from unskilled manual work to more skilled work.

---

[28] These different caste groups will be discussed in the next chapter in the section on caste.

[29] The use of the index of association has been criticized by some, for example Billewicz (1955) and defended by others such as Jones (1975). In this book we use more appropriate and advanced techniques to study patterns of mobility.

Details on the above studies as far as it concerns their use of a schema for the study of mobility as well as studies that use class schemas for other research projects are included in Chapter 3.

As discussed in Vaid (2014: 398), out of the 'studies on social mobility in India reviewed', a few look at 'trends in mobility' but few such as 'Kumar, Heath, and Heath (2002a) and Vaid and Heath (2010) look at the determinants of this mobility', though 'some do mention occupational re-structuring', none analyse the empirical importance of this. In addition, out of the studies reviewed here few look at the differences between absolute and relative rates of mobility. Both absolute and relative rates of mobility are studied in greater detail in Chapters 4, 5, and 6 of this book. The themes explored in the present study will now be discussed.

Themes

This book fills the gap in class mobility research on India by ana-lysing intergenerational social mobility patterns of women as well as men. Furthermore, as this research has been largely motivated by the findings of some recent studies (Kumar, Heath, and Heath 2002a and b) on intergenerational patterns of male mobility in India, we aim to expand on these studies by bringing women into the analysis (taking Vaid and Heath 2010 forward).

There are three major research aspects that this book focuses on: the first concerns the patterns of class mobility of women and men through their own employment; the second concerns the association between caste and class and the influence of caste on class mobility chances; and the third is concerned with the influ-ence of education on patterns of mobility (in addition to these, mobility through marriage is discussed in Appendix B).

As India is a vast country, a national level study would have to be aware of regional as well as rural–urban differences. Within India, according to Raju's (1991: 2827) review of various studies, 'regional characteristics override caste, community and even reli-gion specific behaviour in terms of work participation, literacy attainment, sex ratios, access to health and nutrition and politi-cal participation' . The impact of these regional differences on the mobility experience of women and men are significant. But, rather than any arbitrary regional classification, the focus of this book is on rural–urban differences. One might expect the pattern of mobility to vary by rural or urban area as well, particularly with regard to the large agricultural sector and due to the differing engagement of women and men in the labour market.[30]

The key themes the book explores are:

Class Mobility Patterns

We begin by asking, as did Kumar, Heath, and Heath (2002a) for their study of men, 'How much class mobility is there for *both* women and men in India?'

As discussed in Chapter 2, economic development is believed to influence the lives of women and men differently. Furthermore, as there are vast persisting gender inequalities in Indian society, one would expect to see a different pattern of class mobility for women than for men. This begs the question whether employed women find it harder than men to achieve upward mobility.

Gandhi (1996: 347) concluded in her paper that 'women form a category which crosses caste, class, and ethnic boundaries, yet are divided by these structures, forming a differentiated as well as a common group of people. They are linked not only by their biological characteristics, but also by patriarchal norms, similar oppressions and subordination' . Even though women are believed to be disadvantaged as compared to men, no matter what caste, class, or region; gender need not be a 'leveller', and *within* the same gender there might be variations in mobility chances according to their caste and class origins. It is, thus, interesting to see whether class divides women in the same way that it does men.

For countries of the West, on the one hand, for Heath 'womanhood is a leveller' (Heath 1981: 135) as the restrictions on women's job prospects, especially their concentration in lower white-collar work means that they are much less divided by social origins than

---

[30] However, the nuances within rural and urban, especially the semi-urban, are technically beyond the scope of this book due to data limitations.

men. And, hence, 'Class discrimination divides men, but sexual discrimination brings women together' (Heath 1981: 135). But, on the other hand, according to Goldthorpe (1987), class divides women just as it does men, that is, the effect of class origins is shown to be similar for men and women.[31] For example, according to him, women from service class backgrounds have a greater chance of gaining access to the service class as compared to women from working class families. Thus, as McRae puts it, 'far from "sisterhood" cutting across class inequalities, women are instead divided from other women occupationally much the same way and to much the same extent that men are divided from other men. Class inequalities, in other words, act in ways that are gender-blind' (McRae 1990: 118).

In this book, following Vaid and Heath (2010), we study both absolute and relative rates of class mobility, with a particular emphasis on the relative rates, which are considered a better indicator of the openness of a society, and are 'one of the most important indicators of social inequalities' of opportunity that exist in society (Jonsson and Mills 1993: 229).

Relating to this area, we explore the following main questions:

1. How much mobility is there in the country and what are the patterns?
2. What are the patterns of social fluidity in India? In particular, what are the relative mobility chances of women and men?
3. Has there been any change in social fluidity?
4. Are there any rural–urban differences in mobility and fluidity?

These questions will be answered in Chapter 4.

Caste and Class Mobility

As mentioned previously, caste is expected to play a significant role with regard to class mobility in India especially as certain jatis/castes have been associated with particular occupations.

---

[31] However, it needs to be noted that Goldthorpe is more concerned with relative rates and Heath with absolute rates of mobility. This book will consider both.

Thus, as Kumar Heath, and Heath (2002a) and Vaid and Heath (2010) do in their papers; we will also determine the role caste plays in the process of class mobility by asking 'does membership of the scheduled castes inhibit one's chances of upward class mobility and does membership of an upward caste protect one from downward mobility?' (Kumar, Heath, and Heath 2002a: 2983; See also Vaid 2012). However, this book goes a step further and studies how the influence of caste on class mobility might be different for women. Hence, we also study the interaction of gender with caste to explore the relative disadvantage of women vis-à-vis *other* women and men. Further, we extend the discussion beyond 'Hindu castes' to religious groups such as Muslims and Other Religious Minorities allowing for a more comprehensive account of mobility experiences.

With regard to this area, we ask the following main questions:

1. Is there more congruence between castes and classes at the extremes of the class system, and more movement in the middle?
2. Has the association between caste and class declined?
3. Has there been a decline over time in the relative importance of caste and an increase in the importance of class origins, on class destinations?
4. Do SCs find it harder to take advantage of upward class mobility chances, and conversely, are high castes cushioned from downward mobility?

These questions will be answered in Chapter 5.

Education and Social Mobility

As education is expected to be a significant factor influencing social mobility chances, especially in the context of 'merit selection' under the thesis of modernization, this chapter explores the role of education as a driver of mobility. We ask:

1. How do the patterns of social mobility vary across various levels of education?

2. Does education act as a mediator for social mobility? In other words, do we see any effect of education on social mobility chances?
3. Do we find any support for the 'merit' argument?

This will be the focus of Chapter 6.

Marriage and Class Mobility

As reported, employment for women is low, and marriage is nearly universal in India and still occurs primarily within the confines of caste; in Appendix B of this book we analyse patterns of women's mobility through marriage, and compare those with married men's mobility through employment. Erikson and Goldthorpe (1992) argue that 'the *class* mobility of women tends to be better understood through examination of their experience in marriage markets than in labour markets'. Studying marital mobility of women in India gives us an opportunity to analyse the mobility chances of women who might for various socio-economic reasons have been prevented from entering employment. This will ensure that we are able to include a majority of the women in our analysis, thus providing us with a more comprehensive account of class mobility in India.

With regard to this area, we ask the following main questions:

1. Are women in India more upwardly mobile through marriage than men are through employment?
2. Is women's 'class fate' (Heath 1981) more loosely linked to their class of origin than a man's class fate?
3. In light of caste endogamy, are there caste differences in marital mobility patterns?

These questions will be answered in Appendix B.

Method: The Empirical View

As a book that explores patterns and trends in mobility, the use of quantitative techniques is essential. However, to enable the non-quantitatively inclined reader to follow the arguments and discussions—each empirical chapter (Chapters 4–6) follows a similar structure—with a section setting out the key questions, followed by sections dedicated to the statistical data analysis for those interested in following the technical discussion. The final sections of these chapters provide a discussion of the key findings.

Previous studies in India have tended to use simple statistics like cross tabulations, chi-square tests, and techniques like the index of association which are seldom able to capture the complexities of the Indian case. This book uses fairly standard techniques for the measurement of social mobility and for the inferential analysis (see Vaid and Heath 2010 for a brief overview). We discuss these methods briefly here, and each empirical chapter takes this basic discussion forward. The key technical aspects studied are:

1. Structural change: Social mobility rates are contextualized within a particular occupational structure (Chapter 4), or caste (Chapter 5), or educational structure (Chapter 6) as the case may be. Hence, the empirical chapters begin with an overview of the existing structures and the changes over time in the distribution of occupations, caste, and education as the case may be.

2. Absolute mobility rates: Absolute mobility can be understood as the movement either vertically or horizontally between class origins (parent's class)[32] and class destinations (respondent's class). Vertical movement implies upward or downward movement when compared to class origin,

[32] Some authors have argued for the use of mother's occupation for the study of sons and daughter's occupational mobility (see, for an example, Rosenfeld 1978; Aschaffenburg 1995; and Miller and Hayes 1990). Whereas, Breen and Whelan (1995) argue that if the focus of any work is on 'class' and not occupational attainment, then it is not useful to include mother's occupation. Here, for the most part, class origins are indexed by father's class as information on employment of 'mothers' is limited in the NES data. While the 2009 and 2014 NES surveys have inquired about mother's occupation, as the Appendix in Chapter 4 shows, the small sample sizes make any major analysis difficult—though some broad conclusions are drawn.

whereas horizontal mobility implies moving among occupations placed at similar levels of the class structure. There
are three types of measures that make up absolute mobility rates—inflow, outflow, and total mobility (Chapter 4
discusses these different measures; Chapters 5 and 6 take
the discussion of total mobility rates further). These three
rates are calculated from a simple cross-tabulation of class
origins (father's class) and class destinations (respondent's
own class). This is referred to as a mobility table. These rates
summarize the per cent of people who move into an occupational class, or out of a class, and the total number who are
socially mobile (vertically and horizontally). These are hence
useful summary measures of change and movement.

3. Relative mobility rates: Relative mobility differs from absolute mobility as it measures the movement between origins
and destinations *net* of structural changes that might take
place in an economy. For example, due to industrialization
there might be an increase in non-manual jobs and a decline
in agricultural or manual jobs; this would make more 'room at
the top' if these jobs are hierarchically placed (with non-manual higher placed than manual and lower agrarian jobs). This
room at the top would lead to an increase in absolute rates of
mobility, with people moving into these newer jobs. However,
this structural change need not have the same impact on fluidity or relative mobility patterns. Relative mobility rates, due
to their very nature, require more advanced statistical modelling. However, the core data for this comes from the cross-tabulation of the Origins and Destinations, that is, the mobility
table. Odds ratios lie at the heart of these rates—and help capture the relative risk of someone from a particular origin 'making it' to a specific destination while avoiding another one
(Heath and Payne 2000). Chapter 4 discusses these in more
detail. As many odds ratios can be calculated from one cross-
tabulation of origin and destination, we also use log-linear
modelling to summarize whether all odds ratios possible in a
table are common across gender, caste, or levels of education.
This enables us to see whether any particular group suffers a
disadvantage with regard to relative mobility or equality of

opportunity. A series of summary statistics are used in log linear modelling which are explained in more detail in Chapter 4—and similar models with caste and education extensions are applied in Chapters 5 and 6, respectively.

4. Class attainment: As a final measure, this book looks at the attainment of specific class destinations along with the factors that could influence this attainment including class origins, caste, education, and locality. Logistic regression modelling is conducted in this regard and discussed in more detail in Chapters 5 and 6.

On a final note, in order to capture change over time, this book draws briefly on cross-sectional surveys over one decade from 2004–14 using the National Election Study datasets from the Centre for the Study of Developing Societies (CSDS), Delhi. As no panel data exists across this period, for more disaggregated analysis we use a birth-cohort approach throughout the volume with the 2014 dataset to trace changes over four decades. This approach is discussed in Chapter 4. Finally, to capture locality wise differences, key results in all chapters are discussed by rural and urban location.

Book Layout

Chapter 2 discusses the Indian context for the study of mobility, including discussions of both caste and gender, two significant aspects of this book. This chapter also looks in detail at participation of women in employment as well as the changes in the Indian economy, especially with regard to workforce participation that may be expected to lead to a change in mobility patterns.

Chapter 3 includes a discussion of some of the major debates surrounding the definition of class. Here we discuss our conceptualization of social class and its operationalization in terms of a class schema.

Chapter 4 analyses the patterns of absolute and relative rates of class mobility as well as the trends in these patterns over time. It also provides a rural–urban perspective of these patterns.

Chapter 5 studies caste and its influence on class mobility and analyses in detail the association between caste and class in India.

Chapter 6 explores the role of education as a driver of mobility, and the possible impact of class, caste, gender, and locality in mediating education's role.

Chapter 7 concludes with the main findings of the research and will explore possible directions for future research.

The technical Appendix A provides a discussion of the NES dataset used in this book, as well as a validation exercise of the schema initially used by Kumar, Heath, and Heath (2002a and b) and updated by Vaid and Heath (2010). It also presents the final schema used in this book.

Appendix B provides a discussion on an additional theme which is significant given the possible under reporting of women's work: it explores the mobility of women through marriage and compares those patterns with married men's intergenerational mobility through own employment.

2

The Indian Context

Caste, Gender, and the Labour Market

Social class mobility, as a sociological phenomenon, draws on many features depending on the geographic and temporal context. There are two distinctive features of the Indian context that warrant detailed examination in a social mobility study. These are: caste and gender.[1] Caste, with its 'traditional' link with specific occupations and in the context of preferential or 'reservation policies' to overcome historical inequality, is tied closely to social mobility opportunities and outcomes. Gender difference, especially due to the gender inequalities prevalent in India with regard, for instance, to labour market participation and segregation is expected to influence mobility as well. How these inequalities might translate into inequalities in patterns of employment and in turn into inequality in mobility opportunities is of interest.

In this chapter, these aspects of caste and gender and their influence on labour market participation are discussed in some detail, especially relating to the possible implications on class mobility.

[1] While the focus is on caste, since religion is another domain of differences and possible inequalities in the labour market—this book also broadly provides a look at patterns of mobility for Muslim and other religious minority groups. Other differences such as race and ethnicity, while important, are not part of the present study due to the absence of adequate information in the datasets used.

Given the regional diversity, any analysis of national mobility patterns in India might require the examination of regional differences. However, establishing what comprises a particular region has its own difficulties (and has been attempted elsewhere: Vaid 2007). Rather than disaggregating regional differences, this book looks specifically at differences between rural and urban India—differences in terms of employment opportunities and gendered access—make this distinction an important one to explore. The present chapter provides some state-wise and locality-wise (rural–urban) patterns of employment to provide a context to our study.

In the first section on caste, we briefly discuss its main characteristics, especially regarding occupational continuities and the evolving association. We follow this with a detailed discussion on reservation policies of the Indian State and their expected impact on social mobility. Chapter 5 provides a more detailed look at the debates on caste and occupational mobility.

As this book places an emphasis on women's mobility patterns, in the section titled 'Gender: Women's Mobility', we discuss the gender aspect of employment along with the restrictions placed on women's economic participation due to caste or class pressures. We then discuss the trends in employment participation of women and men overtime and changes in the occupational structure as a result of industrialization and liberalization and its implications for a mobility analysis.

In the final section on 'Regional and Rural–Urban Variation', while reviewing regional variation across India, we discuss the importance of utilizing a rural–urban perspective for the study of social mobility in India.

We end this chapter with a summary of the ways in which the three aspects of caste, gender, and locality relate to employment and the central theme of mobility and lay out the various chapters in which the consequences of these factors on mobility will be discussed.

Caste

Caste is perhaps one of the most widely discussed forms of stratification in India. Its persistence and flexibility, given the debates on the unchanging influence of caste on the one hand, and on the reduction of its role and ultimate death on the other (Srinivas 2003) highlight its adaptive nature (Fuller 1996). In the following discussion on caste, and some of its widely accepted distinguishing characteristics,[2] we discuss in some detail the idea of caste as a system of closed stratification, and follow this with an alternative view of a more fluid system.[3] The Indian government's policy of reservation aimed at the most disadvantaged communities is discussed as this is crucial to contextualize the social mobility of various groups, especially the SCs, STs, and OBCs. In the chapter on caste and class mobility (Chapter 5), we extend this discussion and analyse the changing nature of caste and hereditary occupations. We also extend the discussion in the empirical chapters to include religious groups such as Muslims and Other Minorities. An analysis of this evolving nature of caste will help shed light on the different patterns of class mobility and how these patterns might vary for women and men. The aim of this section is to describe the context and reserve the discussion on the patterns and consequences for social mobility for Chapter 5.

The Caste System

The term 'caste' is derived from a Portuguese term 'casta' meaning breed or race (Jodhka 2012). According to Béteille (1965), a caste is 'a small and named group of persons characterized by endogamy, hereditary membership and a specific style of life which sometimes includes the pursuit by tradition of a particular occupation and is usually associated with a more or less distinct ritual status in a hierarchical system, based on concepts of purity and pollution'

[2] Gist (1954) provides a summary of caste and its various dimensions, particularly caste and marriage and caste and occupations in South India; see also Davis (1949) for a discussion of the characteristics of the caste system. For more recent literature see Fuller (1996), Béteille (1996a), Srinivas (1996b), and Jodhka (2012).

[3] These studies span a wide time spectrum, and show that across time some amount of fluidity in the caste system was always accepted (Fuller 1996). In Chapter 5 we discuss briefly these changes in more recent times, particularly where the relationship between caste and occupation is concerned.

(p. 46). This definition highlights some of the characteristics of caste (Béteille 1969; Kolenda 1986; Jodhka 2012): its hereditary nature, the pursuit of traditional occupations, hierarchical rank, endogamy, and the practice of pollution rites.[4]

According to some scholars' reading of the *Manusmriti*, four varnas[5] make up the Hindu system of caste; these are the Brahmins (primarily priests, doctors, and so on); Kshatriyas (warriors); Vaishyas (businessmen), and Shudras (lowest caste, mainly artisans and manual labourers). The 'untouchables' were those who lay outside this caste system and formed, according to some, a fifth category (see Kumar 2010 for a critique of this). They could not perform ritual activities, as they were considered ritually impure ('polluted'), and any interaction with a higher caste was believed to lead to the latter being 'polluted' by the former.[6] This has been

---

[4] But these characteristics need not have a universal meaning for all castes, or indeed in all parts of the country. For example, Kapadia (1991) challenges the claim that 'purity and pollution are the overriding concerns of all Hindus and that they are the "encompassing" ideology of all the castes' (p. 9), a claim made by Dumont in *Homo Hierarchicus*. Deliege seems to agree with Kapadia as he states that 'caste status is not uniformly understood in terms of relative ritual purity' (in Fuller 1996). Fuller summarizing the results of Deliege's work, says that for the Pallars (a former 'untouchable' caste), 'the defining feature of the Pallars former untouchability was their obligation to do "slave work", thus servitude rather than ritual pollution, was crucial to their status and identity' (Fuller 1996: 14).

Similarly, according to Sheth 'the reality of castes cannot be understood or explored merely with reference to the principle of hierarchy. In reality, castes operate horizontally, producing and reproducing divisions and repulsions, differences and separations vis-à-vis each other and at different orders of grouping. They cannot be viewed as units of any single hierarchy' (Sheth 1991: 333; Gupta 1991). Basile and Harriss-White (2000: 14) in their study of Arni village find that there need not be one but 'several hierarchies based on religion' coexisting.

[5] While Varnas 'are not actual groups. They form an ideological scheme' to classify people (Zwart 2000). However, since jati is the 'operative term' for caste (Deshpande 2002) we use it in this volume to refer to sub-castes.

[6] In some extreme cases even the sighting of an 'untouchable' was believed to lead to impurity. The practice of untouchability has been constitutionally illegal since 1950.

the formal theoretical division of caste, which also extends beyond Hinduism in India and leads to a hierarchy of pollution and ritual status in other religions as well.[7]

In everyday life, the division of caste is neither so clear-cut nor restricted to these five categories; each varna is further divided into jatis. Literally thousands of jatis can exist for each varna, and these jatis too can be ranked by ritual purity at least theoretically. In practice, however, many of these jatis are effectively considered to be at the same level, for the purpose of social interaction and so on, depending on the particular function they perform, the particular setting, and region.[8] Srinivas discusses how the position in the rank order of jatis was not rigid, and gives the example of Brahmins who were in some regions considered 'untouchable', for example, for performing funeral rites (Parry [1980] in his study on Benaras also makes this point). Srinivas (2003: 2) states that 'the fact that the rank order of a jati in the local hierarchy is frequently a matter of doubt and ambiguity is, ..., evidence of the dynamism of the caste system at the macro or all-India level' (see also Raheja [1988] for her study on the Gujjars and a non-Brahmin cantered hierarchy).

Flexibility of Caste

Castes have been considered by some scholars to be a closed stratification system where no mobility is possible. Scholars have focussed on the individual or the group as the unit of mobility. For some researchers like Marnane (1967), individual mobility within the caste system is possible. While others, in particular Mandelbaum (1970) drawing on Srinivas (1966), have concluded that

> individual mobility, by itself, is limited and ephemeral. It is limited because even though a man may become wealthy and personally powerful in his locality, his neighbours of higher rank still deal with him

[7] Dumont ([1966] 1970) and various contributions in Srinivas (1996b) detail the prevalence of caste in other religions.

[8] Mandelbaum (1970) explores the concept of varna, jati, and jati-clusters, as well as kinship relations within jatis in the first volume of his book. In the second volume he moves to the broader study of the village and region, in which he also analyses jati mobility.

according to the ritual attribution of his *Jati*. It is ephemeral because members of a rising family must find brides and grooms for their children from comparably eminent families. Unless other families of their *Jati* have risen in similar proportion, the status gains of one family may fade away after a generation. Hence mobility in rank must be collective if it is to be fruitful and durable. (Mandelbaum 1970: 428)

In this section we draw on Vaid (2014) who has provided a discussion on this theme. As discussed by her, Dumont ([1966] 1970) believed that caste is a system where only the physically and numerically dominant can be mobile, that is, where 'those with wealth and political power can use these resources to move up in terms of status en masse'. However, others have believed that caste is a system where a 'certain amount of fluidity' is possible for most people (Vaid 2014: 395; see also for a discussion Zwart 2000; Fuller 1996; Jodhka 1997; Srinivas 1966, 1987; Béteille 1965, 1996a; Sivaram 1990; Driver 1962; Davis 1949; Ghurye 1932).

As Vaid (2014: 394) discusses, according to Srinivas (1996b) the 'descriptive view of the caste system of a very small region at one point in time leads to the misinterpretation of caste as a hierarchy of immobile groups'. But this immobility of groups is not proven, as can be seen through the process of what he terms Sanskritization. Srinivas put forth this idea of Sanskritization in 'light of the movement that he saw occurring between different ritual positions' (Vaid 2014: 396), that is, a process of 'cultural mobility' (Singh 1994) occurred when lower castes would 'take on the beliefs, rituals, and practices of a higher caste' for reasons of, for example, 'economic and status advancement' (see Srinivas 1966, 1987, and 1996a; Charsley 1998). For example, 'giving up alcohol or turning to vegetarianism considered to be purviews of the higher castes'; were often a part of the process (Vaid 2014: 396).[9]

---

[9] A key outcome of the process of Sanskritization is that it alters the lifestyle of those who have *arrived*, and in particular, it has *radical* effects on the lives of women (Srinivas 1996). This influence of Sanskritization on women's lives will be discussed in more detail in the section 'Gender: Women's Mobility'.

While not explicitly acknowledging its roots, Sanskritization draws on the concept of imitation. There is a suggestion that the notion of imitation, as Charsley points out, begins from the work of French philosopher Gabriel Tarde (1895). From Tarde, Charsley traces the concept of imitation as being picked up by the anthropologist W.H.R. Rivers, who explored, among other things, the introduction of Christianity in the Torres Straits area. Rivers then influenced his student Ghurye, who, in turn, influenced his student Srinivas.

Jodhka, however, has argued that 'attempts to claim a higher ritual status through what Srinivas called Sanskritisation was not a simple process. It could not be achieved only through a ritual and life-style imitation and had to be also negotiated with the local power structure' (1997: 35).[10] Jodhka quotes Dube who gives two reasons why the higher castes or jatis would attempt to stall this process of upward mobility of the lower castes. 'In the first place, such mobility had the potential of threatening its own ambition if not position. Second, it could result in a chain reaction which could then lead to suspension of the flow and services and goods from dependent castes' (Dube 1955: 175–6 quoted by Jodhka 1997: 35). Deliege (2002) mentions how socially upwardly mobile Dalits meet opposition today not due to their traditional status but their 'social ascension'. Furthermore, it is not the Brahmins that oppose their ascent (as they are not 'directly threatened' by it), but it is the castes that are 'structurally close' to them that oppose their upward mobility (p. 2).

Furthermore, according to Jayaram, castes that are Sanskritized 'wish to gain public endorsement' (Vaid 2014: 396), which is a 'slow and tenuous process, and is not likely to be reinforced if the caste concerned does not simultaneously improve its economic status and political clout' (Jayaram, 1996: 79). Hence, mere imitation without a simultaneous change in the economic position would not result in successful upward caste mobility.

[10] According to Karanth (1996), emulation might also be seen as defiance, as these lower castes were formerly strictly forbidden from emulating the higher castes. See Dirks (2001) for other examples of how the lower castes attempt to shed their low status.

This discussion seems to suggest as discussed elsewhere (Vaid 2014: 396) that the process of Sanskritization is not occurring in isolation, and is closely linked to a 'caste's interaction within the political and economic spheres'. In addition, the process of Sanskritization for many castes was 'not only an attempt to claim higher status but also a demonstration of the new economic position of a lower caste household' (Karanth 1996: 94; see also Panini 2001).[11]

In more recent decades, particularly since the introduction of preferential policies by the Indian State for deprived castes, caste identity has been observed to be flexible. Caste is seen to play a 'different role in the political and the private' sphere. 'For example, striving for a higher ritual status in the private 'religious' sphere has been accompanied by the contradictory process of castes claiming a lower status with regard to the State's preferential policies' (Vaid 2014: 405; Karanth 1996; Jayaram 1996; Béteille 1981 and 1992).[12] In other words, as Vaid discusses, certain castes claim 'backward' status in order to benefit from the State's positive discrimination policies (Harriss-White 2003; see the section titled 'Reservation Debates' later in this chapter), that is, with regard to scarce resources like jobs (Karanth 1996: 95). But, in the religious or social sphere a higher status is coveted (Jayaram 1996: 80).[13]

[11] Modernization (or Westernization as Srinivas prefers this to Modernization; for more see Singh [1994]) is another phenomenon believed to be occurring simultaneously with Sanskritization. For Srinivas (1962), Westernization occurs as a result of 'changes brought about in Indian society and culture as a result of over 150 years of British rule, the term subsuming changes occurring at different levels ... in technology, institutions, ideology and values' (1962: 42). Where, Sanskritization is believed to be occurring within the framework of caste, Westernization involves mobility outside the caste system (see Srinivas 1962: 9). According to Jayaram 'Modernisation has reduced the tempo of Sanskritisation and somewhat muted its significance' (Jayaram 1996: 80).

[12] These reservation policies are discussed in the next section titled 'Reservation Debates'.

[13] For more on these 'situation-specific' decisions made by individuals see Karanth (1996); and his use of Srinivas' concept of 'dual culture'; for a study of individuals using false caste certificates to claim lower caste status for job and educational reservations see Gatade (2005); see Kulkarni (1991) for a discussion on the STs and Census enumeration problems.

Fuller and Kapadia have also highlighted this adaptive and evolving nature of caste, as discussed by Vaid (2014: 404), with 'particular reference to the domestic versus public domain, with caste taking on different roles in different spheres. In the private "domestic domain" caste continues to follow the rules of pollution, whereas in the public domain certain higher castes have adapted to the changes occurring and are now not averse to working and interacting with members of lower castes'.[14] The role of castes as interest groups in the political arena 'has also been a subject of many debates and is another indicator of the adaptive nature of caste' Vaid (2014: 404). Srinivas hence suggests that 'for purposes of sociological analysis a distinction has to be made between caste at the political level and caste at the social and ritual level' (1962: 5).[15]

In a review of Shah and Desai's (1988) book Sheth summarizes this evolving nature of caste by highlighting their theoretical argument regarding 'division' rather than 'hierarchy' as the salient principle of caste. He particularly emphasizes the changing role of wealth and education and the evolving nature of caste and goes on to say that:

> In the allocation of status, greater salience is now being accorded to the achieved and inherited wealth of individuals and to the political power of groups, rather than to inherited ritual privileges and dis-privileges. Such criteria of status as education, wealth, power and urban residence, have acquired a degree of legitimacy and prominence which they did not have in the past. In the process the caste system is fast losing its basic character as a ritual-occupational hierarchy governed by the idea of purity and pollution. In its place a different system of stratification is emerging. In this emerging system, units of the caste system are coalescing into new formations and alignments, informed more and more by commonality of material interest and its consciousness and less and less by considerations of the traditional ritual hierarchy.(1991: 334)

[14] Kapadia in her village study showed how Brahmins only adapted to the changes in the public arena, whereas pollution rules were strictly followed by them at home (see also Mayer 1996).

[15] For more on party politics, political participation, and caste among others see Varshney (2000); Jaffrelot (2000); Chandra (2000a and b, 2004); Kothari (1970a and b).

It is important to highlight here an area in which caste and its salience has not declined quite as much as it has in other areas. This is regarding caste marriage. 'One of the key characteristics of the caste system is the closed system of marriage or caste endogamy' (Vaid 2014: 404; see Davis 1941: 380; Jodhka 2014; Ambedkar 1916). In both rural and urban areas inter-caste marriage is still quite rare. As Vaid (2014) mentions, according to Caldwell, Caldwell, Caldwell, and Pieris (1998: 146) even though 'some erosion of arranged marriage has begun ... and an increase has occurred in cross-caste marriage', these marriages still tend to be between 'castes of a similar hierarchical level'. As the prevalence of caste endogamy might lead to a similarity between women's marital mobility and men's class mobility patterns, this aspect will be briefly explored in Appendix B of this book.

This discussion simply touches on the vast literature in this area and highlights the evolution of castes and the caste system over time. While some of its characteristics (such as practicing 'pollution') have all but disappeared from the social sphere (see also Mayer 1996), others (such as its role in the political arena) have led to caste becoming a part of the 'political language' of the day (see the discussion on Dumont and 'substantialisation' in Fuller 1996; see also Parry 1999). All in all, while caste may have evolved over time, it seems to have been 'quite resilient as an institution and has not disappeared altogether' (Vaid 2014: 405).

Reservation Debates[16,17]

The Constitutional Provisions for reservations, understood as a package of protective, preferential and developmental practices, are intended to create conditions for the social advancement of historically disadvantaged groups, their integration into mainstream

[16] In this book, we use the term 'reservation' instead of 'affirmative action', or 'compensatory discrimination' policies (Galanter 1984: 2), to keep up with the common language of the debate surrounding this issue in India.

[17] Galanter (1984) provides a comprehensive account of the discussion of reservation policies in India, the judicial view surrounding the selection of the beneficiaries, as well as the establishment of the policies.

society, and participation in its opportunity structure on equal terms with the advanced groups. (Radhakrishnan 1996: 203)

The historical division of Indian society into various jatis, coupled with the practice of untouchability, and the geographic isolation of certain communities has meant that particular communities have lagged behind others in terms of political participation, educational and occupational attainment, and with regard to opportunities for social mobility. After much debate (see Dirks 2001; Galanter 1984; McMillan 2005 among others) the makers of the Indian Constitution, in 1950, provided for reservation for the most deprived of these groups: the SCs (ex-'untouchables') and the STs (isolated tribal communities).[18] In the early 1990s, amid violent protest these reservations were extended by a Constitutional Amendment to the OBCs, a group believed to be relatively less 'socially and educationally' deprived when compared to the SCs and the STs, but, nonetheless, disadvantaged when compared to the 'forward' or high caste.[19] Reservation proposals right from when they were initiated pre-independence have met with protests and violent outbreaks. The controversial aspect of these reservation proposals was made shockingly apparent after the tabling of the provisions of the Mandal Commission Report in the early 1990s (see assorted articles in Srinivas 1996b), and again, more recently after the government's bid to increase reservation (see debates in Seminar [1990, 2005]; and discussions in *The Times of India* [2006, Caste cauldron Mandal II] and *Hindustan Times* [2006 Mandal 2 Muddle] to name a few).

[18] Reservation policies for certain backward groups were introduced before Independence in a few southern states like Mysore in the 1920s (See Dirks 2001: 282). In addition, in 1935 reservations were made for the 'depressed' classes in provincial legislatures. And '[t]he scheduled castes were allowed 8.5 per cent reservation in central services and other facilities for the first time in the history of India in 1942' (Das 2000: 3833). For a historical view of electoral reservation in India see McMillan (2005: especially ch. 1).

[19] These disadvantaged groups of SCs, STs, and the OBCs have also been collectively called the 'depressed' or 'backward' classes (see Chitnis 1997). In this book we use the terminology of 'high' caste to mainly separate the non-reserved category from the reserved categories.

As Chitnis (1997: 91) states 'caste riots in the issue of reservations have grown to be a common phenomenon of Indian life since the mid-seventies' (see also Yagnik 1981). More recently, groups that are not considered 'backward' socially or economically have begun to demand OBC status; for example, the Patels and Gujjars and the demand for reservation which continues.

It was believed that reservation policies would help in the upward social mobility of the 'depressed' sections of Indian society. In light of the recent continuing debate surrounding the extension of these reservations, this issue has gained importance, especially with regard to how existing reservations might have benefited these communities. Due to the vastness of the reservation debates, we discuss the major groups eligible for these policies and highlight some of the issues surrounding reservations, especially in light of their relevance to social mobility opportunities.[20]

Scheduled Castes

Scheduled Caste is an 'official euphemism' for the ex-'untouchables'[21] (Galanter 1984: 122). They have also, at various points in their history, been called Harijans or Dalits.[22] According

---

[20] See Galanter (1984: especially Chapters 5–8) in which he discusses the Constitutional Articles and various provisions made for the SCs, STs, and OBCs. According to Galanter the Constitution does 'prescribe an agency and a method for designating' the SCs and STs, but not in the case of the OBCs (1984: 121; see also footnote 6). This lack of a clear definition, especially of the OBCs, has had consequences that are being felt to this day, as we will see in the following section.

[21] Article 17 of the Indian Constitution abolishes the practice of untouchability.

[22] 'Harijan' (meaning 'children of God') was Gandhi's term to denote the former 'untouchable' castes, but this term was rejected by these groups because it was deemed to be patronizing or denigrating. They instead prefer the use of the term 'Dalit'. According to Pande '... the term "Dalit" (literally, "crushed", "downtrodden" or "oppressed"), widely used as a term of description of those at the very bottom of the social, cultural, economic heap, is also now used as a term of militant self-assertion on the part of many of those so oppressed' (2006: 1779).

to Galanter the selection of SCs 'has proceeded primarily on the basis of "untouchability"—measured by the incidence of social disabilities 'but, this criterion has been combined in varying degrees with economic, occupational, educational, and residential and religious tests' (Galanter 1984: 134). These ex-'untouchable' groups were included under a Constitutional 'schedule' or list in 1936 by the British government. After Independence a Presidential Scheduled Caste Order of 1950 used the same list with only two changes: four Sikh castes were added to the schedule, as were lower castes from areas that had not been included in the 1936 list. The next revision to this list was made in 1956 with the inclusion of all Sikh 'untouchables' (Galanter 1984: 132; Chitnis 1997: 103). In 1990 converts to Buddhism from the 'untouchables' were also included in the list (Das 2000: 3833).

As of the last Census (2011) SCs account for 16.63 per cent of the Indian population. The highest concentration of SCs is in the states of Punjab, Himachal Pradesh, and West Bengal, whereas Nagaland and the islands of Lakshadweep and Andaman and Nicobar have no SCs.

For these SCs, as discussed by Galanter, seats have been reserved in legislative bodies (in the lower houses of Parliament (Lok Sabha) and state legislatures (Vidhan Sabha) but not in the Upper House (Rajya Sabha) proportional to their population in each state;[23] they also have 15 per cent reservation of places in government-funded institutions of higher education (especially government run technical and medical colleges); and in all government employment posts 'recruited directly on an all-India basis by open competitive examination' (Galanter 1984: 86; see also Chapter 3). In addition to

---

[23] 'Unlike the general authorisation of special treatment and the provision of unreserved posts in government service, the reserved seats in the legislature are subject to a constitutional time limit' (Galanter 1984: 46). The initial time limit for these reservations was for ten years till 1960, which has over the years then extended according to Constitutional Amendment Acts. Any demands to de-schedule the groups that have advanced and are no longer in need for reservations has been met with resistance (Chitnis 1997: 92–3; Dirks 2001: 280) and no such de-scheduling has taken place.

reservations, various other concessions (such as age waiver, reduction in minimum qualifying grades, and so on) are also made for the recruitment of these SCs (Galanter 1984: 87).

Scheduled Tribes

Scheduled Tribes, sometimes referred to as 'Adivasis', which comes from the Sanskrit meaning 'original inhabitants' (Bhengra, Bijoy and Luithui 1998), are the tribal groups that receive reservation due to their historical geographical and cultural exclusion.[24] According to the 2011 Census they make up 8.63 per cent of the Indian population. Defining the term 'tribe' itself has been problematic. Some (Ghurye, in Gupta 1991) have referred to them as 'backward Hindus', while others (Xaxa 2003 provides a detailed review) have attempted an identification of characteristics that would constitute tribes especially with regard to Constitutional provisions.

According to Bhengra, Bijoy, and Luithui '[e]xcept in the North-East, they are not evenly distributed throughout India but are essentially found in pockets across the country—mainly the forested, hilly and mountainous areas—in approximately 20 per cent of India's geographical area .... As a percentage of regional population, their concentration is highest in the North-Eastern region (Arunachal Pradesh, Assam, Manipur, Meghalaya, Mizoram, Nagaland and Tripura) and lowest in the Southern region (comprising Karnataka, Kerala and Tamil Nadu)' (1998: 5). Certain states and Union Territories like Delhi, Punjab, Haryana, Chandigarh, and Pondicherry have no tribal populations (Ministry of Tribal Affairs 2004–5 annual report).

On similar lines to the SCs, STs too receive the same provisions of reservations in the legislature, government employment, and government-funded educational institutions. The number of seats reserved for the STs is set at 7.5 per cent.[25]

---

[24] According to the annual report (2004–5) from the Ministry of Tribal Affairs, Government of India, the Human Development Indices are lower for the STs as compared to the rest of the population, as they seem to suffer from both 'geographical and cultural exclusion'.

[25] For more on the various provisions made for the Scheduled Tribes including educational and occupational provisions, land reform, protection

The total combined reservation of 22.5 per cent of seats for the SCs and STs does not preclude them from applying to the *general* or *open* unreserved seats.

Other Backward Classes[26]

The Other Backward Classes (OBCs) are a more heterogeneous category than the SCs or STs; this list contains some non-Hindus, including tribal groups not included in the ST list, as well as SC converts to non-Hindu religions (Galanter 1986). The OBCs are, to an extent, made up of Shudras or the lowest caste groups that are marginally higher in the 'traditional' hierarchy than the 'untouchable' castes, but are socially, educationally, and economically deprived communities.

As their name suggests, OBCs are not strictly castes but are constituted of the 'socially and educationally backward classes of citizens' (as mentioned in Article 15 of the Constitution of India). Thus, while the enumeration of communities that were considered eligible to be included under the SC and ST list was relatively clear-cut, this was not the case where establishing a list of the OBCs was concerned (Sheth 1997: 231; Shah 1996: 175).[27] The definition of the OBCs has thus been fraught with many problems, a major one of which was the use of *castes* rather than *classes* as a defining criterion. This issue according to Dirks (2001: 277) was debated as early as the 1930s when J. H. Hutton, the Census commissioner, attempted to define untouchability using various criteria ranging from 'pollution' to 'poverty'. According to Zwart (2000: 231) the two Backward Classes Commissions of India did

---

of tribal art and so on: see the National Commission for Scheduled Tribes Report available at https://www.tribal.nic.in/DivisionsFiles/NCST-RM/NCST/18SplNCSTReport(mainReport).pdf (accessed 3rd October 2017)

[26] For a Central list of the OBCs, see http://ncbc.nic.in/User_Panel/CentralListStateView.aspx (accessed 3 October 2017).

[27] According to Galanter (1984: 135) the SCs 'have been chosen ... on the ground of their low social and ritual status in the traditional social hierarchy'; a criterion that the courts have maintained should not be used as the sole criterion for the demarcation of the OBCs.

not 'begin with caste as the criterion of selection' (p. 241), but due to various reasons (cf. 241–2) in their final reports they used caste as one of the basic criterion of backwardness.[28]

Under Article 340 of the Constitution, the government has set up two Backward Classes Commissions in order to compile a list of all the OBCs across the country. These Commissions were also empowered to suggest measures for uplifting these sections of society. The first of these Commissions was the Kalelkar Commission (report published in 1955) and the second was the Mandal Commission (report published in 1980).[29] The Kalelkar Commission listed 2,399 communities as Backward. The report of this commission was not unanimous and its recommendations were rejected by the government at that time. Even the Chairman of the Commission, Kaka Kalelkar withdrew his support from the Report, due 'especially [to] its acceptance of caste as the basis of backwardness and [its] recommendations for reservation in public services' (Radhakrishnan 1996: 205–6).

Over two decades later the Mandal Commission or the Second Backward Classes Commission was established by the ruling Janata Party in 1979 under Morarji Desai. The Mandal Commission identified 3,743 communities as belonging to the OBCs (a much higher figure than the Kalelkar Commission). The findings of this report were shelved for a decade, till the V.P. Singh government, in the early 1990s, decided to implement the recommendations of the report to reserve 27 per cent of the seats for the OBCs (bringing the total reserved seats for SCs, STs, and OBCs in the country to just under the Supreme Court stipulated 50 per cent). This was widely believed to be a political ploy and was followed by widespread protest by the upper castes.

[28] For more on whether caste or class was meant to be the criteria for the demarcation of the backward classes, see Galanter (1984) who discusses the legislative debates of the time, as well as recommendations by various governments (see especially Chapter 7). Das also lists various cases in the High and Supreme Court dealing with whether caste should be the sole criterion for reservation or some form of economic backwardness should be included (see Das 2000: 3834).

[29] For a review of these two commissions see Radhakrishnan (1996) and Zwart (2000).

Radhakrishnan, in his critique of the Mandal Commission Report, states that it

> does not contain any substantive data on the socio-economic, educational and occupational conditions of the different castes/communities, measured in terms of educational attainments, admissions to professional courses, employment in state and central services, and educational, economic and occupational background of parents. From these data alone could the Commission have made an overall assessment of castes and communities as advanced or so backward as to be brought under the Constitutional provisions. (1996: 207; see Bhalla and Jain [2006] and Shah [1996: 189] for further critiques of this Report)[30]

As no Indian Census between 1931 and 2011 had collected information on caste (other than information on the SCs and STs) there are no figures for the proportion of the OBC population (the 2011 caste census data has not been released). The Mandal Commission set the OBC population at 52 per cent of the Indian population (among which the Hindu OBCs were enumerated at just under 44 per cent). This figure, as mentioned, has been much disputed especially by other national surveys. According to the National Sample Survey (NSS 2006) and National Family and Health Survey (NFHS 2000) the figure for the OBCs, including Muslim OBCs, is somewhere between 32 per cent (NFHS) and 41 per cent (NSS). This problem with the 'over' enumeration of the OBCs is important as reservations are meant to be made on the basis of population size.

Whether the old reservation policies have indeed met their aims and should hence be extended to the OBCs, is still being questioned. There has been much work that shows that despite the State's positive discrimination policies, not all members of these lower castes have benefited equally. The *forward* sections, also called the *Creamy Layer*,[31] of these 'backward' castes are believed to have gained from these policies, while the most

---

[30] Refer to Radhakrishnan (1996) for further critiques of the methodology, the data collected and the conclusions of this Commission.

[31] The term 'creamy layer' refers to the more advantaged position that a small minority of the caste has vis-à-vis the most disadvantaged sections of the same castes (see Chaudhury 2004).

deprived sections remain so (see Chitnis 1997; Dushkin 1979).[32]
McMillan's (2005) analysis

> supports studies which have shown that the quotas for employment
> of Scheduled Castes and Scheduled Tribes in all sectors of govern-
> ment are still far from being achieved. Scheduled Castes are over-
> represented in the lowest classes of government employment, par-
> ticularly in jobs as "sweepers", whereas the Scheduled Tribes are
> under-represented in all levels of government employment .... The
> ability of Scheduled Caste and Scheduled Tribes to attain the higher
> levels of the government sector are restricted to a tiny minority
> (2005: 315).[33]

This has been a brief history of caste and reservation policies in
India.[34] In this book these three constitutionally recognized major
caste/community groupings (SCs, STs, and OBCs) will be studied
to analyse the mobility patterns of these groups as well as to see
if they are indeed disadvantaged as compared to the upper castes
as well as Muslim and other religious minority groups with regard
to mobility opportunities. As discussed in Chapter 5, a division

---

[32] See Karanth (1996) where he discusses how despite these reservation
policies, the ex-'untouchable' castes are still dependent economically
on the dominant castes. See also Mandelsohn and Viczny (1998). But,
Weisskopf (2004) with reference to reservation of SCs and STs in educational
institutions believes that even though these preferential policies tend to
benefit a creamy layer of the SCs and STs, this does not imply a failure of
the policies as they do increase the access of these deprived communities
to education and elite occupations (see also Weisskopf (2006)). For more on
this creamy layer see Galanter (1984); Sivaramayya (1996).

[33] For discussions on the upward mobility of lower castes and their
access to the middle class as well as the continued dominance of the upper
castes in the middle class see Sheth (1999).

[34] For more on the issue of caste and reservations as well as reservation
and politicization of caste see debates in India Today (1991); Radhakrishnan
(1996); Dirks (2001). For discussions on reservations, especially with a
focus on various backward classes commissions, see Radhakrishnan (1990)
and Dirks (2001). For discussions on the consequences of reservations see
Weiner, Katzenstein, and Rao (1981) and Weiner (1989).

of caste/community groups will be used in as much detail as is possible in the empirical analysis to study patterns of mobility (including the separation of the creamy from the non-creamy layer). While a detailed examination of jatis is not possible at this stage due to data limitations, these major categories do capture the major constitutional divisions recognized by the Indian government for its reservation policies (see also Gist 1954; Deshpande 2001: 132).

Gender: Women's Mobility

Stratification research has been criticized for its 'intellectual sexism' (Acker 1998) relegating women to subsidiary roles within the family and undervaluing women's labour. Some of the criticisms of the more male-centric approach in social mobility research stem from the emphasis on the *family* as the unit of stratification analysis with the class position of all the members of the family deriving from the occupational status of the head of the household, often a male member (Acker 1998; Crompton and Mann 1986; Szelenyi 2001). Social mobility research in India too has mostly ignored women's labour force participation and focused on patterns of male mobility (for example, Kumar, Heath, and Heath 2002a).

Not only is it important to study the experience of women, it is especially important to study women's mobility *alongside* men's mobility, given the vast gender inequalities in India as well as due to the observation that women experience social and economic changes and modernization in ways distinct from men (discussed further; see also Momsen 1991). In this context, we study whether these gender differences also translate into greater inequality of opportunity in terms of mobility chances for women. We discuss the influence of modernization, industrialization, and liberalization of the economy on both women and men. In this respect, we highlight the changes in education and employment participation which will have implications for mobility opportunities and outcomes.

Women's Social and Economic Status

Research across a wide range of disciplines has covered the position and experiences of women vis-à-vis different aspects of their lives: their employment, health, education, and marriage. The diversity of the country implies equally diverse experiences of women in different parts of the country and from different backgrounds.[35]

Many activists from the nineteenth century onward, referred to as social reformers, fought against the low status accorded to women (Forbes 1996; Devi 1993; Liddle and Joshi 1986). Due to their efforts and the subsequent efforts of the women's movement and post-Independence feminist movements, the Indian Constitution and various amendments have accepted the statutes for the equality of all people, and also include special provisions for the equality in employment for women.[36] While this history is well known, it is important for understanding the theory of modernization and subsequent context of the modern Indian nation-state. While 'in

[35] Devi 1993; Kishwar and Vanita 1996; Srinivas 1996b; Davis 1949, among many highlight this diversity. For a detailed discussion of status of women in India see the Government of India 'Towards Equality' report of the Committee on the Status of Women in India (Guha, Kara, Shyam, Dogra, Mahajan, Dube, Hasan, Sarkar, and Mazumdar 1974), and Devi (1993) for a brief historical look at the status of Indian women; for a look at post-independence India and women's status in the political, economic, and social spheres see Forbes (1996), refer to Liddle and Joshi (1986) for the impact of colonial rule on women, and Srinivas (1996a) for an anthropological look at women in India and the evolution of different aspects of their lives. See also Srivastava (2003) for an empirical summary of indicators of women's status like maternal mortality, employment, and education, and Giele and Smock (1977) for a discussion on factors that influence women's relative status.

[36] The Convention on Elimination of All Forms of Discrimination against Women (CEDAW) (2000) details the most significant constitutional provisions and amendments vis-à-vis equality and the status of women regarding employment and other facets of life. See also Devi (especially endnote 1). See the section on 'Women and Work' from the annual report of the Ministry of Labour (2005–6: especially p. 76: Box 11.1), which has a list of protective legislatures regarding employment of women in India.

the *documents* of the new Indian state the past had been undone, modernity was triumphant, and women were no longer subordinate to men' (Forbes 1996: 224, emphasis mine; see also Srivastava 2003), this is true on paper alone. The myth of 'modernity' is exposed[37] when we observe the discrimination against women which starts before birth and continues through their life in one form or another. The persisting low female to male sexratio is one glaring example. There are also large gender inequalities in inheritance of property, in women's access to healthcare; high maternal mortality rates; inequality in household decision-making; inequality in education, unequal labour force participation, with women clustered in the more precarious, lower paying jobs with few decision-making opportunities. We now briefly discuss the process of marginalization of women by a *modernizing* economy (Kishwar 1996: 38).

Modernization and Women

For the 'champions of modernization', increasing industrialization and technological advancement was believed to lead to an improvement in the lives of both genders. They also believed that women would experience 'economic change in the same way as men' (Forbes 1996: 237), but this has clearly not been the case (Harriss-White 2003; Kapadia 1991; Sharma 1996).

Firstly, it is believed that as the economy modernizes and new technology and industrialization follow, women's status would improve. As most recent research shows, however, the outcome of technological change has not been that clear-cut. There are many examples in the literature of the marginalization of women with technological growth. Taking the post 'green revolution' period after the 1960s as an example, a period in which the government

[37] India is one of the few countries shown to have a very low female to male sex ratio (FMR). According to Agnihotri (2000) 'the larger demographic behaviour reflected in the sex ratios has its origins in gender inequalities that operate at micro and macro level' (p. 89). For more on this adverse sexratio see Drèze and Sen 2002; Kynch and Sen 1983; Visaria 1967, 1971; Dyson 2006.

introduced high yielding varieties of crops with the resultant effect of an increase in mechanization, Parthasarathy and Nirmala (1999), among others, observe that women were often not allowed access to, or use of, agricultural machines such as ploughs (Hirway and Unni 1990; Forbes 1996).[38] The tasks that they had formerly performed manually, like threshing and harvesting, are now performed increasingly by men; women hence lose out on their jobs.[39] Similar findings in terms of industrial labour and the service industry are seen. Hensman (1996) gives an example from the pharmaceutical industry, with the resulting displacement and concentration of women in the lower level jobs an offshoot of the mechanization that has taken place (see contributions in Papola and Sharma [1999]; for discussions on possible employer prejudice against women see Hensman [1996]; Anker and Hein 1985). Marginalization of women in the workforce with mechanization and modernization is not a phenomenon unique to India, but has been observed in almost all developed countries (Varghese 1993).

Secondly, there has been an assumption that with economic progress the social bias against women would diminish, but this has not been the case as is depicted through the worsening trend in the female to male sex ratio (see Agnihotri 2000). Talking about this adverse sexratio Kynch and Sen state that 'indeed with economic and social progress, as the absolute position of both men and women has improved, the relative position of women seems to have fallen behind. If we judge well-being in a poor country like India by capability to live long, women's well-being has fallen vis-à-vis men's, even though absolutely both have increased substantially' (Kynch and Sen 1983: 371).

---

[38] '[O]perating a potters wheel ,... which is a symbol of power and skill, is almost exclusively a male monopoly' (Kishwar 1996: 20).

[39] In a separate but related vein, Kishwar (1996) also shows how the processes like deforestation as well as privatization of previous communal land adversely affect women, as the job of survival and care of the family often rests with women, and women now need to trek larger distances for food and fuel. The brunt of modernization is thus faced most often by women. For an example of how urbanization and industrialization have an adverse effect on women, see the account of the Baoris by Kishwar (pp. 25–6).

Thirdly, prosperity also has a different effect on women than it does on men. With economic development and the increase in newer job opportunities come changes in the economic position of the family. There has been a shared assumption that women would gain from increasing prosperity, but literature shows otherwise. It has been seen that paradoxically in prosperous families, instead of an expected decrease in gender discrimination (with an increasing allocation of resources to girls), there may be an increase in discrimination (Carswell and De Neve 2013).[40] Further, for poorer households, women's labour is necessary for survival. But as one moves up in wealth and prosperity, and survival is no longer an issue, women are withdrawn from work[41] (due to reasons of 'status production' (Agnihotri 2000) and 'reproduction' (Caplan 1985),[42] and women's work outside the house is seen as dispensable.[43] With this withdrawal from labour and decrease of women's contribution to family income, comes the loss of women's autonomy and power to make decisions (Liddle

[40] An example is the adverse sex ratio seen among the prosperous. For more on this paradoxical positive relationship between wealth and women's disadvantage see Heyer 1992; Harriss-White 2003: chapter 5; Drèze and Sen 2002 and Agnihotri 2000; for peasant households see Kishwar 1996. Kynch and Sen (1983) also note that some of India's richest states for example Punjab and Haryana have some of the lowest female to male ratios (see also Miller 1981).

[41] But, 'the economic aspects alone, however, do not explain why it is the women who withdraw from outside work. It is the sexual aspect, the control of women's sexuality for the maintenance of property within the group ...' (Liddle and Joshi 1986: 91). Thus, the cultural aspect then has a material/economic basis.

[42] Women play a significant role in class and status reproduction. Their withdrawal from work not only enhances the status of a family, they also play a powerful role in the 'construction and perpetuation' of the class system, with regard to the labour they provide at home and through the socialization of the next generation (see Caplan [1985] for a study of women's role in class reproduction in India).

[43] As we will see in the discussion on gender and employment, this *withdrawal* of women from *visible* work for *status* reasons has led to an under-enumeration of women in national survey data.

and Joshi 1986). With this decline in autonomy, it is argued, comes further discrimination.[44]

For women, who are economically active and do contribute towards the financial aspect of the family, their position within the family tends to be different, especially with regard to their decision making role.[45] Agnihotri (2000) in his work on the sex ratio patterns in India shows that rather than prosperity itself being the 'crucial variable' in improving the position of women, it is the 'female contribution to prosperity', that is, their contribution to the family income that plays a more significant role (Bhan 2001; Papola and Sharma 1999). As Bhan (2001: 13) states, 'many have argued that the labour participation of women is one of the most important indicators of women's empowerment, access to resources, and decision making ability'. Vaid (2017) looks at women's narratives on the significance of their work for decision-making.

Kapadia (1991: 32) gives an example of this from her village study where she shows that on one hand, women's economic positions differ sharply, as upper caste women are more dependent on men and have no jobs. Whereas, on the other hand, the ex-'untouchable' 'Pallar women are breadwinners who often contribute even more than Pallar men towards the support of their families'. In addition, she adds that 'their economic independence has made Pallar women resolute and enterprising, and this economic independence has led to a corresponding weakening of the upper caste ideology of female subordination'. For Kapadia then '... in the lowest castes the discourses of female subordination lack

---

[44] In addition to this loss of earning power and autonomy in household decision-making, the prevalence and spread of norms such as *dowry* makes the family view women as an even bigger 'burden'. Many see dowry as a 'symptom' of the devaluation of women (Kishwar 1996: 14), but dowry also feeds into their further devaluation. As with increasing dowry demands, parents' begin to view their daughters as an increasing burden—which further increases the discrimination against them and affects adversely their status. See Heyer (1992) for more on the relationship between dowry, prosperity, and female neglect.

[45] According to Mies as well (1980: 292) 'The new economic role of women seems to be a more important cause of the change in the intra-family relationships than the new inheritance rights of women'.

a material foundation in everyday practice' (Kapadia 1991: 32).
Similarly, Kishwar observes that

> unlike the family structure in the peasant land owning castes, among
> the landless poor the family is relatively less restrictive for women.
> One of the key reasons for this is that the landless female agricultural
> labourer, however much she is exploited, is at least recognised as a
> wage earner, as someone who contributes to the upkeep of the fam-
> ily by her earnings. (Kishwar 1996; See also Ramu [1988] for work on
> women as wage earners and their power of negotiation in the family).

As Mary and Lalita (1995: 10) conclude in their study, and which
is applicable here 'the biggest single implication of the analysis
offered here is that it is necessary to pay attention to the specific
circumstances of different women, since caste, communal, class
and other divisions mediate the way in which women suffer from
gender discrimination'.

This review of gender issues has not only discussed gender differences and divergent outcomes of the modernization process, it
has also highlighted the fact that women do not form a homogenous group: their caste, class origins, education, husband's class,
and region all have an important impact on their own economic
participation and quite possibly their class mobility chances too
(see also Raju 1991). This underlines the need to use a gender perspective in analysing mobility.

As one of the main aims of this book is to study how modernization and industrialization might influence mobility chances
and make society more fluid, in the next section, we discuss two
areas where the modernization thesis expects there to be substantial changes. The first is with regard to education and the second
with regard to employment and structural changes in the economy. The first of these is discussed briefly here and then in more
detail in Chapter 6; and, the latter is discussed in more detail here
due to its overall relevance to class mobility patterns, especially as
discussed in Chapter 4.

Gender and Education

The 'modernization theory' purports that increasing economic development will lead to a decline in importance of ascribed characteristics

(that is, caste, class, gender) and an increase in achieved characteristics as the determining factor for attaining a particular class destination. Hence, an expansion of the educational system would lead to consequent changes in attitudes and opportunities available both for women and men. A decline in gender inequality in access to education would then have significant outcomes with regard to employment opportunities, and, in turn, social mobility. Whether this has been the case in India is explored in Chapter 6.

Table 2.1 and Figure 2.1 show the crude literacy figures for India, while Table A2.1.1 in the Appendix displays the *effective* literacy figures for specific age-ranges. Literacy rates in India have increased for both women and men in the last century; but, so has the gender gap in literacy in absolute terms approximately till

Table 2.1 Literacy Percentage 1901 to 2011, Census Figures (Crude Literacy Rates)

Year*	Men % of Total Male Population	Women % of Total Female Population	Literacy Gap (Men–Women) *Percentage Points*	Odds Ratio
1901	9.83	0.60	9.23	18.1:1
1911	10.56	1.05	9.51	11.1:1
1921	12.21	1.81	10.40	7.1:1
1931	15.59	2.93	12.66	6.1:1
1941	24.90	7.30	17.60	4.2:1
1951	24.95	7.93	17.02	3.9:1
1961	34.44	12.95	21.49	3.5:1
1971	39.45	18.69	20.76	2.8:1
1981	46.89	24.82	22.07	3.1:1
1991	52.74	32.17	20.57	2.8:1
2001	63.24	45.15	18.09	2.6:1
2011	71.22	56.99	14.23	2.4:1

Source: Statement 21-Crude Literacy Rate by Sex, p. 103; Provisional population Totals, http://censusindia.gov.in/2011-prov-results/data_files/india/Final_PPT_2011_chapter6.pdf (last accessed in July 2016).
Note: Odds ratios are calculated from official government figures. The 1901-41 figures are for undivided India; 1991 figures exclude the state of Jammu and Kashmir where the Census was not conducted.

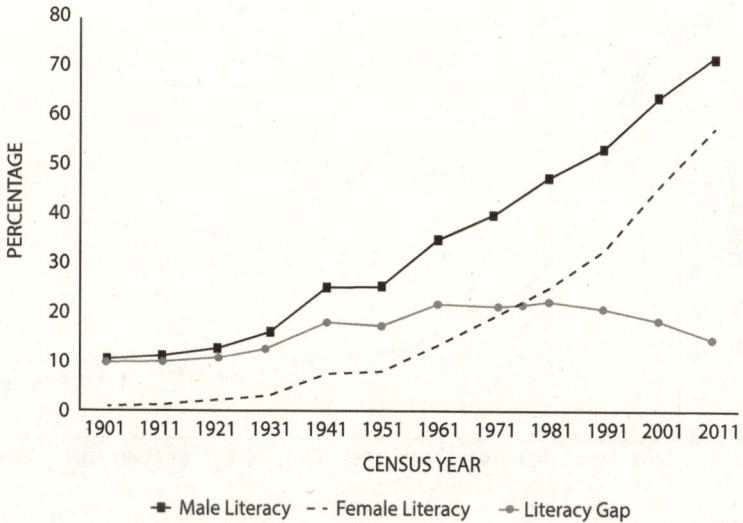

Figure 2.1 Literacy Rates and Literacy Gap, Census 1901–2011

Source: see Table 2.1

1981. The reduction in the literacy gap since 1981 seems to be driven by an increase in women's literacy.

These absolute figures are not sufficient to study how the disparity between women and men or the 'inequality of opportunity' has changed over time as marginal or structural changes like the expansion of the education sector could confound the picture. In order to see the real change minus any marginal changes, that is, to study the relative chances of being literate for women and men one needs to look at the odds ratios. A comparison of the odds ratios shows how the relative chances of literacy have decreased between the two sexes, after allowing for the marginal changes (this can be seen in the last column in Table 2.1).

Figure 2.2 is a graphical description of the odds ratios from Table 2.1. The odds of a man having greater access to education as compared to a woman have clearly declined with a small increase in 1981, indicating a decline in inequality between the two genders; though in 2011, the odds still stand at more than twice for men when compared to women. These figures confirm that since the beginning of the previous century, gender inequality in literacy

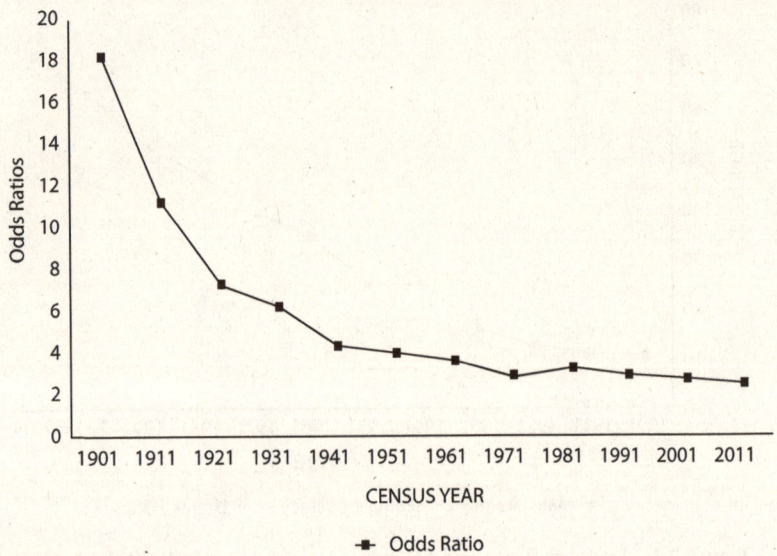

Figure 2.2 Odds Ratios for Men and Women's Literacy, Census 1901–2011
Source: Table 2.1.

has declined, but more importantly, that the relative chances of women and men in terms of literacy have remained more or less stable till the 1980s and began to decline from 1991 though still not equalizing. Hence, despite the rapid expansion of the educational system, the increase in the number of women in higher education, and other government policies, gender inequality in literacy is persisting.

Literacy rates also vary according to caste and religion. In the 1991 Census the combined literacy rate for SCs and STs was 56 per cent as compared to 76 per cent for the other castes (*Education Statistics*, Sub-Table XVIII, DOE website), that is, an odds ratio of 2.5:1. More recent figures from Census 2011 show that for all groups 35 per cent of women, and 19 per cent of men are non-literate; for SCs these figures are 44 per cent and 25 per cent, respectively; and, for STs they are 51 per cent and 31 per cent, respectively. For those with graduate degrees and higher, while the all India average is 6.5 per cent (men 8 per cent and women 5 per cent), for SCs these figures are 3.2 per cent (men 4 per cent and

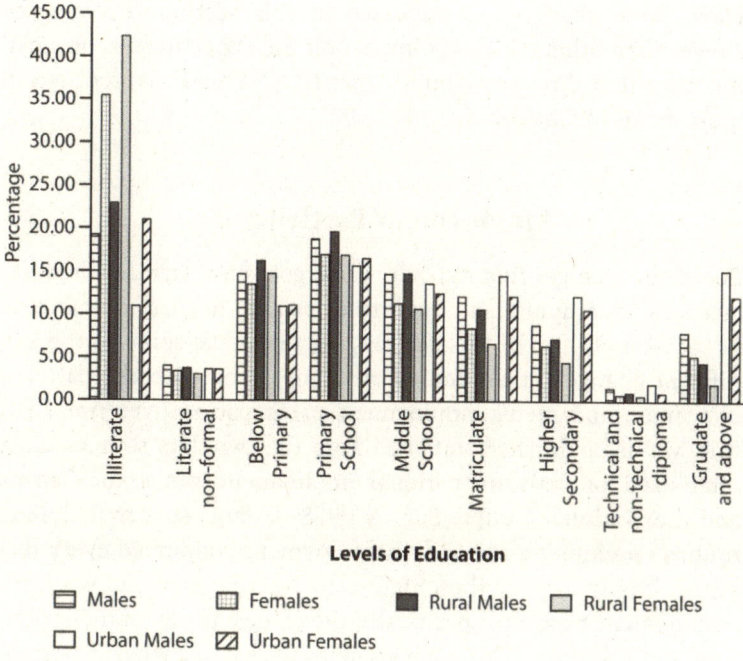

Figure 2.2a Educational Level by Locality and Gender for Age 7+, Census 2011

Source: Available at http://www.censusindia.gov.in/2011census/C-series/C08. html (last accessed on 15 April 2017).

women 2 per cent) and for STs it is 2 per cent (men 2.7 per cent and women 1 per cent). Clear rural–urban differences are found. While SC and ST men and women have more graduates in urban India, as expected, their figures are nearly half of the national average. Muslims are seen to have patterns similar to SCs, who are, in turn, marginally better off than the STs. Hindus were nearly twice the percentage of Muslims in the graduate and above category (tables from author).

A rural-urban dimension is clearly important, as through her analysis of literacy data, Raju (1991) shows that non-SC urban women emerge as a privileged group as compared to the rural men of all categories including non-SC men. She suggests that a distinction needs to be made within women, and research on women cannot ignore social class relations as well (see also Vaid 2004).

Have these changes, as discussed in this section, albeit some
slower than others, had any impact on the opportunities of social
mobility that different groups experience? This is approached in
more detail in Chapter 6.

Employment Participation

Economic changes that a society undergoes have significant repercussions for employment opportunities and, in turn, on patterns
of social mobility. In this section, we underline some of the significant changes in the Indian economy along with the patterns
of women and men's employment participation over time. For
this, we use published statistics from the two data sources most
often used for analysing national employment trends: the Census
and the National Sample Survey (NSS—a large survey including
rounds on employment and unemployment conducted every five
years). Firstly, we use these figures to describe men and women's
employment position, specifically the change in sectoral distribution over the years. This analysis helps to describe what structural
changes have taken place in the Indian economy since independence. Secondly, we outline the economic participation by gender
of the major caste groups which is significant for establishing possible variations in mobility experiences.

Economic Development and Economic Participation

Historically, the Indian economy was, and continues to be, dominated by agriculture where participation in the labour force is concerned. However, agriculture's share in output or gross domestic
product (GDP) has been on a decline, post-green revolution, since
the early 1990s (Dev 2010). The widespread economic reforms and
Structural Adjustment Policies (SAPs) introduced in India in the
early 1990s, often referred to as the *liberalization* period, were an
extension of the reform process set in motion in the 1980s (Nayyar
2006). According to Bhan (2001: 17) 'structural adjustment, by its
very definition, implies an intra-and inter sectoral redistribution
of resources in order to increase the efficiency of the economy and

make it more competitive on a global scale'. These SAPs hence influence how and where goods are produced in addition to a change in 'sectoral break-up of the economy'. But, despite the enthusiasm surrounding the economic reforms and the celebrated high rate of growth of the economy, which continued till 2010 before declining (Sen 2016), its effect on employment generation particularly in the organized sector (Papola 2010) has been minimal. This is because of two reasons. Firstly, most of the economic growth has been in sectors that do not require an extensive labour force but rather are skilled labour intensive industries, like the IT software industry (Harriss-White 2003). Secondly, the decline in the size of the agricultural sector, a major employer in India (Chadha and Sahu 2002; Dev 2010; McNay, Unni, and Cassen 2004) has led to the slowing down of employment generation and an increase in 'casualisation' (Papola 2010), which has been felt the most by women (Bhan 2001). Employment generation has actually slowed down in both rural *and* urban areas, though the impact has been more pronounced in rural India (Chadha and Sahu 2002). Moreover, women have felt the impact of this slowdown more than men, with an increasing marginalization of the female workforce (Chadha and Sahu 2002; Bhan 2001).[46] Some research (contributions in Papola and Sharma [1999]; especially the paper by Parthasarathy and Nirmala [1999]) has argued that 'technological change, in recent years, has not led to the decline in women's employment in aggregate, though it has led to a change in occupational and status structure of women's workforce' (p. 15). According to these authors, due to these changes the opportunities that women now have are restricted to the jobs that require lower skill levels and have worse working conditions. The increase

---

[46] Authors like Mathur (1994) have studied the U-shaped relationship between economic development and female workforce participation. Using district level data he concludes that the 'oft referred to inverse relationship between female work participation and economic development emerges to be true in initial states of development in the rural segment, but not so in the case of the urban segment' (p. 466). But he also shows that the declining work participation in the early stage of development is 'reversed at higher levels of development' both for women and men (p. 498), thus, leading to a U-shaped curve.

in casual labour is higher for women than for men. 'The lack of female mobility between sectors renders them even more vulnerable to policy change. Various factors like socio-cultural barriers, lack of adequate skills, gender bias in hiring etc. may be responsible for this lack of mobility' (Bhan 2001: 18). As Bhan emphasizes, this 'lack of labour mobility' is detrimental to women since they may not be able to access credit resources or, due to social/cultural reasons, may not be able to set up their own enterprises.

Liddle (1988: 7), while comparing women's participation in India to that of women in more developed countries, concludes that rather than there being a majority of women in any particular industry, women in India are concentrated in the least secure employment within most industries. In terms of job segregation, Liddle (1988: 16) mentions that even though in the 'Western' sense there isn't job segregation, that is, no occupation is more than 50 per cent female, there is still job segregation if one looks at occupations in which there are more women than their 'overall share in employment' (see also Anker and Hein 1986). Hence, we are able to observe occupations that have high female clustering such as: school teachers, nurses, sales, clerical work, and so on. These are highlighted by Liddle as being lower-level jobs.

Kundu (1999: 68) agrees that there has been an increase in 'feminization' (though the use of this term is debated among scholars) especially in urban areas, where the informal sector has grown, especially as women accept the lower paying jobs with the worse working conditions that men are no longer willing to perform. In rural areas too a similar structural change is witnessed. Here, a shift from agriculture to non-agricultural employment has led to an increase in work for men, but this has not been the case for women (Chadha 1999). Women in these rural areas seem to take on the low-level seasonal agricultural jobs when men move into non-agricultural employment.

At this point it becomes important to underline the distinction in India between the informal and formal economy, or the unorganized and organized sectors. According to Harriss-White (2003: 4–5) 'the informal economy is the economy not covered by the official data on registered enterprises', and this accounts for 83 per cent of the working population; 92 per cent of women workers and 80 per cent of male workers are in the informal sector.[47] McNay, Unni, and Cassen (2004) stress that unorganized sector workers are characterized by having unstable employment 'contracts', lower income than organized sector workers and hardly any social security benefits (p. 164). In recent years employment growth has been the highest in the informal or unorganized sector (McNay, Unni, and Cassen 2004); and according to the authors 'a process of informalisation of employment has occurred and the unorganised sector is absorbing labour more quickly than it is generating output compared to the organised sector', and hence, they conclude that 'these trends imply an overall deterioration in employment quality during the 1990s' (McNay, Unni, and Cassen 2004: 165).

The organized or formal sector has had two divergent trends in employment generation in the past few decades. On the one hand, the organized *public* sector, with the most secure job contracts, pension benefits, and so on has been contracting its jobs since the 1980s due to reforms introduced by the International Monetary Fund (IMF) and the World Bank.[48] The organized *private* sector, on the other hand, has had larger female employment growth, but this has been restricted to the lower level jobs. Total female employment was growing faster than male employment in the organized sector (at 3.07 per cent per year versus 1.12 per cent for men between 1981–96 according to Srivastava [1999]), but the growth has been concentrated more in the private organized sector rather than in the more 'secure' public organized sector. The overall impact of these trends has been an increase of women in regular waged employment, but this has been primarily in lower

[47] Due to the very nature of the informal sector, figures on the employment participation in this sector are disputed (Harriss-White 2003). See also McNay, Unni, and Cassen (2004: 163) who state that according to the Indian Planning Commission (2002), 92 per cent of the employment in India is in the unorganized sector.

[48] According to Srivastava [2003] (p. 135) the organized public sector has provided more jobs than the private sector. But this is problematic for women in light of the reduction and withdrawal of the public sector in recent decades which is expected to continue (see also Bhan 2001).

level jobs requiring less skilled work.[49] This increase in regular
work has, hence, not always been to the benefit of women, as they
not only receive lower pay than men but are also clustered in the
worst jobs (Kundu 1999: 68; Papola and Sharma 1999: 1). However,
having regular waged work has its benefits in terms of autonomy
of women within the family as seen in our previous discussion
(Kapadia 1991; Mies 1980; Agnihotri 2000; Vaid 2017).

Despite this increase in regular waged work, there has been
some debate on the growth of *casualization* of the workforce, that
is, labourers working as casual labourers with temporary contracts
rather than permanent benefits, since the introduction of the economic reforms (Papola 2010). Casualization implies an inherent
deterioration in the working conditions of the labour force. Not
all studies are in agreement with the growth of casualization. For
example, while McNay, Unni, and Cassen (2004) seem to argue
that growth has not led to increased casualization, Chadha and
Sahu argue otherwise. According to Liddle (1988: 14) 'casual labour
is an area where it is difficult to collect accurate statistics, because
the labourers do not appear regularly at a fixed place, and because
female casual labourers turn into domestic workers on days when
there is no work' (see also Srivastava 2003: 127). National Sample
Survey figures show that casualization had declined for women in
urban areas, but increased in rural areas; whereas it has been on
a rise for men in both rural and urban areas (Visaria 1999). This
declining casualization and increasing regular salaried employment for women, especially in the urban areas (Kundu 1999: 63),
seems to have occurred simultaneously. But according to McNay,
Unni, and Cassen, in spite of a decline in casualization of women
and an increase of regular salaried jobs for them, 'the female workforce continues to have a higher proportion of casual workers and
lower proportion of regular wage workers than the male workforce' (p. 168).

[49] See Gupta (1988) for examples from the labour bureau and other
research that shows that women in the formal sector too are in the least
skilled work. Also see Anker and Hein (1985) where they show that
women are rarely managers and supervisors, mainly due to the traditional
sexual division of labour.

This review covering literature from a broader time period has discussed the impact of liberalization on women and men's employment in India. In the rural sector, a key policy that is expected to have important repercussions where employment generation is concerned is the Mahatma Gandhi National Rural Employment Guarantee Act (MGNREGA) (Basu, Chau, and Kanbur 2010). The Act launched in select districts in 2006 was expanded to all rural districts two years later. Carswell and De Neve (2013) have reported on the positive outcome of this Act for rural women in Tamil Nadu, beyond employment generation in terms of 'wages, independence, dignity' (p. 90). Pankaj and Tankha (2010) have similar findings in their four state study. They find that,

> women workers have gained from the scheme primarily because of the paid employment opportunity, and benefits have been realised through income-consumption effects, intra-household effects, and the enhancement of choice and capability. Women have also gained to some extent in terms of realisation of equal wages under the NREGS, with long-term implications for correcting gender skewness and gender discriminatory wages prevalent in the rural labour market of India. (Pankaj and Tankha 2010: 45)

Hence, labour force participation and the effects of such participation, as influenced by the MGNREGA, is a significant context for the study of social mobility of women and men. We may however not be able to capture the full extent of the impact, or lack thereof, of this policy in our study on mobility since the time lag may not be sufficient.

In the next section, we study patterns of workforce participation using published statistics from the NSS and the Census.

Workforce Participation

Since 1911 the Indian Census has been collecting data on employment status, but due to changes in the definition of what comprises 'work' and 'worker' in each subsequent round of the Census, it is a difficult task to compare these figures over time. See Liddle (1988) and Visaria (1999) for summaries of the changes in the definition of the term 'worker' in each subsequent Census. For the pre-independence period it is also hard to separate rural and urban areas (Visaria 1999: 24).

In addition to these problems, reliable figures on women's employment are hard to find as most official figures have been disputed as under-representing women. For example, both the Census and the NSS interview the head of the household, who due to cultural reasons, usually happens to be a male member, even if he is not the most economically active member of the family. Moreover, in regions where it is considered more 'acceptable' for a woman to be a housewife and not go out to work, the actual employment status of women is often under-reported (Liddle 1988; Srivastava 2003; Mukhopadhyay 1981; Visaria 1967). Also, as a large proportion of the Indian population is engaged in the informal (unregistered) sector, which is especially the case for women, the under-enumeration of the working population is an important issue. Liddle (1988: 9) argues that this is because national survey (NSS and Census) figures are 'androcentric and women's work is subjected to a process of marginalisation because it does not fit into male patterns'. In an agrarian economy like India, both domestic and productive work are very closely related (Bardhan 1986, Liddle 1988) and many women have a dual work role 'producing both economically and for subsistence' (Liddle 1988: 9). But, home-based work and farming on own land are not always included in national figures (see also Srivastava 2003), and hence, women are under-enumerated due to the nature of their work. This is true for more than just the agrarian sector as Liddle goes on to give instances of this from other research, for example, in the garment sector, where women often produce at home, and hence, the Census tends to exclude them and counts this as 'domestic' rather than productive work. These problems of enumeration are discussed with regard to the Census and the NSS in the next section.

Figure 2.3 displays the Worker Population Ratios (WPRs) from 1911–2011 (the accompanying Table A2.1.2 is included in Appendix A2.1). These WPRs can also interchangeably be called the Work Participation Rates (Chadha and Sahu 2002). The WPR is the ratio of the number of workers to the total population for each Census year. In this case the WPR is for both 'main' and 'marginal' workers together as surveys before 1971 did not make this

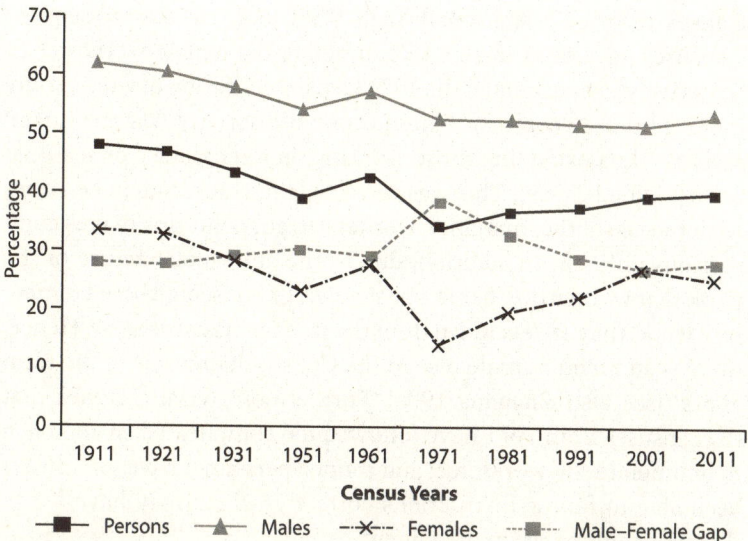

Figure 2.3 Worker Population Ratio (WPR) Women and Men, Census 1911–2011

Source: see Table A2.1.2 in Appendix A2.1.

distinction explicit. According to the Census *main* workers are those employed for a major part of the previous year, whereas *marginal* workers are those that worked at any point in the previous year; this includes women working on a seasonal or temporary basis. If one separates the two (main and marginal workers) then according to McNay, Unni, and Cassen (2004) there has been a decline in 'main workers' and an increase in 'marginal workers' according to the Census figures. We must note, however, that the WPR shown here is the *crude* WPR, as the age composition of the population has not been included (Visaria 1999).

Figure 2.3 displays a lower WPR for both women and men when compared to the early part of the last century. The sharpest decline for women according to these figures seems to have occurred in the 1970s, since when the WPR has been on a rise, levelling off in 2011. The female WPR in 2011 was at 25.5 per cent. The male–female gap (barring 1971) has been roughly around 30 percentage points.

The reason for the sharp decline in the women's WPR between 1961 and 1971 according to Visaria (1999) is not because the 1961

Census reported a spuriously high WPR, but because subsequent Censuses have been unable to enumerate the female workforce as 'effectively'. For example, the 1971 Census definition of worker only included those people for whom economic activity was the 'main' activity, thus excluding those working on a temporary or seasonal basis (Liddle 1988: 9). This was corrected for in subsequent censuses with the use of the 'marginal' worker category. But this makes comparisons difficult. In addition, due to the ambiguous nature of the work that women do, that is, subsistence or household based temporary work, they are excluded from the *main* worker category. Hence, there is an inherent male bias in the Census definitions of the term 'work' (see also Chanana 1996). Furthermore, Visaria argues that the censuses from 1971 have followed too complicated an approach to enumerate the workforce, and trained personnel have not always been able to follow instructions correctly, which may have led to the under enumeration of women.

As Visaria and others (McNay, Unni, and Cassen 2004; Liddle 1988; Jacob 2001) seem to suggest that the census is not perhaps the ideal data source to observe employment rates, and the NSS is considered a better source to compare over time changes (Chadha and Sahu 2002: 2000), we compile figures for WPR arrived at by using the NSS data available for the period 1972–2012. These are displayed in Figure 2.4 (Table A2.1.3 in Appendix A2.1).

Till 2004–5, the NSS data consistently showed higher rates of work participation by women than the Census (however, for the two rounds after that, women's WPR is lower in the NSS than the Census). This has been, it is argued, both due to more adequate training of investigators as well as due to the use of a broader and more gender sensitive definition of work in the NSS. Rather than separating the workers into 'main' and 'marginal' categories like the Census does, the NSS collects information on what it calls 'usual' and 'current' status work. 'Usual status' work is meant to capture the amount of employment of the respondents over the past year, whereas 'current status' work looks at employment over the previous week. Under these two approaches usual status is considered a better means for capturing the workforce participation of women rather than the current status approach due to the seasonal and temporary nature of women's work (Chadha and Sahu 2002; Seal 1981).

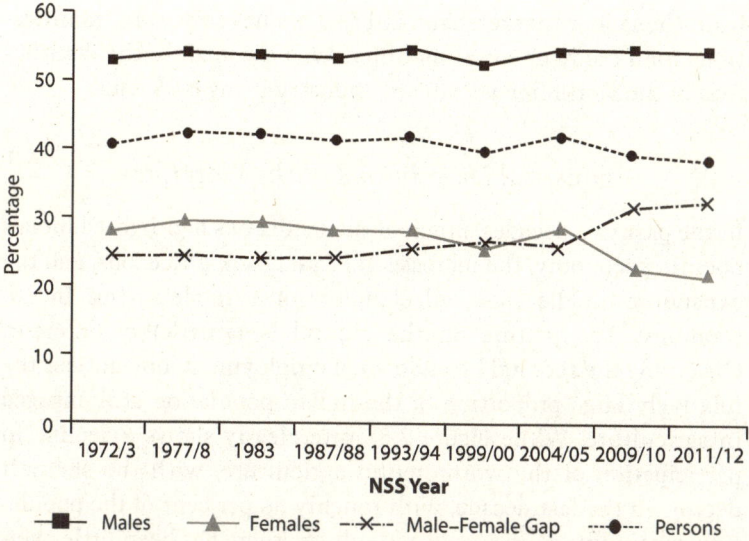

Figure 2.4 Worker Population Ratio (WPR) for Usual Status Workers—Women and Men, NSS 1972–2012

Source: see Table A2.1.3 in Appendix A2.1.

One possible reason for a rise in WPR in the Census and a decline in NSS figures for the same period towards the end of the 1990s (and more recently) could, it has been argued, partly be because Census figures here include both 'main' and 'marginal' workers, and the number of marginal workers has increased significantly in recent years (McNay, Unni, and Cassen 2004).

Through Figure 2.4 not much change can be observed in the WPR for men and women since the 1970s till the end of the 1990s. The WPR for women has been consistently under 30 per cent in the four decades being analysed, and has declined in the last few rounds of the NSS, a phenomenon that has been a cause of concern. Much research has gone into assessing the patterns of decline in women's labour force participation (Andres, Dasgupta, Joseph, Abraham, and Correia 2017). This decline in the female WPR is of significance where discussions on social mobility opportunities are concerned. Some have argued that it is the improvement in economic status levels that has led to the withdrawal of women

from the labour market (Saha 2017). This has important ramifications for a study of social mobility. We now analyse the distribution of the workforce in India by industry using NSS data.

Industrial Distribution of the Workforce

In the past two decades, much of the media has highlighted India's
booming economy, the increase in IT and back-office jobs, and the
expanding middle class, all elements of a 'modernizing' Indian
economy. The picture on the ground is remarkably different.
Observing the sectoral breakdown of employment, one notices the
relatively large proportion of the Indian population still engaged
in agriculture. While Figure 2.5 quite clearly shows a decline in
participation of the workforce in agriculture, with the sharpest
decline in the last decade, with roughly 50 per cent of the population continuing to engage in agriculture, there has been little overall dramatic shift of the working population from agriculture to
industry. These figures are from the NSS for the years 1972–2012

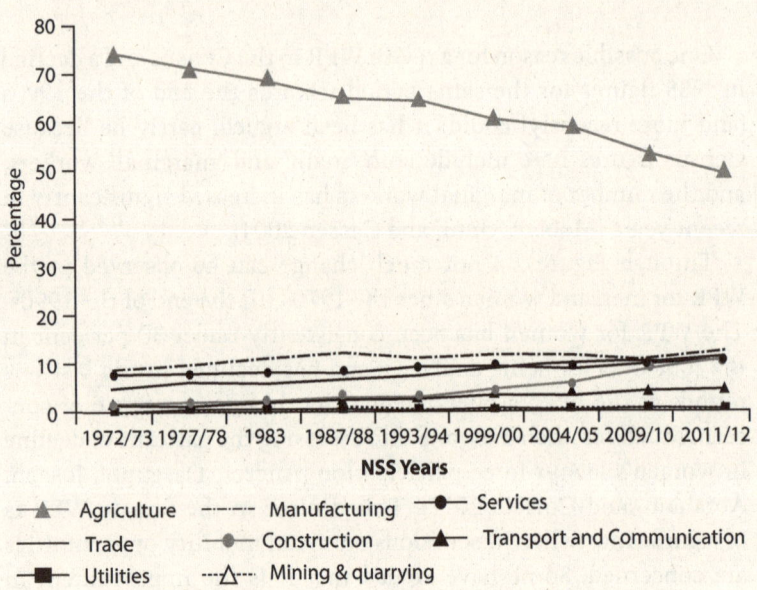

Figure 2.5   Industrial Distribution of All Persons, NSS 1972–2012

Source: see Table A2.1.4 in Appendix A2.1.

(the accompanying Table A2.1.4 in Appendix A2.1 also displays this information by rural and urban areas and by gender). Hence, though employment growth in the agricultural sector has declined, it is still by far the major employer in the country. In Figure 2.5, since the other non-agricultural sectors are close to each other in terms of participation rates, and in order to study any change in these sectors we display the graph for industrial distribution of *non-agricultural* workers (Figure 2.6) separately.

The proportion of Indian labour engaged in trade, manufacturing, and services has risen quite considerably since the early 1970s whereas those engaged in the mining sector and utilities have remained quite stable. We look at the graphs separately for women and men in order to analyse any gender differences in these patterns (Figures 2.7 and 2.8).

With regard to the manufacturing sector, the second largest sector after agriculture (Gupta 1988), it is important to highlight the difference between the organized and unorganized sectors.

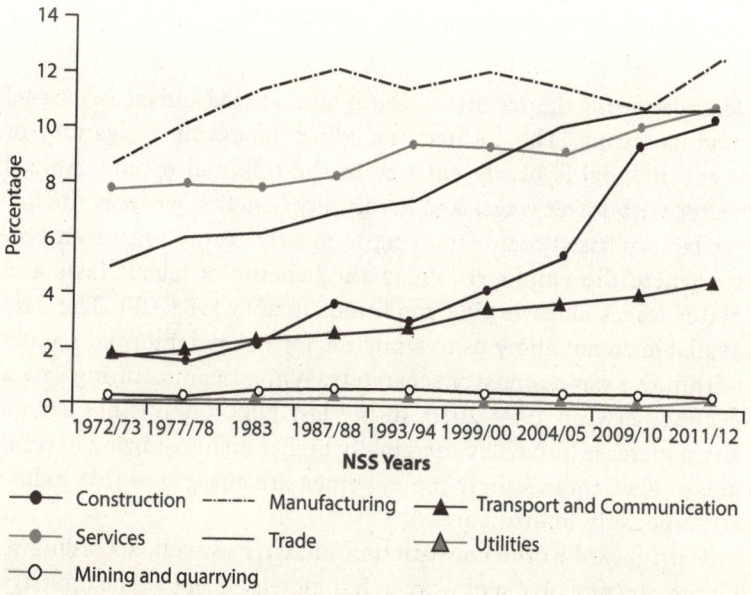

Figure 2.6 Industrial Distribution of All Persons in Non-Agriculture, NSS 1972–2012

Source: Table A2.1.4 in Appendix A2.1.

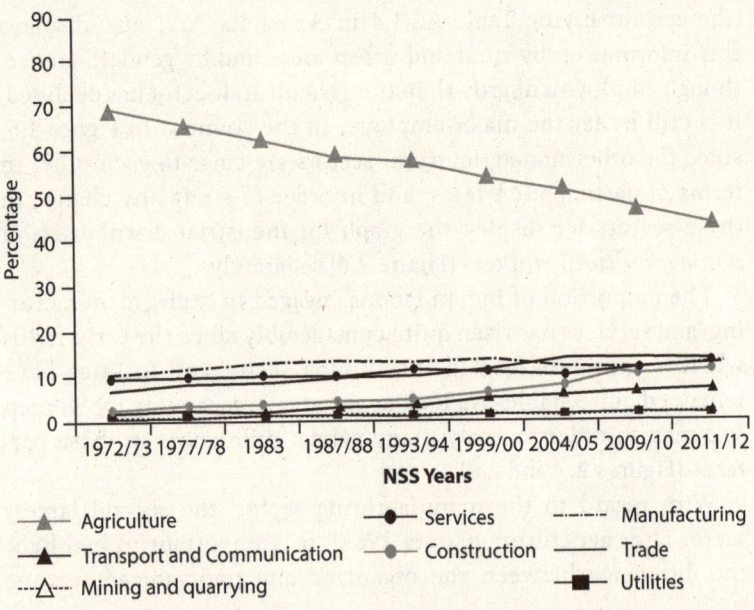

Figure 2.7 Industrial Distribution of Men, NSS 1972–2012

Source: Table A2.1.4 in Appendix A2.1.

Manufacturing figures include both home-based and factory-based manufacturing. The former (including for example cigarette or beedi making) is nearly entirely in the informal or unorganized sector with lower wages and hardly any benefits, whereas the latter factory-based manufacturing is mostly in the organized sector where the employees enjoy the benefits of labour laws and better wages and working conditions (Gupta 1988: 29). The data available do not allow us to study the formal and informal sectors within the same industry separately. While manufacturing saw a decline between 1999–2010, in the last NSS round it has seen a sharp increase (driven by marginally higher manufacturing in rural areas—also, interestingly more women are engaged in this industry, especially in urban areas).

With regard to the construction industry as well, according to Gupta, the proportion of women has increased, but as the industry is 'almost entirely in the unorganised sector, and its wages and conditions are among the poorest' (1988: 28) this is not necessarily a positive development for female employment.

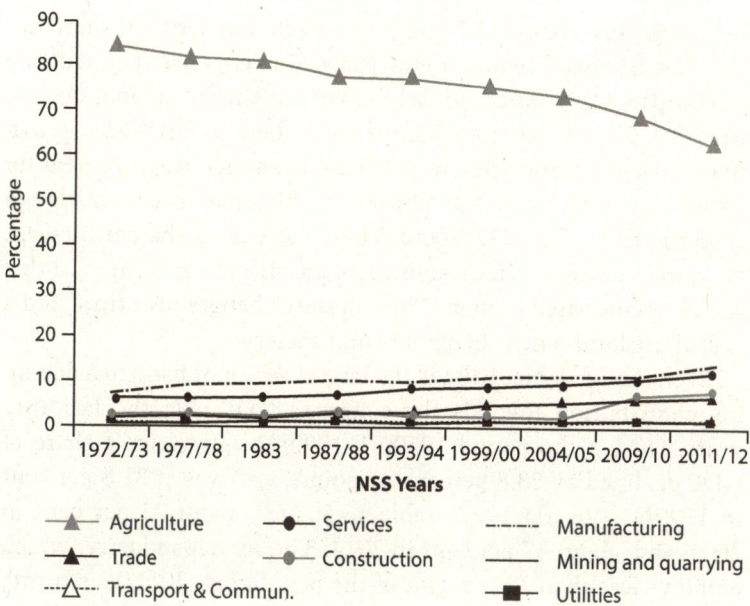

Figure 2.8 Industrial Distribution of Women, NSS 1972–2012
Source: see Table A2.1.4 in Appendix A2.1.

The service sector (made up of trade, commerce, transport, and other services) too has had an increase in participation of women, though the growth in this sector has not been as high as in the West (Gupta 1988). Also, women tend to 'cluster' in certain jobs within these sectors, for example, as nurses or teachers. In the Indian Administrative Service (IAS) women remain mostly in, what Gupta calls, 'nurturing' departments like social welfare. Thus, even though the participation of women in the professions has increased slightly since the 1960s, they are concentrated in clerical work, or as school teachers; jobs, which, according to Liddle, are mostly performed 'under male supervision' (1988: 23; see also Deshpande and Deshpande 1999; Liddle and Joshi 1986).[50]

---

[50] In urban India, according to Deshpande and Deshpande (1999: 234) women are concentrated in three occupations: as 'technical professionals' like teachers and nurses; in service occupations such as maids and cooks; and as farmers.

Comparing Figures 2.7 and 2.8, we see that for men there has been a substantial decline in the proportion engaged in agriculture as compared to women, for whom we see a more gradual decline till 2004–5 with a sharper decline since then. In 2011–12 approximately 44 per cent of men were engaged in agriculture, whereas for women the figure stands at 63 per cent (12 percentage points lower than the figure for 1999–2000). There has been a sharper increase of women in the services—but there are still fewer women in this sector as compared to men. Thus, despite changes over time, India is still predominantly an agricultural society.

Even though agriculture is the largest sector, it has had a declining contribution towards the country's GDP over the last fifty years. During the period 1950/51–1990/91 agriculture's share of GDP declined by 23.8 percentage points, and was at 31.6 per cent in 1990/91 (Visaria 1997, Table 13.8: 278), about 22 per cent in 2004; and, about 17 per cent in 2014. The service industry, which employs less than 11 per cent of the population (2011/12 figures), contributes towards over 50 per cent of the GDP (Sen 2016). As discussed previously, this has led many pundits to emphasize that the Indian growth success story is of a 'jobless variety' (McNay Unni, and Cassen 2004: 169) which might lead to a spurt in unemployment in the future. This might have an impact primarily on women (McNay, Unni, and Cassen 2004), as jobs in the service and manufacturing sector require a particular level of skill and education and a vast number of the population, especially women, are unable to take on these jobs. As mentioned earlier, with modernization and the creation of more mechanized and specialized jobs, it is the women who lose out. Therefore, women are increasingly engaged in agriculture, especially lower agricultural jobs, 'not because more work (is) available, but because of the non-availability of work in other sectors as indicated by a decline in the number of days of work available' (Papola and Sharma 1999 summarizing Unni: 5). This information only underlines the irony of growth. While the world media commends the Indian success story, a large proportion of the population is unable to avail of these benefits.

Since this book aims to study mobility opportunities open to different castes and communities, we briefly discuss the economic participation of different caste groups in India.

Gender, Caste, and Employment

This section looks briefly at the participation rates of different caste groups by gender over time according to NSS data. As information on the OBCs was only collected from the 1999–2000 round onward of the NSS and not in any of the rounds before that, we use the information on the combined 'other' category that included both OBCs as well as the higher castes up till 1999–2000 and then at OBCs separately since then. The graphs for these Worker Population Ratios are displayed here (Figures 2.9–2.12), and the accompanying Table A2.1.5 is provided in Appendix A2.1.

We observe that though all WPRs were declining till 1999–2000 they seem to have stabilized for men since then. The WPR for ST men in rural areas is consistently higher than that for the other caste groups, including the SCs. Other than ST men it is hard to differentiate between the WPRs for the other caste groups. However, we observe that the WPR for the 'other' category is the lowest till 2000, and then rises sharply. This seems to be due to

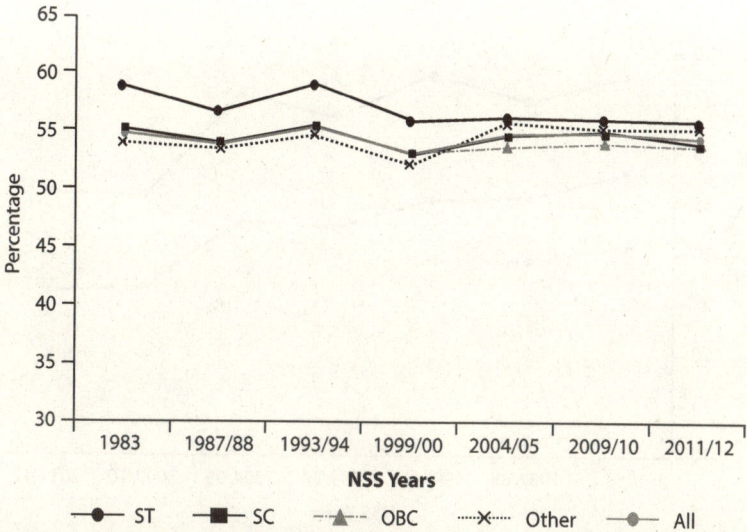

Figure 2.9 Worker Population Ratio (WPR) for Men by Caste for Usual Status Workers, NSS 1983–2012: Rural India

Source: Table A2.1.5 in Appendix A2.1.

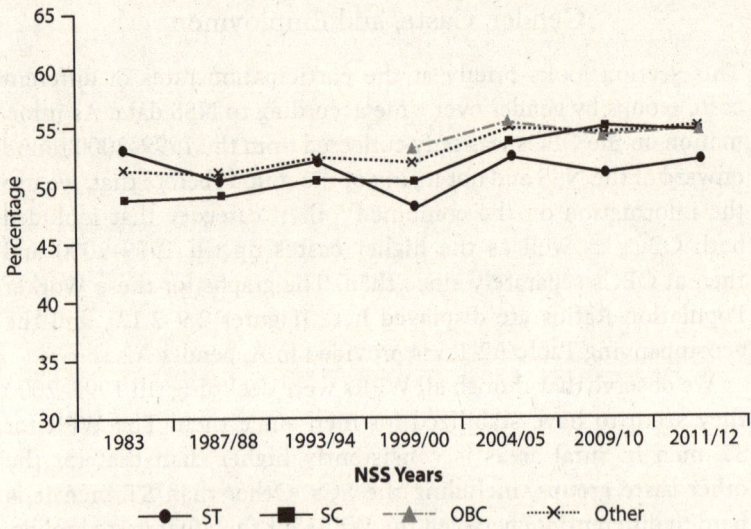

Figure 2.10 Worker Population Ratio (WPR) for Men by Caste for Usual Status Workers, NSS 1983–2012: Urban India

Source: Table A2.1.5 in Appendix A2.1.

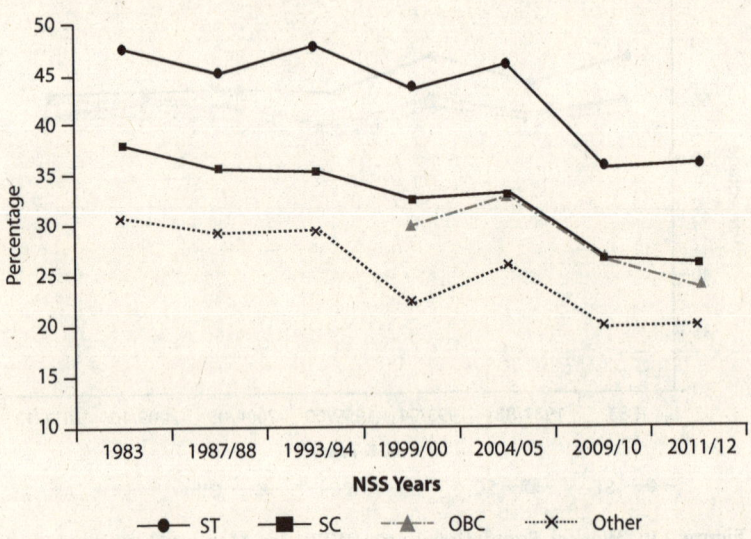

Figure 2.11 Worker Population Ratio (WPR) for Women by Caste for Usual Status Workers, NSS 1983–2012: Rural India

Source: Table A2.1.5 in Appendix A2.1.

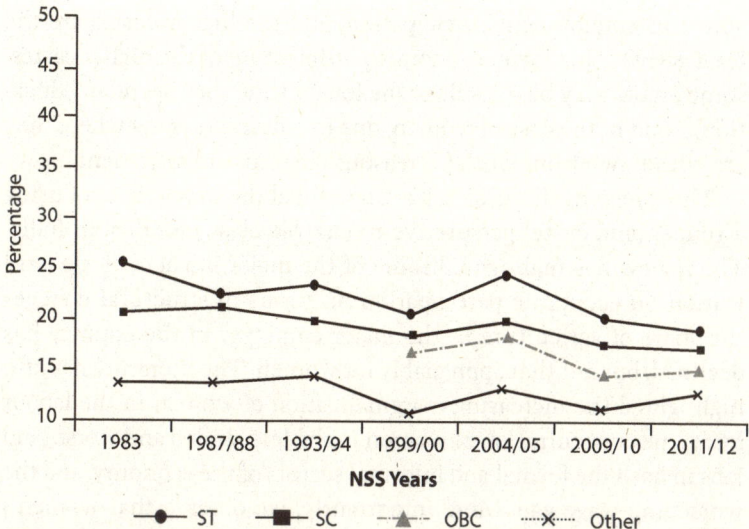

Figure 2.12 Worker Population Ratio for Women by Caste for Usual Status Workers, NSS 1983–2012: Urban India

Source: Table A2.1.5 in Appendix A2.1.

the separation of the OBCs from this category from 1999–2000. Concurrently, the slight increase in the OBCs may have been due to their separation from the 'other' category. For urban areas, the WPRs for all caste groups are gradually rising.

In the case of women, the pattern is slightly more distinct. The WPR for STs is higher in both rural and urban areas, followed by that of the SCs. The gap between the two WPRs is higher in the rural setting. Also, more significantly, the WPR for the 'other' caste category women is lower than the average WPR in both rural and urban areas.[51] The WPRs are lower for both women and men in urban areas when compared to the rural areas. For women we find an increase in WPR for all groups in 2004–05—most so for SC women, followed by a levelling off in 2011/12.

These graphs provide support for the literature that showed that the SCs and STs, especially in the case of women, are the most

---

[51] In Figures 2.9–2.12 for the y-axis the percentage scale has a different starting point, as there are many more men than women in employment.

active in employment participation; and the higher castes are the least active. This lower economic participation of the higher castes, some argue, may be a result of the longer time they spend in education,[52] and in the case of women, due to cultural reasons where they are withdrawn from work for reasons of status enhancement.

The foregoing discussion has underlined the importance of using a gender (and caste) perspective to analyse class mobility in India. The review has highlighted some of the major impacts of modernization on economic participation. In terms of structural changes the share of agriculture as the major employer in the country has declined, but not that appreciably for women. The literature has also highlighted the increasing marginalization of women in the labour force, the concentration of women in the less skilled and worse paid jobs in both the formal and informal sectors of the economy, and the worsening wage gap. More importantly, we observe that women's economic participation is constrained by various factors, both social and economic, for example, caste and economic status of the family are some of these factors. More recently we observe a decline in women's workforce participation (Anders 2017). In the empirical chapters we will study the impact these forces have on the mobility patterns of women and men, especially with regard to differences in equality of opportunity across various groups. We now move on to a discussion on regional and rural–urban variation.

Regional and Rural–Urban Variation

An understanding of the Indian economy has to be informed by an adequate recognition of deep seated regional diversities and heterogeneities. (Drèze and Gazdar 1997: 3)

This final section summarizes the discussions in this chapter in light of regional differences, while highlighting how these differences might affect class mobility patterns across the country.

---

[52] Though authors like Srivastava (2003), using NSS data, have shown a decline in WPR for all age groups and not just for the school going ages, which she concludes is because of a decline in work opportunities rather than an increase in time spent in education.

India is a large and diverse country, and it is expected that the amount of social fluidity will vary in different regions due to differences in their historical social and economic development, and in particular due to differences in the economic participation of women. Moreover, as demographic changes such as fertility and mortality rates, level of urbanization, and changes in rural/urban and regional population have an influence on socio-economic aspects such as education and employment (Dyson 2006: 11); and as these demographic changes vary across regions, the implications of this regarding education and employment, and hence, mobility, will be varied.

Besides, or rather along with, this regional diversity there are also strong rural/urban differences in the country. Given the size of the country and the breadth of diversity, it is difficult to study mobility patterns by each state using datasets currently available. Vaid (2007) provides an example of this comparison by clustering states into 'broader' regions. However, as different disciplines have 'problematized' region differently (Misra and Niranjana 2005) and to avoid any problematic generalizations, this book, rather than looking at north-south differences, looks instead at differences according to rural–urban location (referred to as 'locality').

In terms of gender participation in employment, regional differences are observed and these have implications for our mobility analysis. Figure 2.13 (and the related Table A2.1.6) displays these figures according to the NSS for the year 1999–2012.[53] The southern states have higher female labour force participation than the northern states.[54] Cultural reasons have been emphasized as possible causes of this variation, for example the use of Purdah

---

[53] These are figures for the Labour Force Participation Rate (LFPR), that is, the proportion of people in the labour force, that is, the proportion 'offering themselves for work' (Chadha and Sahu 2002: 2001). We are unable to study the WPR as we do not have access to the raw data and have had to rely on secondary sources that have this information.

[54] According to the 1991 Census only four of the eleven northern states had a WPR of more than 20 per cent for women. These were Gujarat, Rajasthan, Himachal Pradesh, and Madhya Pradesh. Of the seven southern states four had higher than 20 per cent WPR, and these were Goa, Karnataka, Andhra Pradesh, and Tamil Nadu (see also Table 11.3 of ILO report).

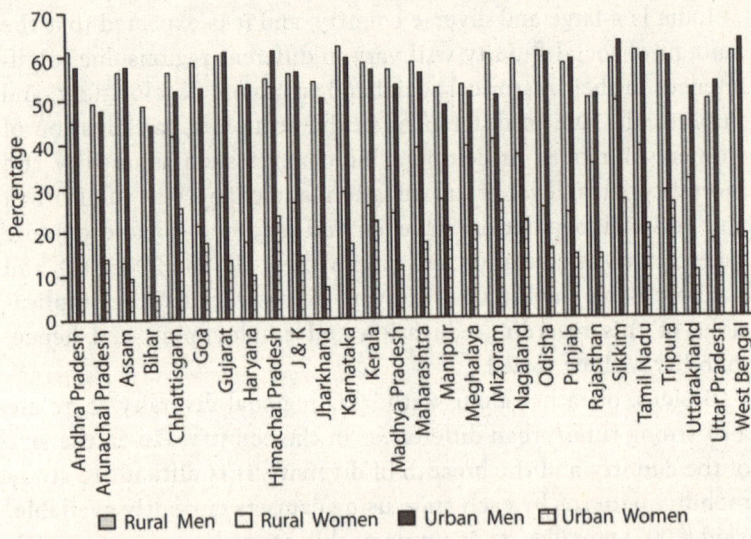

Figure 2.13 LFPR for Men and Women by State, for Usual Status Workers, NSS 1999–2012

Source: Table A2.1.6 in Appendix A2.1.

(see Boserup (1970 and 1990) for more on women's participation in employment in the context of development). Others like Miller (1981) have argued that the regional differences are an outcome of the prevailing agricultural economy or differing cultivation patterns in the northern and southern states. The states in the south are predominantly rice-growing regions, and rice cultivation requires intensive labour which has 'traditionally' been considered a female occupation. In contrast, the northern states are wheat growing states which do not require intensive labour, and hence, women are not that actively involved in these cultivating jobs and can be easily withdrawn from work.

More critically for our discussion on social mobility—rather than these macro-regional differences—we will be looking at differences within the same state according to rural and urban areas. These, as seen through the figures in the previous section of this chapter, are critical differences between the rural and the urban when it comes to employment, especially for women.

* * *

This chapter has discussed in detail the two aspects of caste and gender that are central to our analysis of class mobility in India. The rest of the book focuses on the influence of these aspects on the patterns of mobility and fluidity in the country. Throughout the book the mobility of women will be analysed alongside that of men.

In Chapter 4, we focus on class mobility of men and women through their own employment and analyse these patterns over time. In particular, in light of our literature review we utilize a 'locality' perspective to analyse any variations in these mobility patterns.

In Chapter 5, on caste and class mobility, we extend the discussion on caste and its association with 'hereditary' occupations. We also analyse the observed declustering of castes in certain occupations, as well as the alternative hypothesis of continued clustering. Hence, we study the role of caste with regard to class mobility chances, particularly in the context of the 'reservation' debates; especially whether certain castes are protected from forces of downward mobility, while others are unable to take advantage of upward mobility chances.

Previous research in the area of caste and class mobility using an empirical perspective has included work by Kumar, Heath, and Heath (2002b) and McMillan (2005). Both these authors have used NES datasets (for 1971 and 1996), restricting themselves to men in the first instance, and combining both women and men in the second. McMillan's work focuses specifically on SCs and STs, and compares them with the larger 'other' caste category. While Kumar, Heath, and Heath separate this amorphous *other* category, their classification of *community* is still quite general, and there are certain inconsistencies in the coding of the variables. In Chapter 5, we take this research forward by using the newer NES (2014) dataset that has a more detailed categorization of community taking forward Vaid (2012). Due to the sample size of the NES, this detailed research is possible in some instances without the problem of very small sample sizes.[55]

---

[55] We do not, as the authors mentioned here did, use the 1971 round of the NES to study mobility patterns as it is quite problematic in this data to separate out the women, not only due to small sample sizes, but also due to the differences in the collection of the samples from year to year. See Appendix A on Data and Validation of this book for more. However, Chapter 7 provides a brief analysis of the 1971 NES.

In Chapter 6, we focus on the effect of education on social mobility allowing us to explore the processes of mobility expanding on work published in Vaid (2016).

Appendix B of this book provides a brief look (using NES 2009 data, since the 2014 NES does not have spousal information) on marriage and avenues of mobility open to women. We briefly focus on patterns of mobility of women through marriage rather than through their own employment. Marriage is nearly 'universal' in India (Reddy 1998; Bloom and Reddy 1986), and as we observed in our discussion on caste it is an important institution for the perpetuation of the caste system (Ambedkar 1916) through the continued practice of caste endogamous arranged marriages. Moreover, as the figures for economic participation of women show that 'officially' the workforce participation for women is under 30 per cent (though this varies by caste and region), a complete picture of their social mobility requires a study of their mobility patterns by marriage in addition to their own class mobility.

Appendix A2.1: Tables for Figures in Chapter 2

Table A2.1.1   Effective Literacy Percentage 1951 to 2011, Census Figures

Year*	Men % of Total Male Population	Women % of Total Female Population	Literacy Gap (Men-Women) *percentage points*
1951	27.16	8.86	18.30
1961	40.40	15.35	25.05
1971	45.96	21.97	23.99
1981	56.38	29.76	26.62
1991	64.13	39.29	24.84
2001	75.26	53.67	21.59
2011	82.14	65.46	16.68

Source: Figures for 1951–2011 are from p. 102 from: http://censusindia.gov.in/2011-prov-results/data_files/india/Final_PPT_2011_chapter6.pdf.

Note: *1991 figures exclude the state of Jammu and Kashmir where the Census was not conducted. Figures for 1951–71 are for those aged five and above; figures for 1981–2011 are for those aged seven and above (*effective* literacy as defined by the Census).

Table A2.1.2 Table for Figure 2.3: Worker Population Ratio, Women and Men, Census 1911–2011

Census Year	Persons	Males	Females
1911	48.2	62.0	33.9
1921	47.0	60.6	32.8
1931	43.6	57.9	28.4
1951	39.1	53.9	23.4
1961	43.0	57.1	28.0
1971	34.0	52.7	13.9
1981	36.8	52.6	19.8
1991	37.5	51.6	22.3
2001	39.1	51.7	25.6
2011	39.8	53.3	25.5

Source: 1911–91 figures from Visaria 1999: Table 1, p. 24; 2001 figures from the Census of India website at www.censusindia.gov.in; Figures for 2011 are from: http://www.indiastat.com/table/labourandworkforce/380987/workparticipation/299/6321/data.aspx (last accessed in March 2017).

Table A2.1.3 Table for Figure 2.4: Worker Population Ratio, Usual Status Workers, Women and Men, NSS 1972–2012

NSS Year	Persons	Males	Females
1972/3	40.7	52.7	27.8
1977/8	42.3	54.3	29.7
1983	42.0	53.8	29.6
1987/88	41.2	53.1	28.5
1993/94	42.0	54.5	28.6
1999/00	39.7	52.7	25.9
2004/05	42.0	54.7	28.7
2009/10	39.2	54.6	22.8
2011/12	38.6	54.4	21.9

Source: NSS figures; Sarvekshana (2001–2) Statement 6, p. 8, figures are for all *usual status* workers Figures for 2004–12 are from NSS 68th Round, July 2011–June2012 (NSS Report No.554 [68/10/1], Employment and Unemployment Situation in India 2011–12, Statement 5.2, p. 99).

Table A2.1.4: Table for Figures 2.5, 2.6, 2.7, 2.8: Industrial Distribution of the Workforce, NSS 1972–2012: Men Only

		1972/73	1977/78	1983	1987/88	1993/94	1999/2000	2004/05	2009/10	2011/12
Agriculture	Rural	83.3	80.7	77.5	74.6	74.1	71.4	66.5	62.8	59.4
	Urban	10.7	10.6	10.6	9.1	9.0	6.5	6.1	6.0	5.6
	Total	68.8	65.6	62.2	58.7	57.4	53.6	50.8	47.1	43.6
Mining and quarrying	Rural	0.4	0.5	0.6	0.7	0.7	0.6	0.6	0.8	0.5
	Urban	1.0	0.9	1.2	1.3	1.3	0.9	0.9	0.7	0.9
	Total	0.5	0.6	0.7	0.9	0.9	0.7	0.7	0.8	0.6
Manufacturing	Rural	5.7	6.4	7.0	8.1	7.0	7.3	7.9	7.0	8.1
	Urban	26.8	27.5	26.8	29.6	23.5	22.4	23.5	21.8	22.4
	Total	9.9	11.0	12.8	13.3	12.7	13.0	12.0	11.1	12.3
Utilities	Rural	0.1	0.2	0.2	0.3	0.3	0.2	0.2	0.2	0.3
	Urban	0.9	1.1	1.1	1.2	1.2	0.8	0.8	0.7	1.4
	Total	0.3	0.4	0.4	0.5	0.5	0.4	0.4	0.3	0.6
Construction	Rural	1.6	1.7	2.2	3.7	3.2	4.5	6.8	11.3	13.0
	Urban	4.4	4.2	5.1	5.8	6.9	8.7	9.2	11.4	10.7
	Total	2.1	2.2	2.9	4.2	4.2	5.7	7.5	11.3	12.3
Trade	Rural	3.1	4.0	4.4	5.1	5.5	6.8	8.3	8.2	8.0
	Urban	20.1	21.6	20.4	21.4	21.9	29.4	28.0	27.0	26.0
	Total	6.5	7.8	8.1	9.1	9.7	11.4	13.4	13.4	13.3

Transport and	Rural	1.0	1.2	1.7	2.0	2.2	3.2	3.8	4.1	4.2
Communication	Urban	9.1	9.8	10.0	9.7	9.7	10.4	10.7	10.4	11.7
	Total	2.6	3.1	3.6	3.9	4.1	5.2	5.6	5.9	6.4
Services	Rural	4.8	5.3	6.1	5.5	7.0	6.2	5.9	5.5	6.4
	Urban	27.0	24.3	24.7	21.9	26.4	19.0	20.8	21.9	21.4
	Total	9.3	9.4	9.3	9.5	10.5	10.2	9.6	10.2	10.8

Source: Chadha and Sahu 2002: Table 6 page 2008: Sectoral distribution of usual (principal and subsidiary status) workers in India by workers' sex and residence: NSS data 1983/1999–2000, Table 8 from Visaria (1999): 40 for NSS years 1972–2/1977–8; also Statement 12 and 13, p. 14, Sarvekshana 2001–2.

NSS 61st Round, July 2004–June 2005 [NSS Report No.515 [61/10/1], Employment and Unemployment Situation in India 2004–5, Statement 5.9.2, p. 140–5, Table 28, p. A-252–A-263].

NSS 66th Round, July 2009–June 2010 [NSS Report No. 537 [66/10/1], Employment and Unemployment Situation in India 2009–10, Statement 5.9.1, pp. 139–44, Table 29, p. A-298–A-332].

NSS 68th Round, July 2011–June2012 [NSS Report No.554 [68/10/1], Employment and Unemployment Situation in India 2011–12, Statement 5.11, p. 115–16, Statement 5.11.1, p. 167, 170–3].

Table A2.1.4 contd. Table for Figures 2.5, 2.6, 2.7, 2.8: Industrial Distribution of the Workforce, NSS 1972–2012; Women only

		1972/73	1977/78	1983	1987/88	1993/94	1999/00	2004/05	2009/10	2011/12
Agriculture	Rural	89.7	88.2	87.5	84.7	86.2	85.3	83.3	79.4	74.9
	Urban	32.9	31.9	31.5	29.3	24.7	17.6	18.1	13.9	10.9
	Total	84.3	81.8	81.1	77.4	77.5	75.4	73.8	68.7	62.8
Mining and quarrying	Rural	0.2	0.2	0.3	0.4	0.4	0.3	0.3	0.3	0.3
	Urban	1.4	0.5	0.7	0.8	0.6	0.4	0.2	0.3	0.3
	Total	0.3	0.2	0.4	0.5	0.4	0.3	0.3	0.3	0.3
Manufacturing	Rural	4.7	5.9	6.4	7.2	7.0	7.6	8.4	7.5	9.8
	Urban	24.6	29.6	26.7	28.3	24.1	24.0	28.2	27.9	28.7
	Total	6.6	8.5	8.9	10.0	9.5	10.4	11.2	10.8	13.4
Utilities	Rural	0.0	0.0	0.0	0.0	0.1	0.0	0.0	0.0	0.1
	Urban	0.1	0.1	0.2	0.2	0.3	0.2	0.2	0.4	1.0
	Total	0.0	0.0	0.0	0.0	0.0	0.0	0.0	0.1	0.3
Construction	Rural	1.1	0.6	0.7	2.7	0.9	1.1	1.5	5.2	6.6
	Urban	2.7	2.2	3.2	3.7	4.1	4.8	3.8	4.7	4.0
	Total	1.3	0.8	1.0	2.8	1.4	1.6	1.8	5.1	6.1
Trade	Rural	1.5	2.0	1.9	2.0	2.1	2.0	2.5	2.8	3.0
	Urban	9.6	8.7	9.5	9.7	10.0	16.9	12.2	12.1	12.8
	Total	2.3	2.8	2.8	3.0	3.1	3.8	3.9	4.3	4.8

Transport and Communication	Rural	0.0	0.1	0.1	0.1	0.1	0.1	0.2	0.2	0.2
	Urban	1.4	1.0	0.6	0.9	1.3	1.8	1.4	1.4	2.7
	Total	0.1	0.2	0.2	0.2	0.3	0.4	0.3	0.4	0.7
Services	Rural	2.8	3.0	2.8	2.9	3.4	3.6	3.9	4.6	5.2
	Urban	27.4	26.0	26.7	27.1	35.0	34.2	35.9	39.3	39.6
	Total	5.1	5.7	5.5	6.1	7.8	8.0	8.6	10.2	11.7

Source: Chadha and Sahu 2002: Table 6 page 2008: Sectoral distribution of usual (principal and subsidiary status) workers in India by workers' sex and residence: NSS data 1983/1999–2000, Table 8 from Visaria (1999): 40 for NSS years 1972–2/1977–8; also Statement 12 and 13, p. 14; Sarvekshana 2001–2.

NSS 61st Round, July 2004–June 2005 [NSS Report No.515 [61/10/1], Employment and Unemployment Situation in India 2004–5, Statement 5.9.2, p. 140–5, Table 28, p. A-252–A-263].

NSS 66th Round, July 2009–June 2010 (NSS Report No. 537 [66/10/1], Employment and Unemployment Situation in India 2009–10, Statement 5.9.1, pp. 139–44, Table 29, p. A-298–A-332].

NSS 68th Round, July 2011–June2012 (NSS Report No.554 [68/10/1], Employment and Unemployment Situation in India 2011–12, Statement 5.11, p. 115–16, Statement 5.11.1, p. 167, 170–3].

Table A2.1.4 contd. Industrial Distribution of Workforce, NSS 1972–2012, All Persons

		1972/73	1977/78	1983	1987/88	1993/94	1999/2000	2004/05	2009/10	2011/12
Agriculture	Rural	85.6	83.4	81.3	78.1	78.4	76.3	72.7	67.9	64.1
	Urban	14.8	15.2	14.6	13.5	12.3	8.8	8.8	7.5	6.7
	Total	73.9	71.0	68.6	64.9	64.0	60.4	58.5	53.2	48.9
Mining and quarrying	Rural	0.3	0.4	0.5	0.6	0.6	0.5	0.5	0.6	0.5
	Urban	1.0	0.8	1.0	1.2	1.2	0.8	0.8	0.6	0.8
	Total	0.4	0.4	0.6	0.7	0.7	0.6	0.6	0.6	0.5
Manufacturing	Rural	5.4	6.2	7.1	7.6	7.7	7.8	8.1	7.2	8.6
	Urban	26.3	27.9	29.1	29.5	26.2	25.1	24.6	23.0	23.6
	Total	8.8	10.2	11.5	12.2	11.6	12.2	11.7	11.0	12.6
Utilities	Rural	0.1	0.1	0.1	0.2	0.2	0.2	0.2	0.2	0.2
	Urban	0.8	0.8	0.9	1.0	1.0	0.7	0.7	0.6	1.3
	Total	0.2	0.3	0.3	0.4	0.4	0.3	0.3	0.3	0.5
Construction	Rural	1.4	1.3	1.7	3.3	2.4	3.3	4.9	9.4	11.1
	Urban	4.1	3.7	4.7	5.3	6.3	8.0	8.0	10.2	9.3
	Total	1.9	1.7	2.3	3.8	3.2	4.4	5.6	9.6	10.6
Trade	Rural	2.5	3.3	3.5	4.0	4.3	4.5	6.1	6.4	6.5
	Urban	18.2	18.8	18.0	18.8	19.4	23.7	24.6	24.3	23.4
	Total	5.1	6.1	6.3	7.1	7.6	9.0	10.3	10.8	11.0

Transport and Communication	Rural	0.6	0.8	1.1	1.3	1.4	2.1	2.5	2.9	3.0
	Urban	7.7	8.0	8.1	7.8	7.9	8.7	8.6	8.7	10.0
	Total	1.8	2.1	2.5	2.7	2.9	3.7	3.8	4.3	4.8
Services	Rural	4.1	4.5	4.4	4.9	5.1	5.2	5.0	5.4	6.0
	Urban	27.1	24.8	22.6	22.9	25.4	23.5	24.0	25.2	25.0
	Total	7.9	8.1	8.0	8.4	9.6	9.5	9.3	10.3	11.1

Source: Chadha and Sahu 2002: Table 6 page 2008: Sectoral distribution of usual (principal and subsidiary status) workers in India by workers' sex and residence: NSS data 1983/1999–2000, Table 8 from Visaria (1999); 40 for NSS years 1972–2/1977–8; also Statement 12 and 13, p. 14; Sarvekshana 2001–2.

NSS 61st Round, July 2004–June 2005 (NSS Report No.515 [61/10/1], Employment and Unemployment Situation in India 2004–5, Statement 5.9.2, p. 140–5, Table 28, p. A-252–A-263].

NSS 66th Round, July 2009–June 2010 [NSS Report No. 537 [66/10/1], Employment and Unemployment Situation in India 2009–10, Statement 5.9.1, pp. 139–44, Table 29, p. A-298–A-332].

NSS 68th Round, July 2011–June2012 (NSS Report No.554 [68/10/1], Employment and Unemployment Situation in India 2011–12, Statement 5.11, p. 115–16; Statement 5.11.1, p. 167, 170–3].

Table A2.1.5 Table for Figures 2.9–2.12: WPR of Caste Groups by Gender for Both Rural and Urban Areas NSS (all usual status workers)

Gender	Area		ST	SC	OBC	Other	All
Male	Rural	1983	58.8	55.1	–	54.0	54.7
		1987–8	56.7	53.8	–	53.5	53.9
		1993–4	59.1	55.4	–	54.7	55.3
		1999–2000	55.8	53.1	53.2	52.0	53.1
		2004–5	56.2	54.5	53.7	55.7	54.6
		2009–10	55.9	54.8	54.0	55.2	54.7
		2011–12	55.7	53.9	53.8	55.2	54.3
	Urban	1983	53.1	49.0	–	51.4	51.2
		1987–8	50.4	49.2	–	50.9	50.6
		1993–4	52.0	50.5	–	52.3	52.1
		1999–2000	48.0	50.3	53.0	51.8	51.8
		2004–5	52.3	53.7	55.4	55.0	54.9
		2009–10	51.0	55.0	54.3	54.2	54.3
		2011–12	52.0	54.5	54.6	54.9	54.6
Female	Rural	1983	47.8	38.1	–	31.0	34.0
		1987–8	45.4	35.8	–	29.4	32.3
		1993–4	48.2	35.5	–	29.7	32.8
		1999–2000	43.8	32.5	30.2	22.3	29.9
		2004–5	46.4	33.3	33.0	26.2	32.7
		2009–10	35.9	26.9	26.7	19.9	26.1
		2011–12	36.4	26.2	23.9	20.1	24.8
	Urban	1983	25.5	20.5	–	13.9	15.1
		1987–8	22.5	21.3	–	14.0	15.2
		1993–4	23.4	19.9	–	14.5	15.5
		1999–2000	20.4	18.5	16.9	10.8	13.9
		2004–5	24.5	20.0	18.5	13.4	16.6
		2009–10	20.3	17.8	14.5	11.3	13.8
		2011–12	19.2	17.2	15.1	12.9	14.7

Source: Sarvekshana (2001–2) Statement 33 p. 32;
NSS 68th Round, July 2011–June 2012, Statement 3.17, p. 41 (NSS Report No. 563 [68/10/4], Employment and Unemployment Situation Among Social Groups in India).
Note: For NSS years 1983, 1987–8, 1993–4; no separate category of social group 'OBC' was there. The category 'Others' included 'OBC' for these years.

Table A2.1.6 Table for Figure 2.13: Labour Force Participation Rate, Men and Women by Locality and State, NSS 2011–12.

State/UT	Rural Men	Rural Women	Urban Men	Urban Women
Andhra Pradesh	61.2	44.8	57.6	18.0
Arunachal Pradesh	49.2	28.2	47.5	13.9
Assam	56.4	12.9	57.3	9.7
Bihar	48.7	5.8	44.1	5.4
Chhattisgarh	56.3	41.6	51.7	25.2
Goa	58.6	21.2	52.6	17.4
Gujarat	60.2	27.9	60.7	13.5
Haryana	53.2	16.4	53.5	10.2
Himachal Pradesh	54.7	52.9	61.2	23.6
Jammu and Kashmir	55.9	26.3	56.3	14.5
Jharkhand	54.2	20.4	50.3	7.3
Karnataka	62.0	28.9	59.4	17.1
Kerala	58.3	25.8	56.7	22.2
Madhya Pradesh	56.4	23.9	53.3	11.9
Maharashtra	58.2	38.9	56.0	17.2
Manipur	52.3	27.0	48.3	20.4
Meghalaya	52.9	39.2	51.5	21.0
Mizoram	59.9	40.5	50.7	26.7
Nagaland	59.0	37.1	50.9	22.4
Odisha	60.6	25.1	60.3	15.8
Punjab	57.9	23.7	58.6	14.1
Rajasthan	50.0	34.9	50.7	14.4
Sikkim	58.6	49.2	62.8	27.4
Tamil Nadu	60.7	38.6	59.9	21.1
Tripura	59.9	28.7	59.4	26.0
Uttarakhand	46.5	31.5	51.9	10.8
Uttar Pradesh	49.6	17.8	53.3	10.6
West Bengal	60.2	19.4	63.0	18.6
Andaman and Nicobar Islands	60.3	30.0	63.3	24.8
Chandigarh	56.7	4.7	57.9	13.5
Dadra and Nagar Haveli	48.8	16.1	57.6	11.5
Daman and Diu	69.4	3.4	59.5	15.2
Delhi	54.4	14.6	54.8	10.9
Lakshadweep	59.8	17.7	58.2	17.8
Puducherry	52.1	22.3	56.3	15.3
All India	55.3	25.3	56.3	15.5

Source: NSS 68th Round, July 2011–June 2012 (NSS Report No.554 [68/10/1], Employment and Unemployment Situation in India 2011–12, Statement 4.1.1, pp. 88–9).

3

How Many Classes Are There?

Class Debates and Class Schemas

'What is social class?' Of course class is an essentially contested concept. It is therefore conceptualised and measured in a variety of ways. There is no 'essence' of social class. In offering an account of class and its socio-logic, all one can say is 'here is my conceptual definition of what class is; here is how I propose it should be measured; here is the evidence that leads me to believe it measures what it is supposed to measure; the following research demonstrates the empirical pay-off of analysis using my measure of class; and given my conceptualisation of it, this is how I explain the empirical evidence on the relations between class and my dependent variables'.[1]

Rose (1998)

For the analysis of class mobility in a society, a clear conceptualization of class and a valid class schema are essential prerequisites. The definition of class has been contentious, especially in the Indian context due to the caste system and the fusing together of caste with class in many studies. We discuss the major debates surrounding the conceptualization of class as well as its varied operationalizations. In the context of mobility studies, we look

---

[1] According to Wright (2005a) different uses of the term class are 'embedded in very different theoretical agendas involving different kinds of questions and thus different sorts of aspects' (p. 717).

briefly at the status attainment approach and explain why we prefer the class schematic approach for our study. As no standardized class schema has been used in research on mobility in India, we provide a conceptualization of class in the Indian context as well as its formulation in terms of a class schema. A statistical validation of the schema is discussed in the Appendix A of this book.

The conceptualization of class in India has varied with the research agenda of the study. For Marxists (for example, Chaudhuri 1987; Patnaik 1976) class is an arena for struggle between the landed and the labourers, whereas for some other sociologists (Jain 1969; Jorapur 1971; Kaistha 1987) exploitation is but one aspect of the debate and for them class, status, and prestige overlap.[2] Prior to discussing some class schemas used in Indian research on mobility, we summarize a few of the key debates on 'class'.

Class Debates

Different theoretical *conceptualizations* of class have led researchers down different paths in terms of using class for their analysis, especially in social mobility research (Rose 1998). Anthony Heath's summary of the major treatments of class in the study of social mobility is a useful place to begin and we quote him at length.

> Any discussion of social mobility necessarily requires us to distinguish a set of categories between which mobility is to take place. This problem has received all kinds of treatments. Pareto was most interested in movement between the governing elite and the non-elite; Sorokin was more concerned with movement between occupational groups which were differentiated according to their social honour; Lipset and Bendix focussed on movement between manual and non-manual occupations, which they tended to equate with movement between the middle and working classes (classes being seen as broad social groupings with shared identities, consumption

[2] Some sociologists merge the objective measures of class with the subjective. The major emphasis of this book is to construct and use a measure of 'objective' class situation and not 'subjective' class identity (Driver and Driver [1987] provide an example of a subjective study of class in India).

patterns and political attitudes); Blau and Duncan in contrast saw
the occupational structure as 'more or less continuously graded in
regard to status rather than being a set of discrete status classes'
and hence rather than looking at movement between discrete categories focussed on occupational achievements as measured on a
continuous scale of socio-economic status (Blau and Duncan 1967:
124); Glass and his co-workers looked at movement between seven
'status categories' distinguished in terms of their social prestige and
based on the assumption that 'the community consists of strata
arranged in the form of a hierarchy' (Glass 1954: 29); and finally John
Goldthorpe, in his report of the Oxford project, looked at movement
between seven social classes differentiated according to the market
and work situations of their incumbents.   (Heath 1981: 49)[3]

In later work, Erikson and Goldthorpe delineate and use an
eleven-class model along with various possible combinations of
collapsed categories for analysis with smaller N data (Erikson and
Goldthorpe 1992).

Given the range of class categories to study social mobility, a
brief look at some of the major discussions on class formulations
and their use in mobility research allows us to contextualize the
choice of the schema used in this book. As the debate in this area
has been vigorous, we are forced to limit ourselves to a few of
the major theories and classifications that are important for our
formulation and representative of the field. We, thus, intend to
provide a basis on which to explain our conceptualization of class
as well as its more practical formulation in terms of a schema,
but we do not intend to provide an exhaustive discussion of the
research in this area.[4]

---

[3] See Appendix B in Reid (1998) for discussions on class schemas used
officially and otherwise in Britain including the Registrar General's Social
Class, the Hall-Jones scale on a more subjective social grading, and the
Hope-Goldthorpe scale.

[4] For a more detailed look at the individual theories and some
discussions a good starting point is Grusky's book on *Social Stratification*
(2001). For an introductory level book see Saunders (1990). Breen and
Rottman (1995) provide a good summary of prominent stratification
theorists (see ch. 2: especially 22–48); Wright (1998) includes a range of
debates on class from various theoretical paradigms.

The Marxist theory of class is often taken to be the starting point for the debate on class; and this is where we begin our discussion as well, before touching briefly on the work of Erik Olin Wright, a neo-Marxist.[5] We then move on to the work of Max Weber. Where neo-Weberians are concerned we highlight in particular the work of John Goldthorpe.[6] We will then move on to a discussion of why the schema employed in this book is categorical in nature and closer to the Weberian idea of market and work situations rather than being based on any form of antagonism among classes.

Though Marx did not explicitly and systematically discuss the definition of class, his work and that of many neo-Marxists has been primarily shaped by it. For Marx, at the broader level, there was a twofold division of society into owners (the bourgeois or capitalists) and workers (non-owners or proletariat), that is, the conflict between the capitalists who were the owners of means of production and the working class was 'the driving force behind further social development' (Grusky 2001: 15). For Wright what 'most sharply distinguishes the Marxist conceptualisation of class from other traditions is the concept of exploitation' (2005b: 5). Thus, under the Marxist framework there exists an exploitative relation between the two groups; this is based on the exploitation of the workers by the capitalists or the owners of the means of production.

Neo-Marxists also seem to share a basic commitment to a 'polarised' concept of class relations (though Wright [2005b] provides a

[5] Though not explicitly talking about Wright in his work, Parkin did once famously say that 'inside every neo-Marxist there seems to be a Weberian struggling to get out' (1979: 25) and for Wright, on the other hand, 'inside every left-wing Weberian there's a Marxist struggling to stay hidden' (1997: 35).

[6] Goldthorpe has argued against being labelled a neo-Weberian (see Erikson and Goldthorpe 1992: 37), but according to Breen (2005) there is some justification in labelling his schema 'neo-Weberian' 'inasmuch as it shares the Weberian focus on life chances and the Weberian modesty about the scope of class analysis' (p. 42). In the *Constant Flux*, Goldthorpe claims that his schema is in inspiration quite eclectic (Erikson and Goldthorpe 1992: 35).

more nuanced approach).But, according to Grusky (2001: 15) 'This simple two-class model should be viewed as an ideal type designed to capture the developmental tendencies of capitalism'. He goes on to state that 'whenever Marx carried out concrete analyses of existing capitalist systems, he acknowledged that the class system was complicated by the persistence of transitional classes (e.g. landowners), quasi-class groupings (e.g. peasants), and class fragments (e.g. the lumpen proletariat)'.

Over the decades there have been many criticisms of Marxist class theory,[7] but the persistence and rapid growth of the middle class has provided 'the critics of Marxism with one of their principal arguments against class theory' (Wright 2001b: 116). Wright attempts in his work to deal with the problem of 'locating the "middle class"[8] within the class structure' (1997: 19) and moves beyond the polarization between capitalists and workers.[9] Using the concept of contradictory class locations, that is, positions that fall between the three classes of capitalists, proletarians, and the petty bourgeoisie,[10] he proposes a neo-Marxist schema.

---

[7] For a particularly informative and amusing critique see Parkin (1979). In an introductory level book, Saunders (1990) summarizes some of the drawbacks of Marxism as '... the insensitivity to systems of stratification other than those based on class, the failure to theorise divisions grounded in gender and ethnicity, the inability to explain the growth of the middle class within capitalism, and the unwillingness to consider actual forms of class consciousness as opposed to idealised ones—all fundamentally undermine Marxist approaches to social stratification. These are not the only problems with the approach—the theory of exploitation, for example, can be challenged, as can the view that capital and labour represent inherently irreconcilable interests' (p. 19). For a discussion on some of the major drawbacks of Marxist class theory from the point of view of a neo-Marxist see Wright (2005a).

[8] The middle class are seen as 'People who do not own their own means of production, who sell their labour power in a labour market, and yet do not seem part of the "working class"' (Wright 1997: 19).

[9] For a discussion of various ways in which Marxists have attempted to deal with the problem of the middle class see Wright (2001a).

[10] Wright includes the Petty Bourgeoisie as for him, along with the capitalist mode of production, simple commodity production (carried out

These contradictory locations for Wright are the supervisors and managers (as they both dominate the proletariat and are, in turn, dominated by the capitalists); the small employers (who share characteristics of the capitalists and the petty bourgeoisie) and the semi-autonomous employees (who fall between the working class and the petit bourgeoisie). In his original formulation he, thus, created six classes and as can be seen they are distinguished on the basis of the concepts of exploitation and domination.[11] In his later formulation Wright expands and reassesses his schema (creating a twelve-class typology) based on exploitation as the primary thrust and not domination. This concept of exploitation for Wright 'is seen to operate in contemporary societies along three dimensions: ownership of means of production, ownership of organisational assets that permit control and co-ordination of technical processes of production, and ownership of skills and credentials' (Breen and Rottman 1995: 65; also Wright 1985, 1997). Wright's class schema has thus evolved overtime.[12]

The second classical theorist whose work on class has had a significant impact on social mobility analysis is Max Weber. For Weber (1958), different economic classes were defined by groups of people who shared differing 'life chances', which were determined

---

by the self-employed) too exists simultaneously (see Breen and Rottman 1995: 63). Wright uses what he calls five 'anchoring questions' to deal with these different agendas of class analysis (see Figure 1: p. 719; see also, for a discussion, his conclusions in his book [Wright 2005b] entitled 'If "Class" is the Answer, What is the Question?' [pp. 180–92]).

[11] In his book on Classes (1985) Wright had argued that the control of 'organisational assets and skill assets' were the basis for a distinctive form of exploitation and was, thus, his *rationale* for considering authority and skills as dimensions of the class structure (see 1997: 19, see also 1985). But in other work he claims that he no longer found this way of looking at the middle class satisfactory (1989, 1997) and lays down a revised version of his Marxist class 'typology'.

[12] For a discussion on the operationalization of these classes see Wright (1985). For a critique of the schema see Rose and Marshall (1986), also Marshall (1997, particularly p. 83); Mills (1994) also critiques Marxist theories of social class.

by the individual's position in the labour market, that is, by the different goods, 'material' resources, and skills that they might bring to the labour market. And those who shared a position in the labour market by virtue of possessing these resources would share a common class situation. Hence, for him 'class situation' was equivalent to 'market situation'; thus, his emphasis on the market as the determinant of the life chances of the people.

For Weber (1953: 21):[13]

> We may speak of a 'class' when 1) a number of people have in common a specific causal component of their life chances, in so far as 2) this component is represented exclusively by economic interests in the possession of goods and opportunities for income, and 3) represented under the conditions of the community or labour markets. [These points refer to 'class situation', which we may express more briefly as the typical chance for a supply of goods, external living conditions, and personal life experiences, in so far as this chance is determined by the amount and kind of power, or lack of such, to dispose of good or skills for the sake of income in the given economic order. The term 'class' refers to any group of people that is found in the same class situation].
>
> (square brackets in original)

He also distinguishes between classes on the basis of their relationship to property, that is, ownership and non-ownership. Within these two categories he distinguishes the ones with property as the 'petty bourgeoisie' on the one hand and the large proprietors on the other. Moreover, within the non-propertied category he distinguishes the 'intelligentsia' who own no independent property but have different skills and credentials than the 'working' class (see Weber 1978; as well as Breen and Rottman 1995: 28–9).[14]

[13] Weber also differentiated between three kinds of classes: the *property class*, the commercial or *acquisition class*, and the *social class*. Social class for him was made up of different class situations between which 'an interchange of individuals on a personal basis or in the course of generations, is readily possible and typically available' (Weber 2001: 142).

[14] Weber had his fair share of criticisms from neo-Marxists among others, who, according to Saunders, 'claim, for example, that Weberian

Much has been made over the years of the differences between Marxist and Weberian traditions of class analysis. The essential difference lies in the concepts of exploitation (for Marxists) and life chances (for Weberians). Unlike Karl Marx according to whom 'it is ... the position which the individual occupies in the social organisation of production, that indicates to which class he belongs' (Bendix and Lipset 1953: 8), for Max Weber 'class is defined not by relationship to means of production, but by sharing of common market positions leading to shared life chances' (Marshall 1998: 700). In *Class Counts* Wright states that 'the reason why production is more central to Marxist than to Weberian class analysis is because of its salience for the problem of exploitation; the reason why Weberians give greater emphasis to the market is because it so directly shapes life chances' (1997: 31).[15]

Despite their differences there are many similarities in their work as 'they both reject simple gradational definitions of class; they are both anchored in the social relations which link people to economic resources of various sorts; they both see these social relations as affecting the material interests of actors, and accordingly they see class relations as the potential basis for solidarities and conflict' (Wright 2005a: 719). Marshall, Newby, Rose, and Volger (1988) too attempt to see whether Marxist and Weberian theories are inherently incompatible and conclude that at least on the basis of their empirical results the two approaches were similar or in their words 'indistinguishable' especially where the ownership and production dimensions of social class relations were concerned (1988: 17).

In light of this discussion, in the section on *Conceptualization* we discuss what recommends one approach over another for an Indian mobility study.

---

approaches fail to understand the structural basis of class antagonisms and overemphasise the division between economic and political power in advanced capitalism' (1990: 24).

[15] For a further discussion on Marx as well as on the contrast of Marx and Weber's conceptualization of class see Bendix and Lipset (1953), Giddens (1973), and Parkin (1979), as well as Wright (2005a and b), Breen and Rottman (1995) among others.

As mentioned previously, Weber maintained a distinction between class situation and status situation. In *The Black-coated Worker*, Lockwood (1958) developed this distinction further where he argued 'that the position of clerks had to be considered in terms of three aspects—their market situation, work situation and status situation'. Lockwood states that 'under "class position" will be included the following factors. First, "market" situation, that is to say the economic position narrowly conceived, consisting of source and size of income, degree of job-security, and opportunity for upward occupational mobility.[16] Secondly, "work situation", the set of social relationships in which the individual is involved at work by virtue of his position in the division of labour.[17] And finally, "status situation" or the position of the individual in the hierarchy of prestige in the society at large is a separate element' (Lockwood [1958] 1989: 15).

This work by Lockwood developed Weber's theories further. However, it is Goldthorpe (who worked with Lockwood and others on the Affluent worker series [Goldthorpe, Lockwood, Bechhofer, and Platt 1969]) who has been credited with bringing this theory to a high degree of conceptual refinement. Goldthorpe originally based his class schema on Lockwood's use of the Weberian idea of market and work situation (Goldthorpe 1980, 1987) but in subsequent retellings he refines and modifies it even further (Erikson and Goldthorpe 1992; Goldthorpe 2000).

This original seven-fold class schema was created by aggregating categories from the collapsed (thirty-six-category version) of the Hope-Goldthorpe occupational scale.[18] For Goldthorpe

---

[16] Erikson (1984: 501) regards the 'market situation more generally as life chances as they stem from the individual's occupation and position in the division of labour. The market situation then will have consequences also for consumption level and housing standard ....'

[17] The *work situation* refers to the extent to which clerks can 'exercise autonomy and discretion in their work, whether or not they come into contact with their boss, and the skills they need in the office' (Saunders 1990).

[18] In one of his earliest classifications Goldthorpe's (1980) construction of his seven-fold schema was based on the previous more subjective Hope-Goldthorpe scale, but the theory behind the schema was based on

a distinctive feature of these categories is that they provide a relatively high degree of differentiation in terms of both occupational
function and employment status: in effect the associated employment status is treated as part of the definition of an occupation ....
On this basis, then, we are able to bring together, within the classes
we distinguish, occupations whose incumbents will typically share
in broadly similar *market* and *work* situations, which following Lockwood's well known discussion, we take as the two major
components of class position. That is to say, we combine occupational categories whose members would appear, in the light of the
available evidence, to be typically comparable, on the one hand, in
terms of their sources and levels of income and other conditions
of employment, in their degree of economic security and in their
chances of economic advancement; and, on the other hand, in their
location within the systems of authority and control governing the
processes of production in which they are engaged.

(Goldthorpe 1980/1987: 39/40)

In his work with Erikson a more theoretically elaborated version of the schema was put forth, where the placement of an occupation in a particular class position was determined by more than
just market and work situation. Their revised formulation differentiates positions within *labour markets* and *production units*,
or more specifically, differentiates such positions in terms of the
'employment relations that they entail' (Erikson and Goldthorpe
1992: 37). Under the theory of social class put forth by Goldthorpe
which has been developed with the class schema derived by him
and his colleagues 'class positions are seen as deriving from social
relations in economic life or, more specifically, from *employment
relations*. It is therefore, in economic life that the implications for
individuals of the class positions that they hold should be most
immediately apparent' (Goldthorpe and McKnight 2004: 1).

---

the Weberian idea of market and work situation. This scale will not be
discussed here, as it was not a measure of social class as we conceptualize
it, where the respondents were asked to rank the occupational titles
according to their 'social standing'. For more on this scale see Goldthorpe
and Hope (1974).

For the operationalization of class in practical terms, this has implications for how employees are differentiated. Hence, what this then means is that

> since class positions are taken to derive from employment relations, the positions of employers, self-employed workers and employees represent an initial level of differentiation. However, in modern societies major importance will attach to the further differentiation that is obviously required *among* employees, who make up the large majority of the active population. This can be achieved, in a theoretically consistent way, by reference to *the mode of regulation of their employment* or, in other words, to the form of their employment contracts, due account being taken of both explicit and implicit features.
>
> (Goldthorpe and McKnight 2004: 3)

The main contrast for Goldthorpe (2000: 208) then occurs between 'labour contracts' (primarily for manual and lower grade non-manual workers) and the 'service relationship' (a contract for professional or managerial employees). See also Erikson and Goldthorpe (1992: 41–2).[19]

Though Goldthorpe's theoretical formulations have evolved over the years, for Breen (2005: 42) this change from early to later formulations of the Goldthorpe schema has had no 'operational consequences'. He also suggests that the different formulations of Goldthorpe's schema can be theoretically reconciled as well, 'since it was differences between positions in the nature of the employment contract that gave rise to the variations in the market and work situation that were relevant in the earlier version' (Breen 2005).

The Goldthorpe class schema has had its fair share of criticisms,[20] but the most vigorous critics have been the researchers at what has been called the *Cambridge school* (discussed further).

---

[19] For more detail on the theory behind his schema, see Goldthorpe (2000). The NSSEC—National statistics socio-economic classification in Britain (introduced in 2001) presents another version of the schema (see Rose and Pevalin [2003] for more details).

[20] For a discussion see contributions in Clark, Modgil, and Modgil (1990).

Despite these criticisms Goldthorpe's schema has been empirically validated on a number of occasions (Evans 1992, 1996, 1998; Evans and Mills 1998) by looking at both its construct and criterion validity and has been shown to be a valid and robust schema for the measurement of social mobility. Marshall, Newby, Rose, and Volger, who tested the explanatory power of three class schemas in Britain—The Registrar General's, the revised Erik Olin Wright typology, and Goldthorpe's schema—on outcomes such as voting, class mobility, and so on, concluded that Goldthorpe's schema was the most appropriate (Marshall, Newby, Rose, and Volger 1988, especially chapter 3).

Social Mobility Approaches and Class Classifications

While class classification is critical for mobility analysis since it helps delineate the categories between which mobility is observed to occur, there have been two major theoretical approaches to the study of social mobility itself, as discussed briefly in Chapter 1. The first is the class schematic approach which uses some of the class formulations elaborated in the previous section (especially the Goldthorpe classification); and, the second is the status attainment approach.

'The status attainment model ... postulates a hierarchical structure of socio-economic positions and attempts to assess which individual characteristics, such as education or family socio-economic background, lead to higher or lower attainment in that structure' (Prandy 1998b: 344). One example of this is the model used by Blau and Duncan (Blau and Duncan 1967: 19) in their study of the *American Occupational Structure* which asks the basic question of 'how the status individuals achieve in their careers is affected by the statuses ascribed to them earlier in life, such as their social origin, ethnic status, region of birth, community and parental family' (Heath 1981). Path analysis using a path model is the method by which they study the strength of these background characteristics. The use of a continuous scale of occupations is particularly associated with the status attainment model.

Some of the studies of status attainment also follow a *reputational* approach which obtains a measure of social standing

or prestige by asking respondents to rank occupations according
to the criteria (for example, prestige) chosen (see Prandy [1998a]
for a critique). According to Prandy the main problem with this
approach is that its concept of socio-economic status is over sim-
plified and ignores 'all issues of social processes' (1998b: 344).

Prandy recommends the Cambridge scale as an alternative to
this measure. It is a scale based on social interactions and 'inte-
grates the economic and the social, class and status, rather than
trying to distinguish them'. He adds that the

> theoretical basis (of the scale) is that incumbents of an occupation
> vary in the average resources of various kinds to which they have
> access and which they can utilise both in enjoying a particular life-
> style and in reproducing their situation. Common lifestyles, based
> on similar resources, are associated with higher levels of sociation:
> people will choose to interact more frequently with those to whom
> they are socially most similar.
>
> (Prandy 1998b: 346)

In effect, this scale captures social status as social interaction
here implies social acceptance. In the construction of this scale
the authors use information on friendship and marriage pattern,
that is, of social interaction, to establish any underlying structure. The authors of this study believe that this scale 'presents
a more adequate picture of social reality' (Prandy 1998b: 346, see
also Prandy 1990). This scale has been refined over the years and
a newer CAMSIS (Cambridge Social Interaction and Stratification)
version was introduced. The major difference between the two
scales was that the later CAMSIS version looks solely at marriage patterns while the older version looked at both marriage and
friendship patterns.

By studying the structure of friendship and of marriage the
Cambridge school concluded that there was an 'overwhelming
single dimension, along which occupational groups were ranged
in a near-continuous manner with no evidence of major gaps
at any point' (Prandy 1998b: 345–6). For them this '"complex
kaleidoscope", in other words, appeared to reveal the pattern of
near-continuous, hierarchical ordering, not one of social classes'
(Prandy 1998b: 345–6). They, thus, disagree with the view of

Goldthorpe and others that classes can be separated into distinct categories.[21]

In addition, while Goldthorpe and other neo-Weberians (for example, Lockwood) distinctly separate the class situation from the status situation, as mentioned in Chapter 1, Prandy and colleagues reject this view. In contrast, Goldthorpe sees the Cambridge scale as tapping a status dimension, which is correlated with, but is 'conceptually distinct' from class (see Chan and Goldthorpe 2002).

As can be seen from the above discussion, one major issue in class analysis is the use of either continuous or categorical measures. There is no one accepted way and different research questions require the use of one or the other of these measures. We come back to this when we discuss our choice in the last section of this chapter, but first a discussion on the schemas previously used for mobility analysis in India.

We begin our summary of the various class schemas for India with studies based in the rural areas, moving on to research conducted in the urban areas, and ending with the analyses of a more current national classification by Kumar, Heath, and Heath (2002a and b) along with a discussion of its merits and limitations.

Schemas for India

Studies using schemas for the analysis of mobility in India range from the theoretically tangled (Chekki 1971; Jain 1969; Jorapur 1971; Mehra, Sharma, and Dak 1985) to a few using clear objective theory and methodology coupled with statistical techniques for their analysis, such as Nijhawan (1969), Kumar, Heath, and Heath (2002a and b), McMillan (2005). The lack of clarity in the conceptualization of *class* has led to a confusing array of schemas and measuring instruments, each of which is meant to capture the researcher's concept of class. A brief survey of the studies now follows.

Peasant class differentiation/stratification in village societies was the focus of research about three-four decades ago. The

[21] On the other hand, see Evans (1998) for work that, in the author's opinion, supports the existence of discrete classes.

primary focus was on the political works of Lenin and Mao and classes were seen as based on the concept of the exploitation of labour (see Chaudhuri 1987; Patnaik 1976). In brief, the classes derived from these key studies were summarized by Chaudhuri (Chaudhuri 1987: 2121) into five categories based on their relation with property and any exploitative relations: landlords and rich peasants who mainly hired labour; upper middle peasants who hired occasional labour; lower middle peasants or subsistence farmers; poor peasants who hired themselves out and also cultivated small pieces of rented land; and finally, the agricultural labourers who owned no land or other assets.

Chaudhuri (1987) used the method of cluster analysis to arrive at this schema and divided 'the agricultural population of a village into different classes on the basis of three variables (i) net sale or purchase of labour power; (ii) net sale or purchase of paddy; (iii) caste-tribe rank' (p. 2124). According to Chaudhuri, of the three variables the effect of the third, caste or tribe was the weakest. This, Chaudhuri believes, is because 'nowadays, even in a village society, caste occupations are not strictly pursued' (Chaudhuri: 1987). The use of caste in differentiating classes seems unfortunate, as discussed in Chapter 1, because not only are 'caste' and 'class' distinct conceptually, caste could also be a variable of interest by itself. This merging of the two concepts is quite characteristic of research on class in India.[22]

Mehra, Sharma, and Dak (1985), in their study of social mobility trends in *rural* Haryana, only include four broad categories in their schema (providing little explanation): Farmers, Artisans, Labourers, and Service. But as this study is restricted to the rural parts of two districts in the state, the applicability of these class categories more broadly, or to the urban areas of the state is unclear.

Jain (1969), in his study of a middle sized town in north India, accepts occupations as the main basis of class status (no definition of what *class status* implies is provided—though the operationalization seems to imply some understanding of prestige), since the 'identification of social class on the basis of the prestige of

---

[22] See Yadav, Mishra, and Srivastava (2003: 126) for an example of an exception to this.

occupations is more objective and useful' (p. 1703). Beyond labelling his classes as Class I, II, III, and IV, he does not define these classes at all, other than saying that the classes are formed based on their *'prestige criterion'*. No indication is given as to which occupations belong to which class category or how the prestige criteria would be arrived at. Other studies that use various measures of occupational prestige (including objective and subjective measures) are Kaistha (1987) and D'Souza and Sethi (1972).

Jorapur (1971), in his occupational mobility study of Dharwar city, in Mysore (renamed Mysuru) in Karnataka, orders his classes by 'status' but fails to explain how he came to order them and what the empirical justification was in arriving at the final status schema. His Table 1 (p. 462) reveals the following 'status' categories: Higher and lower admin and professionals, traders, skilled workers, cultivators, unskilled workers. Due to the small sample size and the biases in selection of households, the results of this study, according to the author, are inconclusive.

Chekki's (1971) classification of Brahmin households in Dharwar city (which was studied by Jorapur) uses 'objective and subjective criterion' (p. 370) which are not very clearly laid out. Only on sifting through the dense text one concludes that the author in their interview and analysis looks at variables such as the 'values' of the people, their material possessions, behaviour patterns, expenses on food and on education and luxury items, interaction with other classes, marriage patterns, and so on, all indicators of lifestyle rather than class per se (work somewhat similar to that of the Cambridge school, particularly where social interaction and marriage patterns are concerned). None of these aspects are explained or laid out clearly, nor is it clarified why the author decided to place certain occupations in a particular class and not in another. The final three categories used are the upper class (including 'physicians, engineers, lawyers, professors, businessmen, and a few upper cadres of government service' [p. 370]); Middle class ('white-collar jobs such as clerks, school teachers, middle strata of salaried persons in government or private offices and a few medium scale traders and those in professions with moderate income' [p. 370]), and the lower or working class ('factory workers, artisans, and those with limited means such as priests, astrologers and cooks' [p. 371]). In addition to its rough outline, Chekki's classification is limited to Brahmin households and might preclude any application to other castes.

Staying with studies in Mysore, Ramu and Wiebe (1973) conduct their occupational mobility study using both survey and participant observation techniques in the Kolar Gold Fields. They study aspects of both caste and class, using simple crosstabs and frequency distributions. They arrive at their class schema by asking the respondents to rank themselves occupationally into: executive (high, low) professional (high, low), business (high, low), owner farmers, white-collar (high, low), blue-collar (high, low), and service and other. There are a number of drawbacks when using such a subjective self-ranking technique without clear criteria for the ranking, not least that it precludes any broader application.

A more detailed classification is provided by Sovani and Pradhan (1955) who arrive at their occupational classification for an urban area by ranking occupations according to what they call 'skill-status.' By this they imply the 'weighing (of) social status, economic status and other elements like skill, enterprise etc.' (p. 25). They arrange their ten grades in 'an ascending order of social and economic importance', these are (we quote from their paper—pp. 25–6):

1. Unskilled manual work ('workers who require no sort of skill but only physical energy' [p. 25]—domestic workers, beedi-workers, sweepers, those engaged in agriculture
2. Skilled manual work (their earnings 'represent payment for their labour' [p. 26]) —includes both semi-skilled and skilled workers like the artisan classes, like cobblers, carpenters, barbers, tailors, wiremen, goldsmiths
3. Lowest professions, administrative posts—astrologers, priests, compounders, jugglers, primary teachers
4. Small businesses—hawkers, shopkeepers
5. Highly skilled and supervisory manual work
6. Clerks and shop-assistants
7. Intermediate professions ('absence of manual work and greater emphasis on brainwork and educational attainment' [p. 26])—salaried posts, secondary teachers, sub-inspectors

8. Medium business
9. High professions and administrative posts
10. Owners of factories, large shops

This classification, though more detailed than many others, does not explain the procedure followed to arrive at the particular ordering or possible overlaps among the classes.

A brief survey of these studies only highlights further the confusion regarding the conception of class and the instruments used to measure it. More often than not, authors have merged together the concepts of status and class; prestige and economic situation. In this book, since we strive to maintain a distinction between class and status we do not use any of the measures of status attainment reviewed here. This review has highlighted that the schema used is influenced strongly by the context of the study; hence, some of the previous schemas have had a strong agricultural focus while others have not. As the book employs a national framework, both urban and rural occupations are a part of our analysis.

The studies discussed above have all been limited to small rural hamlets or areas in one city (see also Gist [1954] for a study based on two towns in south India). Not many authors have attempted a national study using class except the following studies by Mitra and Singh (1999), Nijhawan (1969), Kumar, Heath, and Heath (2002a, 2002b), McMillan (2005) and Vaid and Heath (2010); all of which interestingly use national level data from various rounds of the NES conducted by the Centre for the Study of Developing Societies, New Delhi.

For Mitra and Singh (1999), economic classes seem to be conceptually close to social classes. Using the NES, 1996 data (the same dataset used by Kumar, Heath, and Heath and McMillan), they cover a wide range of characteristics, which they then compute to create a scale of economic classes. Their class schema is strictly *hierarchical*. For the construction of their economic classes they take into consideration the expected monthly income of the respondent in addition to their housing, assets, and occupations. Despite covering this wide range, their explanation of how they arrived at their final classes of Rich, Middle, Poor, and Very Poor lacks empirical justification. Their use of the data on expected

monthly income is questionable. The question that they use to
arrive at this amount is, 'Looking at your needs and the needs of
the household, how much income per month do you think you
must have to meet your needs?' This question fails to capture the
actual monthly income of a household. While this index of economic classes might be justified for the purpose of their study on
the analysis of the Indian electorate, it falls short of a detailed class
schema needed for a mobility study.

In the study of social mobility, according to Nijhawan, 'essentially, one is concerned with strata, that is, occupations that seem
to form a unit with relative uniformity in terms of class, economic
opportunities and style of life' (1969: 1554). Using the 1967 edition of the NES data, he divided his classes into agricultural (with
three sub-divisions) and non-agricultural occupations (with five
sub-divisions); he grouped his occupations by 'skills and prestige'
(Nijhawan 1969: 1554). His class schema is as follows:

Non-Agricultural
1. Professionals: administrative, executive, technical, and
   managerial
2. White-collar: clerks, salesmen, and other related occupations
3. Business and trade
4. Skilled and semi-skilled
5. Unskilled
Agricultural
6. Owner cultivators and farmers
7. Tenant cultivators
8. Agricultural labourers

This schema, while fairly delineated, merges concepts of 'style
of life' with 'economic opportunities'. A more recent class schema
is that of Kumar, Heath, and Heath (2002a and b; henceforth called
the Kumar and Heath schema since it draws heavily on the work
of Anthony Heath). Using the 1971 and 1996 (male only) rounds of
the NES, Kumar and Heath arrive at their schema by combining
occupations that they believed shared similar market and work situations and employment relations—in terms of the 'security and
stability of the contract', chances of promotion and so on. Even

though this schema is by far the most clear and concise account of class in India, it has not been statistically validated, not even by the authors. We refer back to this schema in the next section on our conceptualization.

The original Classes according to Kumar, Heath, and Heath (2002a: 2983) are:

1. Higher Salariat = Executives, professional and white-collar employees
2. Lower Salariat = Class IV employees
3. Business = Large and small businessmen
4. Petty Business = Small store owners and road side businesses
5. Skilled and Semi-skilled manual labourer = mechanics, electricians, tailors, weavers, carpenters and craftsmen, and rickshaw puller
6. Unskilled Manual Labourer = Manual labourers, excluding those in the agricultural sector (such as construction workers, chowkidars and sweepers)
7. Farmers = Owner cultivator and tenant cultivators with more than 5 acres of land
8. Lower Agriculturists = Less than 5 acres of land, sharecropper, agricultural labourer, landless labourer, tea plantation worker, dairy farmer, fishermen, shepherds, hunters.

McMillan (2005), using the 1971 and 1996 NES datasets, employs a class categorization, generally similar to that of Kumar and Heath and Nijhawan in its division between the agricultural and non-agricultural sectors; however, his schema does differ from Kumar and Heath's as far as he does not differentiate 'as carefully between the lower Salariat, business and petty business, which have low numbers of Scheduled Caste and Scheduled Tribe workers' which form the focus of his study (177: fn 4; see also Table 4.1: p. 136). His three agricultural categories differentiate between farmers on the basis of size of land-ownership or non-ownership; whereas his three non-agricultural categories are the high classes (including professionals, government employees from Class I and II, and big business), the skilled workers (including Class III and IV government employees) and unskilled workers. According to

McMillan 'the validity of each categorisation was checked by referring to the non-occupational variables available for each year' (2005: 135).

Though, perhaps suitable for their original use, most of the schemas discussed here may not be generally applicable. Furthermore, most are founded on conceptualizations that differ markedly from the one employed in our study. Of the above, Kumar and Heath's (2002a, 2002b) schema is the closest to our conceptualization of class, in addition to having been previously used for a national study of the mobility of men (and adapted for a study of women and men by Vaid and Heath [2010]). This schema provides a starting point for our discussion and operationalization of class.

Conceptualization of Class[23]

A 'neo-Weberian class schema is a set of principles that allocates positions to classes so as to capture the major dimensions of differentiation in labour markets and production units that are consequential for the distribution of life chances'. Breen (2005: 43)

Following the above discussion and our brief review of the debates surrounding class, we turn to our conceptualization of class, especially with the aim of operationalizing it, so that it can be used in the present mobility study.

In this book we will study mobility in terms of movements of individuals between discrete classes, rather than in terms of their status attainment. That is, not in terms of a hierarchical ranking based on a criterion such as prestige. Put another way, as the aim of the book is to study the patterns of class mobility in India, it was considered better to view the study of mobility in *class structural* terms, that is, to discuss mobility rates, and so on in terms of class categories that are 'relational' rather than in terms of 'categories which represent simply levels distinguished within a prestige or status continuum' (Erikson and Goldthorpe 1992: 32).

---

[23] For this section we found it useful to consult Breen's (2005) paper on constructing a neo-Weberian class schema.

Our argument is thus similar to Rose's (1998), that as 'class is a relational and not a hierarchical concept, (something which both Weber and Marx made eminently clear), hence the need for categorical/typological approaches rather than continuous measures' (p. 756, brackets added).[24]

In our view (following Goldthorpe, Heath, and others) in terms of the operationalization of class, it is not occupations themselves that form discrete groups with shared life chances, but classes which are made up of occupations that share *similar market and work situations* (the line dividing classes then can run not only between but through occupations as well). For instance, a self-employed plumber and an employee plumber would both be in distinct classes by virtue of their different employment status. That is, factors such as security and other employment conditions, promotion prospects, income, as well as the employment status (employee, self-employed, or employer), would determine a person's life chances (see Goldthorpe 1980: 39).

We now briefly discuss the practical formulation of this schema for India. We do not directly apply the Goldthorpe schema to India, as it was created specifically for industrialized countries. Any slavish use of a Western class schema might show a warped picture of the divisions in Indian society. What is needed is a schema specifically tailored to the Indian situation, especially keeping in mind the vast size of the agricultural sector and the divisions therein.

As previously mentioned, of the small number of studies on class mobility in India, the Kumar and Heath schema shares a similar conceptualization to ours. As discussed, this schema separates *four* major groupings, which are further subdivided to form their eight classes. These major groupings quoted from their paper are (Kumar, Heath, and Heath 2002a: 2983, emphasis mine):

1. The Salariat (subdivided into high and low), largely consisting of *salaried employees* with relatively *secure and permanent employment* in business corporations and the civil service (although also including *self-employed professionals*).

---

[24] For more on the status attainment approach and its application in rural India see Sharda (1977).

2. The bourgeoisie or business class (subdivided into business and petty business), consisting of *independents who are directly exposed to market forces* and are not cushioned by the bureaucratic employment of the salariat.

3. Manual labourers (subdivided into skilled/semi-skilled and unskilled), with relatively *high risks of unemployment* and *poor promotion prospects.*

4. Agriculture (subdivided into farmers with more than five acres of *land* and 'small' farmers and agricultural labourers).[25]

This schema is not a strictly *hierarchical* one, and in order to study upward or downward mobility in the vertical sense, they put forth an alternative where the salariat and the business class are at about the same level, followed by the lower salariat at a lower level, then come the skilled, petty business, and farming classes, and at the lowest level are the unskilled and lower agriculturalists (Kumar, Heath, and Heath 2002a). Nor do the authors create separate schemas for rural or urban India.

The classes in the schema used are separated quite generally in terms of employment conditions such as security and permanency of employment. A distinction is also maintained between the agriculturalists and non-agriculturalists. Admittedly, it would be theoretically more refined to look at differences by employment status, for example, managerial status, especially within the category of employees, but data limitations do not make this possible. The construction of this class schema has been guided by theoretical ideas, but also as in the case of Erikson and Goldthorpe

---

[25] According to the authors, 'there is inevitably some degree of arbitrariness in the boundaries between these eight classes. For example, five acres of poor land in a remote area with little access to commercial centres will have rather different implications for one's life chances than one or two acres of well-irrigated land close to large markets'. They admit that this is a problem, 'which is intrinsic to large-scale survey research where we have only limited information about the detailed circumstances of individual farmers'. However, they show through their work on male mobility that the divisions they have constructed do demonstrate 'significant differences, on average, between groups in their patterns of social reproduction' (Kumar, Heath, and Heath 2002a: 2984).

(1992: 46), been shaped by *practical* considerations, particularly the type of data that is available.

In the technical Appendix A of this book, we provide a brief outline of the validation exercise we have conducted on the Kumar and Heath schema using tests of predictive validity to see if their classes are being differentiated from each other with respect to a limited range of outcomes (Vaid 2007). This validated schema forms the basis of the more comprehensive schema that we develop using a newer and more detailed dataset. We end the Appendix with our discussion of our validated schema which is used to analyse mobility patterns in this book. Our schema has 11 social classes which are laid out in Table A.7 in Appendix A. It is important to note that while the Kumar and Heath schema was applied towards the study of male social mobility, there is no reason to assume a similar schema would not be applicable to women (indeed this schema has been used by Vaid and Heath [2010] to study men and women's mobility patterns). However, there have been many debates on the exclusion of women from stratification research generally, and social mobility analysis in particular (Acker 1998; Crompton and Mann 1986; Abbott and Payne 1990; Goldthorpe 1983, 1984). The inclusion or exclusion of housewives too has been much debated (Acker 1998). In some of these studies (for example, Payne and Abbott 1990) some distinct criteria such as education are also used to assign married women for instance to manual or non-manual work. Their main reason for this is the concentration of women in certain occupations in the British case. Since there has been little work on social mobility of women in India, we do not create a separate schema for women; but, rather, we study the national schemas and any variations by gender.

This chapter has provided an insight into some of the major debates on class. Needless to say, this has not been a comprehensive account of this much researched area,[26] but, rather, it has set the tone for the discussion about an appropriate class schema for an Indian class mobility study. Thus, the focus has not been on whether one or the other Western theory and class categorization,

---

[26] Nor does it include the possible classification economists and others may have used for their studies (see Chapter 1).

for example the Wright schema, has relevance to empirical sociology per se, but, rather, the focus has been on conceptualizing an adequate measure for Indian class mobility research given the focus of the study. In light of Rose's quote in the beginning of this chapter we end by highlighting that the schema used in this book is considered most appropriate for the study of mobility in India, and we have consciously chosen not to apply a Western categorization to India, though we have used elements of Western theory to create and validate the schema. This decision has, among other things, been influenced by the unique shape of the Indian occupational structure and the economy, where, a vast proportion of the population are still engaged in agriculture and allied activities, with the concurrent increase in the service sector.

4

How Mobile Is India?

Social Mobility Patterns and Trends

Patterns of intergenerational social mobility—both absolute and relative rates—are critical for understanding the opportunities open to, and used by, women and men from different strata. They are useful measures to capture inequality among strata. In the context of increased economic growth, mobility rates indicate whether opportunities have been open to all; and if not, what are the significant criteria of difference across groups. An analysis of these rates over time also helps identify periods of 'change'.

This chapter explores patterns of intergenerational social mobility in India, enabling us to answer the following questions: Firstly, how much mobility is there for women and men, and what are the patterns? Secondly, what are the relative mobility chances of women and men keeping structural changes constant? Thirdly, has there been any change in this social fluidity (or relative mobility) across time? And, finally, are there any locality-wise differences in social mobility? The next chapter discusses these patterns across caste and community groups and Chapter 6 discusses a possible driver of this mobility.

As seen in the discussion on economic growth (Chapter 2), agriculture remains the primary employer in the country, though its share in the industrial distribution of the workforce has declined more sharply in the last decade. In this context, with regard to the first question posed, we would expect this industrial and occupational distribution to be reflected in a fairly high rate of intergenerational stability in India, with some possible indicators of change in the last decade. This expectation is supported by previous research on Indian men's intergenerational stability (Kumar, Heath, and Heath 2002a and b). With regard to women, we would usually expect there to be less intergenerational stability, given that men, rather than women, tend to directly inherit their father's occupations, in turn, pushing women out of their origin classes. However, we take forward Vaid and Heath's work (2010) that showed otherwise. We would also expect the profile of mobility to be different for women within the context of the discussion in Chapter 2 where we observed the marginalization of the female workforce due to increasing industrialization. These changes imply that women's employment has a very specific character. Firstly, women have been increasingly concentrated in the sectors of the economy that require lower skills and have worse pay and working conditions (see Parthasarathy and Nirmala 1999; Liddle 1988). Secondly, the shift from agriculture to non-agricultural employment has occurred predominantly for men, and women have tended to take on the seasonal agricultural jobs that men have moved out of (Chadha 1999). This character of employment implies that when we compare class profiles and social mobility of women with men, we might expect to find a few specific differences. We would expect women to be more concentrated in low level agricultural jobs. Furthermore, regarding non-agricultural occupations, we would expect to find more women in the lower levels of these classes as women are also marginalized here. Thus, in terms of direction of mobility we would expect women to be more downwardly mobile or stable in the lower level occupations than men, and we might reasonably expect there to be less upward mobility for women when compared to men.

The second question posed in this chapter allows us to analyse patterns of social fluidity (or, mobility net of structural changes) and to explore any gender differences in the openness of Indian society. Given the predominance of more patriarchal father-to-son inheritance (for example, Basu 1999), we would expect the association between origins and destinations in terms of employment to be weaker for women than men. In other words, son's class is expected to have closer links with father's class (this leads on from the expectations under the first question above). However, given the specific pattern of women's employment we may expect to see a stronger origin-destination link for women at lower levels of the class structure.

We are further interested in exploring whether there has been any change in these social fluidity rates over time given the economic changes discussed in Chapter 2. We would expect men, rather than women, to display more increasing fluidity across birth cohorts (our proxy for time), because they have been able to benefit more from industrialization (in terms of moving to the expanding non-agricultural sectors or in terms of migration) than women have.

Finally, differences in mobility and fluidity across locality are discussed. In a country with disparate economic development and labour force participation, and with over 60 per cent of the population still categorized as rural, we expect to find differences in labour force participation of women and men across localities— rural and urban. Insofar as this reflects greater 'traditionalism', we would expect to find less female mobility and fluidity in the rural areas than in the urban areas.

Absolute mobility rates will help us to answer the first question posed in this chapter. We use relative mobility to answer the second question on social fluidity in India. As Miles states: 'absolute rates of mobility are sensitive to a range of "exogenous" structural influences, which vary according to time and place, they are an unreliable guide to the "openness" or "fluidity" of social structures; conceived in terms of the relative life chances of individuals from different social backgrounds' (1999: 6), and so relative mobility is a better indicator of the fluidity or openness in society. It is the intrinsic (that is, independent of marginals) pattern of association between origins and destinations.

With regard to which is the best measure of mobility, Breen and Whelan (1996: 33) have following to say:

> ... the only sensible response is that it depends on the particular issue that one is trying to grapple. Social mobility is a complex phenomenon and it is desirable that we should avoid one 'true' number approaches. If the focus is on class formation and elite closure, then what is crucial is the de facto patterns of mobility as reflected in the current composition of each class. In this case we should focus on

absolute mobility. If, on the other hand, concern is with equality of opportunity, then mobility must be assessed in relative terms.

This book aims to draw out, in particular, the equality of opportunity in terms of access to certain class destinations for persons from varied class origins, that is, the openness of Indian society. Hence, relative mobility is an essential component of this exercise and will be discussed in greater detail in this and subsequent chapters.

As discussed previously, one of the few research projects on class mobility of men in India was conducted by Kumar, Heath, and Heath (2002a and b), we will extend this research by including the mobility of women (extending Vaid and Heath 2010) and by using more appropriate statistical techniques to answer the questions posed.

We begin the chapter by reproducing in Table 4.1 the class schema used along with the frequency distribution for the NES 2014 data (discussed in technical Appendix A at the end of this book; the arguments behind this specific schema were covered in Chapter 3). Due to small sample sizes in some of the empirical analysis in this and in the following chapters, in order to avoid empty cells, we also use a collapsed version of this 11-class schema. The five collapsed classes are the Professional Class (made up of the High Professionals, Low Professionals, and the Routine Non-Manual [RNM] Clerical class); the Business class (made of Business and Petty Business classes); the Farming class (comprised of Large and Small Farmers); the Manual class (including the RNM Service, the Skilled, and the Semi-unskilled classes); and finally the Low Agriculturalists. Unless otherwise mentioned the 11-class schema is the primary schema used (the section on 'Total Mobility' later in this chapter discusses the ordering of the schema for calculating mobility patterns). This class schema allows us to compare our findings to Vaid and Heath (2010). Since, locality-wise analysis is critical to our understanding, given the wide differences across the country, this scheme does not differentiate between 'urban' and 'rural' occupations. An exercise that begins with that differentiation would prejudge the types of jobs held across locality.[1] Instead,

---

[1] The data also indicates that there are agrarian occupations in urban areas and many non-agrarian ones in rural areas. This would also vitiate the use of any location-specific class schema.

Table 4.1 The Eleven-Class Schema with Frequency Distributions for NES 2014[2]

Classes with detailed occupations	Frequency Per cent
High Professionals: higher professionals including scientists, engineers, doctors, college and university teachers etc., administrators and officials (Class I)[3]; elected officials (Central/ State level); managers	3.7
Low Professionals: lower professionals, administrators and officials (Class II); elected officials (District level); technicians, supervisors, school teachers	5.6
Routine Non-Manual Clerical (RNM Clerical): High grade routine non-manual employees, other administrators, Class IV (peons), sales executives, sales persons, shop assistants, traditional clerks, Class III (clerical)	4.6
Business: Big business including factory owners and industrial establishments (with 7+ employees), medium business including small scale industries (3–6 employees), small business including saloons, small agencies (1–2 employees or family workers)	8.5
Petty Business: Petty shopkeepers including non-permanent or unauthorised structures, hawkers, vendors, rentiers	2.9
Skilled Manual workers (not in agriculture) including mechanics, electricians, jewellers	8.2
Semi- and Unskilled Manual workers (not in agriculture) including miners, masons, potters	9.1
Routine Non-Manual Service (RNM Service): Low grade routine non-manual employees, waiters, washermen, barbers, ayahs (maids), other service etc.	3.2

(Cont'd)

[2] For a detailed list of all categories see the NES 2014 Handbook (Lokniti CSDS).

[3] In this context Class I, II, III, and IV here are the Indian government classifications for public sector employees.

Table 4.1 (*Cont'd*)

Classes with detailed occupations	Frequency Per cent
Large Farmers: Farm owners with more than 5 acres of land	5.5
Small Farmers: Farm owners with 0–5 acres of land; Tenant farmers (with 5+ acres of land)	17.6
Lower Agriculturalists: Agricultural Labourers and Non-cultivators; Small Tenants (with 0–5 acres of land)	31.1

Source: NES 2014, CSDS Data Unit

the book disaggregates the pattern of mobility by location (rural–urban) to see whether there are indeed different patterns across locality.

Class Mobility and Its Profile[4]

Class mobility rates—both absolute and relative—are calculated from class mobility tables (see Chapter 1: Section titled 'Method: A Brief Note'). A mobility table is simply a cross-classification of class of origin (here, respondent's father's class) and class of destination (respondents own class). Hence, for each respondent, their

[4] In contrast to Western studies where mobility is analysed for respondents usually aged twenty to sixty-four, in this book we set no upper age limit for the analysis. This is because given the large informal sector in India (Harriss-White 2003) there is no 'retirement' age for a majority of the working population, most of whom continue to work all their lives. Setting an upper age limit would not capture all these people, and hence, my analysis includes all respondents aged eighteen and over. This decision might have implications for our results due to the possible effect of differential mortality, especially as mortality is not random with respect to class. We discuss this in more detail in a later section on birth cohort analysis (where an age limit is set). But we maintain that in the Indian case the arguments for observing the whole sample and not just people up till the age of sixty-four seem stronger than the argument for having an upper age limit.

own and their father's classes are mapped into this mobility table. This table then forms the basis for the analysis of social mobility rates and patterns.

Before we calculate the rates of mobility, we begin by studying the class profiles of respondents and their fathers. This class distribution contextualizes and helps in the comparison of structural change over a generation, as well as in the comparison of differences in women and men's current class positions, and finally, in comparing changes over the three survey periods (in subsequent chapters, the 2014 NES data is the primary data used).

After a discussion of the occupational structure we move on to exploring the first question about the patterns of class mobility where we discuss patterns of absolute and relative mobility rates. While this book focusses specifically on father to son/ daughter mobility, given the small number of employed mothers, Appendix A4.1 of this chapter provides a brief outline of mother to daughter mobility.

Class Distribution

Table 4.2 displays the class profiles or column percentages of respondent's *origin distribution* (that is, their father's class) and their own employment information (for those who have retired, information on their last job is included) called *destination distribution* for three survey periods: NES 2004, NES 2009, NES 2014. This allows us to see how many more, or less, people are in a particular class among sons/daughters and their fathers.

We first compare women and men in employment, and then compare their profiles to their fathers. We note that, as expected, the proportion of women in employment, that is, in this case, for those with class destination information, is much lower than the proportion of men in each survey year. This is a reflection of the low rate of employment of women that was highlighted in Chapter 2. Furthermore, as expected and can be seen from the distributions, the agricultural sector in India is much larger than in any of the industrialized nations studied in the social mobility literature (see Breen 2004). These classes together constitute the largest proportion of the population in both generations (while

Table 4.2 Class Profiles of the Origin and Destination Distributions of Women and Men, NES 2004–14

Origin Distribution Column %	2004		2009		2014	
	Men	Women	Men	Women	Men	Women
High Professional	1.8	2.4	1.3	1.2	2.1	2.8
Large Business	7.3	3.6	7.3	3.8	7.0	4.3
Large Farmer	12.0	9.6	6.9	5.4	7.2	5.8
Low Professional	3.8	3.1	3.5	2.9	2.6	2.3
RNM Clerical	4.5	4.1	4.3	3.3	3.8	3.4
Petty Business	2.7	2.2	2.8	1.5	2.2	1.9
Skilled	5.5	4.7	5.4	4.7	4.7	5.0
Small Farmer	22.9	23.3	17.8	16.1	25.2	17.4
RNM Service	4.4	2.4	2.6	2.1	2.0	2.2
Semi-unskilled	7.6	8.3	7.6	6.5	9.4	9.0
Low Agriculturalist	27.4	36.3	40.5	52.5	33.9	46.0
N	11623	4909	15256	6274	7114	2560
Index of Dissimilarity M–W Origin		**10.6**		**12**		**13.3**
Destination Distribution Column %						
High Professional	2.8	2.6	3.3	2.8	3.6	4.1
Large Business	10.4	3.5	10.4	3.4	10.4	3.3
Large Farmer	9.8	8.9	5.6	4.9	5.7	5.0
Low Professional	5.6	5.9	6.2	7.8	4.6	8.4
RNM Clerical	6.8	3.6	6.6	2.8	5.4	2.4
Petty Business	4.9	2.9	4.0	2.4	3.3	2.0
Skilled	7.9	6.2	9.3	6.7	8.9	6.2
Small Farmer	17.7	21.3	13.3	12.4	18.7	14.5
RNM Service	2.7	2.8	3.3	3.3	2.9	3.9
Semi-unskilled	8.5	8.9	8.7	7.7	9.5	8.1
Low Agriculturalist	22.8	33.3	29.3	45.9	27.1	42.1
N	11623	4909	15256	6274	7114	2560
Index of Dissimilarity M-W Destination		**14.8**		**18.2**		**20.4**

Source: NES datasets, CSDS Data Unit.

Note: These indices of dissimilarity are derived from the table above.

	2004	2009	2014
Origin-Destination Men dissimilarity	13.6	17	14.9
Origin-Destination Women dissimilarity	6.2	11.8	10.4

the figures for agriculture combined vary across the survey periods—a distinct pattern can be seen—over 60 per cent of fathers are reported as being in agriculture across the surveys; however, around 50 per cent sons are in these agrarian occupations. For daughters, however, over 60 per cent across the years are engaged in agriculture—this is a lower proportion than seen in the NSS, but the patterns are similar). The largest concentration of fathers and respondents is in the low agricultural class. Moreover, looking at destination distributions there are more women than men in agriculture, particularly in lower agriculture.[5] However, between 2004 and 2009, we see a much sharper increase for women in the low agricultural class, and while this declines marginally for both men and women in 2014, the proportion is still higher than in 2004. This lends support to the discussion in Chapter 2 where we observed a greater concentration of women in lower agricultural occupations. Along with the increase in lower agriculture, we observe a decline (approximately 4 per cent points for men and women and then a stabilizing) in the large farming class. For small farmers there is a decline and then an increase for both men and women. There are also, as we expected, marginally more women in semi and unskilled manual work as compared to skilled manual work across most years. We also observe a marginal increase for men in this category over time, whereas for women, there is no clear pattern. Skilled manual work remains fairly steady for women and men, with a slight increase and then a decrease for men. Similarly, for the RNM service class there is not much of a pattern for men and a slight increase for women. Moving on to the professional categories, we observe a small, but steady, increase in high professional occupations for both women and men. The NES 2014 is distinct, with more women than men in the high professional class. We also see an increase for women in low professional

[5] The low agricultural class, as discussed in Chapters 2 and 3, might be considered to have the worst terms of pay and working conditions: with no contracts and low income based on the seasonal nature of the occupation. Women in this lower agricultural class are, in a sense, seen to be concentrated on the lowest rung of the class schema—with not much possibility of movement out of these classes.

work; for men there is an increase in 2009 and then a decline. Further, in RNM clerical work we observe a decline for men and women. Finally, there is not much change in the business class which remains fairly steady with more than twice more men than women in it. The petty business class, however, seems to decline across the survey years.

Clearly then in some regards the class distribution of men and women is quite distinct. What underlines this difference further is the comparison across one generation. We move to the discussion of this generational or origin-destination change across the survey years as seen in Table 4.2, and more distinctly in Figures 4.1a and 4.1b. In the two figures, the bars above zero show a positive change over a generation, that is, more sons or daughters than fathers, and bars below zero, a reduction over a generation.

We find that:

For the Professional Class:

a. An increase is seen for women and men when compared to their fathers in the higher professional class.

b. While men and women both show a greater proportion in the low professional class across the years than their fathers, the increase for women is not only much greater, but there are consistently more women than their fathers in low professional work across the years. This lower professional class includes a range of occupations, from class II employees to school/nursery school teachers. A disaggregation shows that within the teaching category there are gender differences. Marginally, more men than women are school teachers (as well as university teachers, an occupation included in the higher professional class); but, within nursery teaching there are nearly twice as many women than men.

c. We see an interesting decline for women across all years when compared to their fathers in the RNM clerical category; however, an increase is seen for men. This RNM clerical category includes a range of administrative, clerical, Class III, and IV jobs which are dominated by men.

For the Business Class:

a. We find a slight increase for men across surveys in the business class compared to their fathers, but a decline for women compared to their fathers.
b. A similar pattern is seen for the petty business class, though a marginal increase is seen for women when compared to fathers.

For Manual Work:

a. A much greater increase for women than men when compared to their fathers is seen in the RNM service category.
b. An increase for men and women in skilled work is seen; but, the increase is sharper for men.
c. A marginal increase for men and then a decline in the semi and unskilled work category for women and men, with a much sharper decline for women, is seen.

For Agriculture:

a. Within agriculture we see a decline of large and small farmers for women and men across a generation with a much stronger decline in 2014 for men.
b. For Low Agriculture, we see a decline for men in all surveys when compared to fathers. While there is a decline for women too, it is not as sharp as for men.

While these patterns and changes are fairly complex, a useful summary of the differences and changes in class profiles is provided by the index of dissimilarity. This index (Δ), shown in Table 4.2 below each section, is the percentage of people who would have to change their positions to make the two distributions the same. For example, for Table 4.2, this index is calculated using the following formula and is expressed as a percentage:

$$\frac{1}{2}\sum_i |f_iM - f_iW|$$

Where f_iM is the percentage relative frequency of men in category i, and f_iW is the percentage relative frequency of women in category i.

On studying the index of dissimilarity, we observe that there are smaller gender differences in origin distributions as compared to the current employment distributions (indicated by the Men–Women origin dissimilarity index in Table 4.2). While the distributions are clearly not identical, with a 10 per cent–13 per cent dissimilarity index, the similarity of the origin distributions, as Erikson and Goldthorpe (1992: 242) argued, indicates that there is 'little or no "selection" of women currently in the workforce by their class origins. In contrast destination distributions display wide sex differences'. While the dissimilarity index figures for origin are not insignificant, they are smaller than the figures for destinations.[6] Looking at the men-women destination index of dissimilarity, we see, about 15 per cent of women in 2004 would have to be 'reallocated in order to make their [current] distribution the same as that of men' (Erikson and Goldthorpe 1992: 242, brackets added). This Index of dissimilarity increases across the survey periods–more women would have to move to make their distribution similar to men—standing at roughly 20 per cent in 2014. This data further underlines the highly sex segregated labour market with a deepening of this segregation. However, this level of segregation at the broad class levels in India seems to be less when compared to industrialized countries (see, for example, various contributions in Breen 2004; especially Tables 5.1, 7.2, 8.1, 11.1, 11.2).

Furthermore, the sources of dissimilarity in India are different from those seen in industrialized countries. For example, rather than the RNM Clerical work category (as in Britain), it is the low agriculturalists and, to a smaller extent, the small farmers, low professionals, skilled, and the unskilled manual categories that have the largest number of women. Also, the professional classes in India are quite small compared to the industrialized countries. Table 4.2 shows that there are about the same proportion of women

[6] The origin dissimilarity index in this table is higher than in Vaid (2016) and differs from Vaid and Heath (2010) since here we include working women only. What this seems to indicate is that women who are in the labour market tend to have fathers who are quite distinct from the women who are outside the labour market. This is particularly so for women engaged in low agriculture with fathers in low agriculture, as well as women with business class fathers.

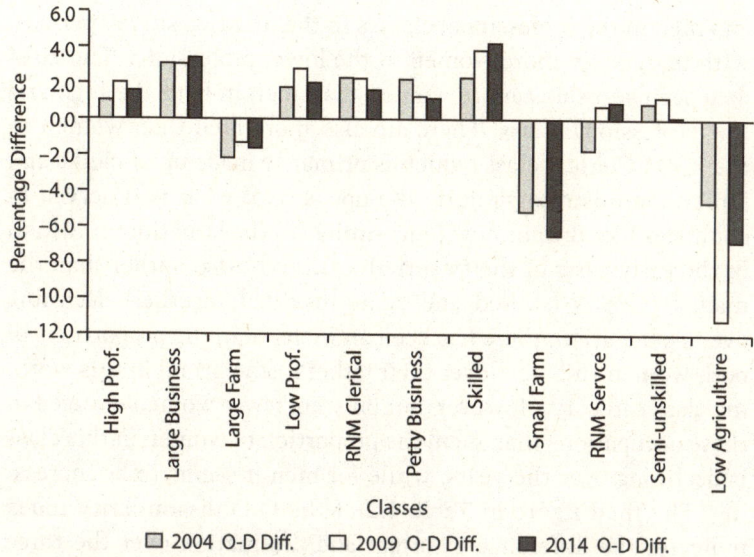

Figure 4.1a Change in O-D Distribution for Men, NES 2004–14
Source: NES 2004–2014, CSDS Data Unit.

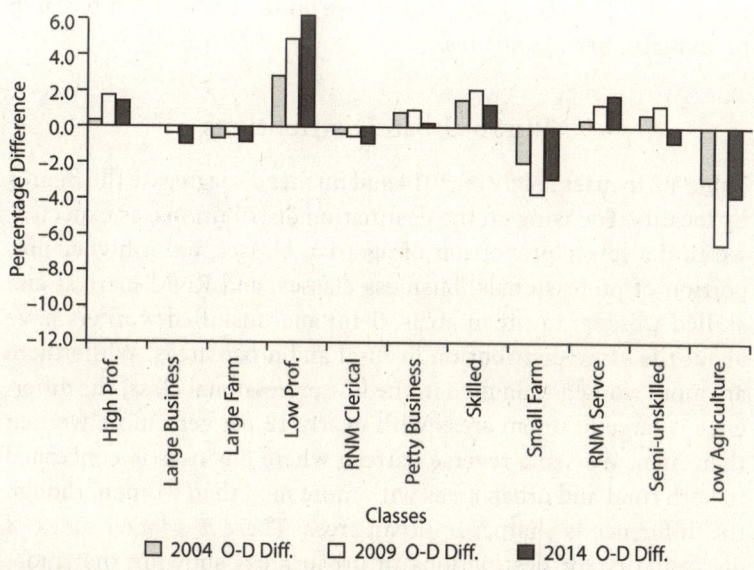

Figure 4.1b Change in O-D Distribution for Women, NES 2004–14
Source: NES 2004–2014, CSDS Data Unit.

and men in the professional classes in the first two survey periods, with marginally more women in the lower professions. The 2014 data seems to show more women than men in both the high and low professional class. There are also more men than women in the RNM Clerical class (which is primarily made up of clerks and junior administrators); quite the opposite of what is observed in countries like Britain now (but, similar to the situation in Britain in the early parts of the twentieth century). Also, rather than the manual classes (skilled and semi-unskilled together) declining over a generation, there has been an increase in the proportions of both women and men (over their father's generation) in this working class category. However, not only are fewer women engaged in these occupations than men; the proportion of women in this class is declining over the years, while for men it seems to be increasing. The final figure in Table 4.2 of the O-D dissimilarity index indicates the difference in origin and destination over the three survey years. We see that men's destination class is more distinct from their origin class (as compared to women). Women's distributions are hence more similar to their fathers as shown by Vaid and Heath (2010)—making the Indian case quite distinct from research on industrialized countries.

Rural–Urban Distributions

Table 4.3 focuses solely on 2014 and further disaggregate the figures by locality. Focusing on the destination distributions, as expected, we find a lower proportion of agrarian classes and a higher proportion of professionals, business classes, and RNM clerical and skilled workers in urban areas. Semi and unskilled workers have about the same distribution in rural and urban areas. While there are more women than men in the low professional class, the difference is large in urban areas with nearly 12 per cent more women than men. We see a reverse pattern where business is concerned in both rural and urban areas with more men than women, though the difference is sharper in urban areas. There is a larger index of dissimilarity for destinations in urban areas showing that more women would need to move to have a distribution similar to men—indicating a more sex-segregated labour market here.

Table 4.3 Class Profiles of the Origin and Destinations of Women and Men across Locality, NES 2014 Only.

	Rural Origin		Rural Destination		Urban Origin		Urban Destination	
	Men	Women	Men	Women	Men	Women	Men	Women
High Professional	1.5	2.4	2.4	3.3	4.2	4.5	7.9	7.9
Large Business	3.2	2.3	7.1	2.3	20.7	13.0	22.6	7.5
Large Farmer	8.5	6.3	6.9	5.6	2.4	3.8	1.0	2.1
Low Professional	1.6	1.5	3.4	5.5	6.3	5.8	8.8	21.1
RNM Clerical	2.2	1.9	3.7	1.4	9.6	9.8	11.4	6.8
Petty Business	1.4	.9	2.7	1.2	5.0	6.4	5.6	5.3
Skilled	3.1	2.7	6.9	4.6	10.7	15.1	16.3	13.2
Small Farmer	29.8	19.9	22.9	17.0	8.4	6.2	3.5	3.4
RNM Service	1.3	1.7	2.3	2.4	4.3	4.7	5.0	10.4
Semi-unskilled	8.7	8.7	9.5	8.3	12.2	10.4	9.5	7.2
Low Agriculturalist	38.7	51.7	32.2	48.2	16.3	20.3	8.5	14.9
N	5585.0	2091	5585	2091	1529	469	1529	469
Index of Dissimilarity	14.3		19.1		12.3		25.4	

Source: NES 2014, CSDS Data Unit.

The distribution of clerical work is unique in India compared to many developed countries where we still see a much higher proportion of men than women and the difference is sharper in urban areas. However, for service work, women surpass men by over 5 per cent in urban India while their proportions are similar in rural areas. Within manual work we see fewer women than men in rural and urban areas, but this category is itself bigger in urban India. The agrarian classes show an interesting pattern, while large farming has declined over a generation, we see fewer women than men in the farm-owning categories (with marginally more women in the category in urban areas). However, in the lower agricultural category which has increased over one generation, we see substantially more women (16 per cent more women than men in rural areas and 6 per cent more in urban areas).

These locality-disaggregated figures only emphasize the difference in the class distribution/labour market further. Women's position, while appearing quite precarious in both rural and urban areas, is also interesting in their being over-represented in low professional occupations (more than men), especially in urban India, thus hinting at possible paths/opportunities open to, and being used by, women to be more mobile. We observe this precariousness through the index of dissimilarity which is the highest in urban areas, where more women would have to move to have their class distribution similar to men.

The discussion in this section has detailed the class profiles across gender and over one generation, painting a picture of occupational change over time allowing for comparison with previous research. We now analyse how much mobility there is in India and the profile of this mobility.

Absolute Mobility Rates

Total mobility rates are an indicator of the amount of mobility in a society. Absolute mobility can be studied by observing inflow and outflow mobility tables along with total mobility rates. Hout (1983: 11) provides one way to understand how outflow and inflow mobility tables differ: 'the outflow percentages record the distribution of destinations for each category of origin; the image is of labour flowing out of the given origin occupation. The inflow percentages record the distribution of origin for each destination; the image is of labour flowing into the given destination occupation'. Both tables together provide a comprehensive picture of intergenerational change.

Inflow Mobility

According to Kumar, Heath, and Heath (2002a) inflow mobility tables show us 'where people currently in the different occupation classes came from. It shows us whether the classes are largely self-recruiting or have been open to an influx from other classes' (p. 2984). Inflow mobility rates are thus concerned with the 'social composition' of classes (see Heath and Payne 2000: 262). These inflow rates can be calculated by observing the column percentages in a mobility table. We expect to find greater inflow into the expanding classes, and less into the contracting classes such as agriculture.

Kumar, Heath, and Heath's (men only) study (2002a) of inflow mobility found that: within the farming classes, large farmers, and the lower agriculturalists were largely self-recruiting. Also, there appeared to be very little recruitment from one farming class into another. Further, both their higher and lower salariat showed the highest levels of inflow mobility. The authors showed that well over half the members of these salariat classes came from other classes, particularly from lower agricultural origins.

Tables 4.4 and 4.5 display the NES 2014 inflow mobility tables (for men and women respectively). Looking at Table 4.4, for men, we find similar results to Kumar, Heath, and Heath: the three farming classes: large farmers, small farmers, and low agriculturalists are the most self-recruiting (with about 88–90 per cent of their members coming from the same class). Moreover, we observe that there is indeed little recruitment from one agricultural class to another: for instance, for men who are large farmers there is little recruitment from the small farmers and low agriculturalists (over 90 per cent of large farmers are recruited from the large farming class itself).

The low professionals followed by the high professionals are the least self-recruiting for men, and hence, show a high amount of

Table 4.4 Intergenerational Mobility Table for Men: Inflow Rates (Column Percentages), NES 2014

Class Origins	Class Destinations											
	High Profn	Business	Large Farm	Low Profsn	RNM Clerical	Petty Business	Skilled	Small Farmer	RNM Service	Semi-unskilled	Low Agric.	Total
High Professionals	30.6	1.8	0.5	3.7	3.1	0.4	0.6	0.5	2.4	0.6	0.4	2.1
Business	11.8	43.4	0	12.9	8.6	2.6	4.2	0.5	5.4	1.6	0.5	7.0
Large Farmers	3.9	3.9	90.1	5.2	4.2	6.0	2.7	1.3	1.0	1.6	0.9	7.2
Low Professionals	11.8	3.0	0.2	21.2	5.2	1.7	1.4	0.6	2.9	1.0	0.4	2.6
RNM Clerical	7.8	6.4	0.5	8.6	20.4	4.3	6.1	1.0	3.4	2.1	0.5	3.8
Petty Business	1.6	1.5	0	2.5	3.7	32.5	2.5	0.4	2.4	0.9	0.4	2.2
Skilled	4.7	3.0	0.2	4.3	3.9	2.1	36.3	0.8	2.0	2.5	0.3	4.7
Small Farmers	14.1	16.6	3.2	21.2	22.2	17.1	12.9	87.8	18.0	6.8	4.8	25.2
RNM Service	0.8	1.2	0	1.5	2.3	1.7	2.7	0.2	35.6	1.2	0.6	2.0
Semi-Unskilled	3.1	5.0	0.2	2.5	7.8	10.7	11.2	1.0	7.3	64.9	1.3	9.4
Low Agriculturalists	9.8	14.3	5.0	16.6	18.5	20.9	19.3	6.1	19.5	16.7	89.8	33.9
N	255	740	403	326	383	234	636	1331	205	675	1926	7114

Source: NES 2014, CSDS Data Unit.

Table 4.5 Intergenerational Mobility Table for Women: Inflow Rates (Column Percentages), NES 2014

	Class Destinations											
Class Origins	High Profn	Business	Large Farm	Low Profsn	RNM Clerical	Petty Business	Skilled	Small Farmer	RNM Service	Semi-unskilled	Low Agric.	Total
High Professionals	48.6	1.2	0.8	4.2	6.5	0	1.9	0	0	0.5	0.2	2.8
Business	7.6	42.9	0	17.7	8.1	2.0	5.0	0	8.0	1.0	0.4	4.3
Large Farmers	1.0	4.8	83.6	3.3	1.6	2.0	3.1	2.2	3.0	0	1.1	5.8
Low Professionals	6.7	1.2	0.8	18.1	0	0	1.9	0	1.0	0	0.6	2.3
RNM Clerical	9.5	7.1	0.8	13.5	22.6	5.9	2.5	2.2	3.0	1.0	0.6	3.4
Petty Business	1.9	4.8	0	5.1	6.5	25.5	1.3	0.5	6.0	1.0	0.3	1.9
Skilled	2.9	8.3	0	5.1	6.5	13.7	44.7	0.8	5.0	3.9	0.7	5.0
Small Farmers	9.5	11.9	7.0	14.4	9.7	13.7	9.4	84.4	4.0	5.8	2.6	17.4
RNM Service	0	2.4	0	2.3	9.7	2.0	1.3	0	37.0	0	0.4	2.2
Semi-Unskilled	1.0	6.0	0	6.0	6.5	13.7	6.9	1.9	13.0	74.4	1.4	9.0
Low Agriculturalists	11.4	9.5	7.0	10.2	22.6	21.6	22.0	8.1	20.0	12.6	91.8	46.0
N	105	84	128	215	62	51	159	371	100	207	1078	2560

Source: NES 2014, CSDS Data Unit.

inflow mobility (with nearly 80 per cent and 70 per cent of their members respectively being recruited from other classes). The RNM Clerical category also shows a high rate of inflow mobility (this was a class that Kumar, Heath, and Heath, due to their data restrictions, were unable to separate out from their salariat).[7] These classes have indeed expanded at a particularly high rate and that explains their low rate of self-recruitment.

In comparison with Kumar, Heath, and Heath's result we observe that rather than the members of the high professional class coming predominantly from the low agriculturalist class (a result explained by them by the fact that the low agricultural class is the biggest of their 7 classes), in our case, the high professional class derives members more often from the small farmers, low professional class, and business class. The recruitment from the low professional to high professional class makes intuitive sense. The recruitment from farm to business ownership indicates the resources that these respondents are able to tap into to move to the high professional class. For the big business class, while self-recruitment is higher, they also recruit from the small farmers and low agriculturalists (and not so much from the petty business). The manual work classes are more self-recruiting than the professional classes (and, in addition, recruit from the small farm and low agricultural classes and from within the manual class).

With regard to the inflow mobility of women (Table 4.5), we see that: firstly, the farming categories are the most self-recruiting for women as well. But, as expected, it is the low agricultural classes that are marginally more self-recruiting (92 per cent) instead of the large and small farmers (84 per cent). Secondly, it is the low professional rather than the high professional class which is the least self-recruiting for women and this could be the result of the pattern of expansion of classes over a generation that we saw in Table 4.2 in which the high professional class has not expanded as much as the low professional class. The low professional class is recruiting quite evenly from big business, RNM Clerical, and small farm

---

[7] It needs to be remembered that the professional classes here are not identical to Kumar and Heath's Salariat. For a discussion of the classes they use see their paper (2002a).

owners. The high professional class is fairly highly self-recruiting (much higher than for men) with nearly 50 per cent of its members coming from high professional class origins. Finally, the remaining members of the high professional class seem to come disproportionately from the low agriculturalists, small farmers, followed by the RNM Clerical class. Given the empty cells in this table, it is important that the small sample sizes are borne in mind for the conclusions drawn.

The results of the inflow mobility analysis have shown us the 'composition' of the different classes. We find some support for Kumar, Heath, and Heath's results as the agricultural classes are found to be the most self-recruiting for both women and men (though for women it is the lowest agricultural class rather than the farm *owner* classes where there is the most amount of self-recruitment); and the professional classes are the most open to influx—high and low professionals and clerical workers for men, and predominantly low professionals and clerical workers for women.[8]

Outflow Mobility

Outflow mobility rates can be derived from the same mobility table, by studying the row, rather than column, percentages. These tables show what 'share of people originating in any particular class are found in any other class' (Breen 2004: 18).

If we look along the diagonal of an outflow mobility table (Tables 4.6 and 4.7), the numbers depicted are those of the sons/daughters who followed their fathers' footsteps occupationally (Heath 1981). Along the diagonal we find more people than would be expected by chance; these are the people who have been intergenerationally stable.

[8] We will not be focusing in great detail on inflow mobility rates in the rest of the book as we are more interested in analysing the chances of people from different class origins of gaining access to various classes (which is better explored through outflow mobility rates and relative rates of mobility), rather than on issues of 'class composition' or indeed, its implications on 'class formation and class actions' that is one of the primary concerns of inflow mobility (Heath and Payne 2000: 262).

Table 4.6 Intergenerational Mobility Table for Men: Outflow Rates (Row Percentages), NES 2014

Class Origins	High Profn	Business	Large Farm	Low Profsn	RNM Clerical	Petty Business	Skilled	Small Farmer	RNM Service	Semi-unskilled	Low Agric.	N
						Class Destinations						
High Professionals	53.4	8.9	1.4	8.2	8.2	0.7	2.7	4.8	3.4	2.7	5.5	146
Business	6.0	64.6	0	8.5	6.6	1.2	5.4	1.2	2.2	2.2	2.0	497
Large Farmers	1.9	5.7	70.8	3.3	3.1	2.7	3.3	3.3	0.4	2.1	3.3	513
Low Professionals	16.3	12.0	0.5	37.5	10.9	2.2	4.9	4.3	3.3	3.8	4.3	184
RNM Clerical	7.5	17.5	0.7	10.4	29.1	3.7	14.6	4.9	2.6	5.2	3.7	268
Petty Business	2.6	7.2	0	5.2	9.2	49.7	10.5	3.3	3.3	3.9	5.2	153
Skilled	3.6	6.5	0.3	4.2	4.5	1.5	68.5	3.0	1.2	5.0	1.8	337
Small Farmers	2.0	6.9	0.7	3.8	4.7	2.2	4.6	65.2	2.1	2.6	5.2	1793
RNM Service	1.4	6.4	0	3.6	6.4	2.9	12.1	1.4	52.1	5.7	7.9	140
Semi-Unskilled	1.2	5.5	0.1	1.2	4.5	3.7	10.6	1.9	2.2	65.3	3.7	671
Low Agriculturalist	1.0	4.4	0.8	2.2	2.9	2.0	5.1	3.4	1.7	4.7	71.7	2412
Total	3.6	10.4	5.7	4.6	5.4	3.3	8.9	18.7	2.9	9.5	27.1	7114

Source: NES 2014, CSDS Data Unit.

Table 4.7 Intergenerational Mobility Table for Women: Outflow Rates (Row Percentages), NES 2014

Class Origins	High Profn	Business	Large Farm	Low Profsn	RNM Clerical	Petty Business	Skilled	Small Farmer	RNM Service	Semi-unskilled	Low Agric.	N
High Professionals	70.8	1.4	1.4	12.5	5.6	0	4.2	0	0	1.4	2.8	72
Business	7.3	32.7	0	34.5	4.5	0.9	7.3	0	7.3	1.8	3.6	110
Large Farmers	0.7	2.7	71.8	4.7	0.7	0.7	3.4	5.4	2.0	0	8.1	149
Low Professionals	12.1	1.7	1.7	67.2	0	0	5.2	0	1.7	0	10.3	58
RNM Clerical	11.6	7.0	1.2	33.7	16.3	3.5	4.7	9.3	3.5	2.3	7.0	86
Petty Business	4.1	8.2	0	22.4	8.2	26.5	4.1	4.1	12.2	4.1	6.1	49
Skilled	2.4	5.5	0	8.7	3.1	5.5	55.9	2.4	3.9	6.3	6.3	127
Small Farmers	2.2	2.2	2.0	7.0	1.3	1.6	3.4	70.3	0.9	2.7	6.3	445
RNM Service	0	3.5	0	8.8	10.5	1.8	3.5	0	64.9	0	7.0	57
Semi-Unskilled	0.4	2.2	0	5.7	1.7	3.0	4.8	3.0	5.7	67.0	6.5	230
Low Agriculturalist	1.0	0.7	0.8	1.9	1.2	0.9	3.0	2.5	1.7	2.2	84.1	1177
Total	4.1	3.3	5.0	8.4	2.4	2.0	6.2	14.5	3.9	8.1	42.1	2560

Source: NES 2014, CSDS Data Unit.

In Table 4.6 we see that a larger proportion of male farmers, businessmen, and manual workers have been intergenerationally stable as compared to people from other classes. In addition, when it comes to the farming sector, one observes hardly any movement at all, for example, low agriculturalists tend not to move into the farm owning category as less than 1 per cent of low agricultural origin respondents end up as large farmers themselves, and only 3 per cent move to being small farm holders (a result observed in the inflow table as well).

Interestingly, while approximately 50 per cent of those from high professional origins remain in this category, nearly the same amount move out, predominantly moving into large business, low professional, and RNM clerical work. Much fewer in number cross the manual-non-manual class barrier falling into the manual work, or agrarian labour, category. A similar indication of movement among the non-manual categories is also seen when we look at the low professional, and to a weaker extent, the RNM clerical class.

For women (Table 4.7), the farming classes are also the most intergenerationally stable. More critically, women with fathers who are in the high and low professions are more likely to be in the same class, and these figures are much higher than the figures for men. Conversely, and contradictory to the figures for men, women do not seem to 'inherit' the RNM clerical work occupations which is the least intergenerationally stable. More than 30 per cent of those from RNM clerical work origins are likely to 'move up' to the low professional class, followed by 12 per cent to the high professionals.

The patterns found in these mobility tables for 2014 are very similar to those found in 2004 (lending greater confidence to the overall persistence of the result).

Total Mobility

We now summarize the *amount* of mobility in the country often referred to as the absolute mobility rate. Mobility tables similar to the ones previously discussed are used to calculate the summary indices of mobility shown in Table 4.8. It needs to be noted that these mobility indices are based on 'table' percentages and not

Table 4.8 Summary Indices of Mobility, Comparison across NES Datasets

Year	Men					Women				
	Stability	Upward Mobility	Downward Mobility	Horizontal Mobility	U/D	Stability	Upward Mobility	Downward Mobility	Horizontal Mobility	U/D
1996	67	19	7	7	2.7	–	–	–	–	–
2004	64	20	11	5	1.8	71	15	11	4	1.4
2009	62	23	10	5	2.3	67	18	10	5	1.8
Rural	67	21	8	4	2.6	72	15	9	4	1.7
Urban	48	31	12	9	2.6	51	27	15	7	1.8
2014	65	21	9	5	2.3	71	16	9	3	1.8
Rural	69	19	8	4	2.3	77	13	7	2	2.0
Urban	49	30	13	8	2.2	46	30	17	7	1.7

Source: 1996 figures are from Kumar, Heath, and Heath (2002a) who use seven-classes to study male-only mobility patterns from the NES 1996 dataset; The 2004, 2009 and 2014 figures are calculated from the NES datasets. The 2004, 2009, and 2014 figures use an eleven-class schema.

Note: Figures are percentages and rounded to the nearest decimal. U/D=upward over downward mobility.

on column or row percentages. Figures lying on the diagonal in a mobility table are summed up and indicate the percentage of those who are intergenerationally stable. Figures above the diagonal are those who are downwardly mobile (for example: they may have moved from high professional class origins to low agricultural class destinations). Conversely, figures below the diagonal have been upwardly mobile.

As the classes in our schema are not 'strictly hierarchical' (as discussed by Vaid and Heath 2010: 140) and the study of mobility involves analysing vertical movement, we depict below the classes that may be considered to be at roughly the same level as each other for the purpose of calculating the amount of mobility. For example, movement between the high professionals, the large business, and the large farming category is considered to be horizontal movement, but the movement from low professional to a high professional class is upward, albeit short range upward, movement. In contrast, movement from the small farming class or low agriculturist class to the high professional class is considered to be long range upward movement. The reason why certain classes were placed together or above another class is both intuitive (regarding life chances or access to resources that one might have by belonging to a particular class) and also due to the differences in the parameters in the class validation exercise (see Appendix A of this book).[9]

The order of classes for the calculation of rates of mobility is:

1. a. High Professionals
   b. Large Business
   c. Large Farmers
2. Low Professionals
3. a. Routine Non-Manual Clerical
   b. Petty Business
   c. Skilled
4. a. Small Farmers
   b. Routine Non-Manual Service

[9] Some classes had parameters similar to others in the validation exercise, and for the purpose of this analysis they are considered to be at a similar level.

5. a. Semi and Unskilled workers
   b. Low Agriculturalists

Table 4.8 summarizes social mobility patterns from 1996 (Kumar, Heath, and Heath's men only study) till 2014, using the expanded class schemas (details in table). The figures are percentages. The figures for 'stability' can be read as 100 minus the amount of mobility, that is, upward, downward, or horizontal together (or put another way: absolute mobility = 100 - stability). The amount of stability seems to have gone down till 2009, but then rose again for both women and men (indicating an increase and then a subsequent decline in social mobility rates). Interestingly, however, the pattern of upward mobility over downward (the U/D column) has stayed constant between 2009 and 2014 (and the pattern of horizontal mobility too is stable across the years for men, though for women we see a slight change). In terms of locality, more or less, similar patterns for men between 2009 and 2014 are seen with more stability experienced in 2014. Urban men experience much higher mobility than rural ones (with the amount of upward mobility exceeding downward to a similar extent—as seen in the column U/D). However, between 2009 and 2014 rural women have seen less movement (stagnated), whereas urban women have experienced more mobility (both upward and downward) over urban men. Horizontal mobility is much higher in urban areas.

Overall, we observe more stability for women than is seen for men. This finding is consistent with Vaid and Heath (2010) and quite the opposite of patterns seen in Western industrialized countries where women are observed to be more mobile (see, for example, Heath and Payne 2000; Erikson and Goldthorpe 1992; and various collections in Breen 2004).

In concurrence with Vaid and Heath (2010: 145), the 'direction of mobility of women is the same as that of men', even though overall there is substantial stability. Thus, we see both women and men experience more upward over downward mobility (as seen in the last column marked U/D in Table 4.8) in India, which is a pattern similar to what is seen in developed countries. It is argued that this 'surplus in upward over downward mobility has occurred due to changes in the occupational structure that have resulted in increasing "room at the top"'. Yet, this surplus is not as high in India as it is in the other countries, and hence indicates the 'slower rate of change in the occupational structure in India' (Vaid and Heath 2010: 145), as shown in Table 4.2. By paying attention to the rates of upward and downward mobility, we can also see that while women are indeed less upwardly mobile than men as expected, both women and men are downwardly mobile to the same extent (except urban women). This implies that the surplus of upward over downward mobility is slightly higher for men than it is for women.

We can conclude that the patterns of absolute mobility reflecting the slower pace of structural changes imply that in absolute mobility terms India shows very high intergenerational stability. In addition, the surplus of upward over downward mobility is much smaller in India due to the 'slow rate of expansion of the non-manual classes and slow rate of contraction of the agricultural classes' (Vaid and Heath 2010: 145). We also observe that men have been able to use the slight expansion in the occupational structure to their advantage as they have been more upwardly mobile than women. However, urban women seem to be an exception, indicating different opportunities (or challenges) faced by women in urban areas—as seen through both the higher upward and downward mobility rates.

Relative Mobility: Social Fluidity

While absolute mobility rates are useful as a summary measure, in order to factor in the implications of structural change on mobility patterns, we turn to the study of relative mobility rates. This will allow us to answer the second question posed at the beginning of this chapter on the openness of Indian society. These relative rates deal with relative chances of people from differing origin classes achieving one class destination rather than another. Relative mobility or social fluidity measures are not influenced by structural changes in the class distributions (that is, changes that occur due to expansion and contraction of certain classes), as are absolute mobility rates. Hence, social fluidity is usually treated as a 'better indicator' of 'inequality of opportunity in a society' whereby lower rates of fluidity imply higher inequality of opportunity (Vaid and Heath 2010: 131). Before exploring whether women and men have similar relative rates of mobility, we should consider the extent of 'stickiness' in Indian classes. Stickiness implies the lack of relative mobility in particular class combinations.

As a 'backbone' of log-linear models, odds ratios are the main measures we use to study relative rates of mobility.[10] An odds ratio is a measure of association between variables that form a table. 'These ratios show us the relative risks of someone from one origin 'making it' to a destination and avoiding another one (Heath and Payne 2000)' (Vaid and Heath 2010: 147). An odds ratio of 1 (one) shows perfect mobility, that is, equal odds between the categories being compared.

Table 4.9 shows that these ratios for most of the class contrasts are extremely large. For example: the farmer: low agriculturalist odds ratio is 237:1 for men. This is in line with the results of the absolute mobility study, which showed the high amount of stability in the farming categories and lack of movement between these categories. Particularly, movement from a low agricultural to a large farming category and vice versa is rare, hence providing the very large odds ratios. In other words, a lot of 'stickiness' exists within the agricultural sector. This may be explained by the ownership of land, which is highly hereditary or by caste (this will be further analysed in the next chapter).

The most fluidity, that is, the lowest symmetrical odds ratios, are to be seen in the professional categories, a result that also makes sense in the light of the findings from the absolute mobility study.

[10] 'An odds ratio is the ratio between the frequency of being in one category and the frequency of not being in that category' Knoke and Burke (1980: 9). 'An odds ratio is an extension of the basic idea lying behind the disparity ratio. But whereas the disparity ratio looks at the relative chances of getting to a *single* specified destination, the odds ratio compares the chances of getting to *alternative* destinations' (Heath 1981: 262). Both ratios are concerned with the measure of relative mobility chances. In this book we discuss odds ratios.

Table 4.9 Symmetrical Odds Ratios, NES 2014

	Men	Log odds (ln)	Women	Log odds (ln)
Farmers: Low Agriculturalists	237:1	5.5	273:1	5.6
High Professional: Large Business	67:1	4.2	232:1	5.4
Business: Petty Business	382:1	5.9	116:1	4.7
High Professional: Low Professional	15:1	2.7	31:1	3.4

Source: NES 2014, CSDS Data Unit.

We find that the highest amount of stickiness is in the business class with 382 to 1 chance that someone from the petty business makes it to the largest business category. However, the least amount of stickiness is seen among the professionals with a 15 to 1 chance for the lower professionals making it to the higher professional class. For women, however, we see a slightly different pattern. While the least amount of stickiness is again in the professionals, the most amount of stickiness is seen amongst the farming categories and not amongst the business class.

In order to make a comparison of the odds ratios easier, we look at the log of the odds. This helps in observing the symmetry of the odds ratios on a log scale. The results are broadly consistent for women and men (with the exception of the business class odds ratios).

As discussed by Vaid and Heath (2010) for the 2004 NES data, when we compare the symmetrical odds ratios for India with those in industrialized countries (as discussed in the concluding chapter) we find much higher stickiness in India. This, Vaid and Heath find, is a sign of firstly, the much higher levels of 'inequality of opportunity' in India and secondly, of the 'closed nature of Indian society' (Vaid and Heath 2010: 150; see Breen 2004 for odds ratios on various countries).

Since from one mobility table numerous odds ratios can be calculated,[11] we use log-linear models to establish patterns and test our hypotheses. For instance, we are able to test, whether the

---

[11] In the present study 100 such odds ratios can be calculated, as in an $r \times r$ table: $(r-1)^2$ odds ratios can be calculated (Hout 1983: 16).

complete sets of odds ratios are common across gender (and later whether they are constant over time and across rural–urban locations). That is, we now move on to answer the question: do women and men have similar relative rates of mobility?[12]

Log-linear analysis is the method most often used to study cross-classified tables and is particularly useful for the study of mobility tables such as those discussed this far. In order to evaluate which of the log-linear models introduced best fits the data we compare some summary statistics (for a discussion see Breen 2004: 25–7; we use models similar to those employed by Vaid and Heath 2010: 163 with suitable modifications). In brief these statistics are as follows:

The goodness of fit of the model is observed by studying the G^2 or likelihood ratio χ^2 statistic. The formula for this is $2\sum F(\log F - \log E)$ where F is the Observed cell Frequency and E is the Expected cell Frequency.[13] But, as the sample size of the present data is quite large one might expect the χ^2 or G^2 to remain significant (at the 5 per cent level). Therefore, to provide a further test of the model fit we look at the Index of Dissimilarity (Δ). This index, introduced in the section 'Class Mobility and Its Profile' of this chapter, can also be interpreted as depicting the 'percentage of cases misclassified', that is, the number of cases that are allocated to wrong cells by the model being studied (Erikson and Goldthorpe 1992: 89). It follows that the lower the Δ, the better the fit to the data provided by the model. In addition to studying the Δ, we also look at the Bayesian Information Criterion or BIC. The BIC is calculated using the formula: $Bic = G^2 - d.f. \times \log(N_{ij})$. The lower the BIC the better the fit to the data. Some authors have shown reservations about using the BIC particularly because 'using the Bic generally leads to a preference for simple models that reflect the broad contours, rather than the details of the social fluidity regime' (see Breen 2004: 27 for a discussion). But, as an additional fit statistic we present the BIC along with the G^2 and the Δ to help us select the preferred model.

---

[12] While writing this section Breen (2004), particularly chapter 2, and Erikson and Goldthorpe (1992), particularly chapters 3 and 7 were very useful.

[13] See Hout 1983: 15 for a discussion of the G^2 or L^2 as it is called there; see also Breen 2004: 24.

To analyse whether women and men have similar relative mobility chances or whether we observe any gender differences, we fit a number of the standard log-linear models. In the first model (in Table 4.10) called the complete independence (or perfect mobility) model: origins, destinations, and gender are hypothesized to be independent of each other—that is, we hypothesize that there is no stability—but rather perfect mobility irrespective of gender. The notation for this model is $\log_m = \lambda + \lambda_i^O + \lambda_j^D + \lambda_k^S$.[14] In Table 4.10, according to the classical goodness of fit (G^2) test this model does not fit the data well (as the p-value is 0.000), and also misclassifies 52 per cent of the cases (the Δ). We, thus, have to reject the hypothesis that there is perfect mobility, which is not surprising.

As this model is not a good fit, we move onto the second model, that is, the conditional independence model, where the origins and destinations are postulated to be independent of each other within each gender, but the class distributions of fathers and their sons/daughters are postulated to vary by gender. The notation for this model is $\log_m = \lambda + \lambda_i^O + \lambda_j^D + \lambda_k^S + \lambda_{ik}^{OS} + \lambda_{jk}^{DS}$. This model again provides a bad fit to the data. It misclassifies over 51 per cent of the cases. The *BIC* for this model is also very large.

The third model is the Common Social Fluidity model (CmSF). This model postulates an association between origins and destinations, but it is presumed to be common for women and men; that is, there are hypothesized to be identical relative rates of mobility for women and men, and hence, no gender difference. As can be seen through the notation an additional origin destination (OD) term is added to the conditional independence model: $\log_m = \lambda + \lambda_i^O + \lambda_j^D + \lambda_k^S + \lambda_{ik}^{OS} + \lambda_{jk}^{DS} + \lambda_{ij}^{OD}$. This model fits the data well despite the G^2 not providing a significant fit, as it only misclassifies 2.4 per cent of the cases. Also, the *BIC* of the model is low. This CmSF model, thus, indicates that there are similar relative rates of mobility for women and men in India. This is similar to the results of the research on developed countries (see, for example, Erikson and Goldthorpe 1992).

---

[14] Where O = origins, D = destinations, and S = gender; (λ) is a constant term in the models.

As the CmSF is a fair but not a perfect fit to the data by classical standards, it leaves open the question whether there are overall differences in fluidity between women and men and particularly what form these differences take. That is, is the origin-destination association weaker for one gender rather than another as we would expect, given the large gender inequality in India. In order to answer this question, we use the uniform difference or Unidiff model—the last model in Table 4.10.

Unidiff models (Erikson and Goldthorpe 1992, also called a log-multiplicative layer effect model, see Xie 1992) are used to study the 'difference in "vertical mobility" between two mobility tables' (Xie 1992: 380). In the current analysis for both women and men this table-specific parameter refers to the strength of the association between origins and destinations that 'is specific to one sex against the other' (Erikson and Goldthorpe 1992: 246)—that is, it compares the male and female mobility tables. The formula below for the Unidiff model is reproduced from Erikson and Goldthorpe (1992: 246, footnote 24) and it can be seen that it is an extension of the CmSF model shown in the previous section.

$$\log F_{ijk} = \lambda + \lambda_i^O + \lambda_j^D + \lambda_k^S + \lambda_{ik}^{OS} + \lambda_{jk}^{DS} + \beta_k X_{ij}$$

Table 4.10   Log-linear models of Social Fluidity for Women and Men, NES 2014

	G^2	d.f.	p	Δ	*Bic*
Complete Independence O, D, S	15723.44	220	0.000	51.75	13704.45
Conditional independence OS, DS	15150.23	200	0.000	51.00	13314.79
CmSF OD	137.51	100	0.008	2.35	−780.21
Unidiff OD|S	140.80	99	0.004	2.28	−767.74

Source: NES 2014, CSDS Data Unit.

Note: N=9674; d.f.=degrees of freedom; eleven-class schema; O=origins, D=destinations, S=gender (models in text). These figures are based on an eleven-class scheme that has some small sample sizes for women. These results should be read along with the later results on the collapsed scheme.

In the equation, X_{ij} refers, in this case, to the pattern of association between origins and destinations for women and men and β_k is a 'table specific multiplier that raises or lowers the overall strength of all the odds ratios in a uniform manner' (Breen 2004: 34).

Using Jeroen Vermunt's statistical programme *Lem*, we fit the Unidiff model to the tables for women and men. As seen in the last row of Table 4.10, the Unidiff model does not improve on the fit of the CmSF model. This shows that even though the CmSF does not fit perfectly (according to classical tests) the Unidiff model fails to improve its fit further, suggesting there is no general tendency for women's class fluidity to be different from men's. Thus, the hypothesis that the strength of the association between origins and destinations would be weaker for women rather than men does not seem to hold, rather the Unidiff parameter for women is marginally stronger than for men.[15] This provides support for the absolute mobility results, where we see a fairly high amount of stability for women—slightly more so than for men.

Hence, it can be concluded that the difference between the two mobility tables for women and men has a more specific character, it may well be that the association is stronger in some regions of the table than in others. As the CmSF or Unidiff models do not provide a perfect fit (and misclassify over 2 per cent of the cases), in order to see whether there is any clear pattern of the inadequate fit of the model, we observe the adjusted residuals of the CmSF model (see Appendix 4.2). The adjusted residuals do not display any coherent or clear pattern of differences between men and women (any figure over 1.96 shows disproportionally more (if positive), or less (if negative) people in that cell than chance alone would dictate). For example, in most developed countries one possible difference is seen to be in the petty business inheritance, but we do not seem to see that in India.

Regarding relative mobility rates we conclude that women and men seem to have similar chances of relative mobility in India, which might imply that privileged fathers are preserving their privileges for their sons *and* daughters—though the mechanisms

---

[15] Unidiff for women is 1.0249, slightly stronger than the parameter for men 1.000.

of how this privilege is secured may be distinct. We discuss this in the concluding section of this chapter, in Chapter 6, and in Appendix B of this book.

Trends in Social Mobility and Fluidity

We now move to the third research question regarding the trends in mobility and fluidity, especially whether there has been increasing fluidity in India over time, as would be expected under the modernization hypothesis. Before we discuss the results of this analysis it is important that the drawbacks of using a birth cohort approach (particularly given the current dataset)[16] to study over-time change are highlighted. This birth cohort analysis allows us to extend on and compare our results to Vaid and Heath (2010).

'A cohort is any group of individuals linked as a group in some way—usually by age. And cohort analysis is a method of investigating the changes in pattern of behaviour or attitudes of such groups' (Glenn 1977: 5). For the analysis of mobility trends over time we conduct a birth cohort analysis. For such an analysis as Vaid and Heath (2010: 162) mention, it would be ideal to have datasets collected through the same sampling procedures and using the same questions over different time points (Heath 1981: 81) rather than to use a cross-sectional dataset. But, as discussed by the authors, due to data restrictions, particularly the lack of data on women as well as differing procedures followed in the various National Election Studies, such an overtime comparison is difficult in India (though some overtime results across surveys are presented in Table 4.2

---

[16] For an over time analysis on India it was not possible to use surveys conducted at different time points (as for example, Heath and Payne [2000] do) as the older versions of the NES (1967 and 1971 versions) do not adequately cover women. And though the NES 1996 does cover women it uses different survey and occupational coding procedures. Hence, we are forced to restrict ourselves to the 2004–14 datasets, and for this section instead of the different measures in the datasets, we follow a birth cohort approach using the 2014 data (see Erikson and Goldthorpe 1987; Heath and Payne 2000, for examples of other studies that follow this approach). See Breen (2004: 4) for a discussion on the disadvantages of using a birth cohort approach.

and 4.8). In the absence of such data, Heath suggests a division of respondents into 'birth cohorts' (1981: 81). There are numerous disadvantages of employing this procedure, namely, 'individuals in the same age group do not necessarily present a representative sample of all those born in those years due to deaths, selective migration, and so on. Moreover, differential mortality may be an important issue, given that mortality is not random with respect to class and older cohorts might be a selection of people who have been upwardly mobile' (Vaid and Heath 2010: 162). So we might not see too much downward mobility due to this differential mortality and a selection bias may be introduced. Moreover, 'those born in earlier cohorts will have spent longer in the labour market, hence, many young people who might seem downwardly mobile now, may be quite successful later on in their lives (see also Heath and Payne 2000: 258; also Breen and Jonsson [1997] for issues of recall bias in reporting parental occupations especially for older birth cohorts)' (Vaid and Heath 2010: 162).

But, as mentioned previously, access to repeated consistent cross-sectional surveys is somewhat limited, such as those used by Goldthorpe and Mills (2004); and we have had to make do with the datasets available. In this regard, the results of this birth cohort analysis should not be exaggerated, but they should be seen as providing a general indication of trends in mobility.

As for Vaid and Heath (2010), our birth cohort analysis is similar to Erikson and Goldthorpe's (1992) 'quasi-cohorts' since the people we are able to study are those that have been left when others have died or moved on. In practical terms, the data asks the respondents at one point about their job, rather than say ten years after they entered the labour market, as Heath (1981) did in his study of mobility. Nor does it have information on mobility from class of origin to class of first employment that Erikson and Goldthorpe (1992: 71) had available, which allowed them to focus attention on quite a specific life cycle phase. Instead, we treat all the respondents aged thirty-five and above to have reached 'occupational maturity' (Erikson and Goldthorpe 1992: 71)—though we also include those in their mid-20s and 30s for comparison. Similar to these authors, we too 'take results for cohorts of this age (35 years) or older as giving a reasonably reliable indication of the "completed" pattern of the collective class mobility of their members' (Erikson and Goldthorpe

1992: 71, brackets added). The caveats regarding differential mortality mentioned before need to be kept in mind.

To study birth cohorts, due to small sample sizes in some classes, we use the collapsed 5-class schema. In addition, we collapse the birth years into four 10-year groups. We do not show the results for the cohorts born before 1950 (that is, those aged sixty-five and above), as the sample sizes were too small to make adequate comparisons.

Birth Cohort Patterns

Absolute Rates

Figure 4.2 provides the pattern for the all India average—while Figure 4.3 disaggregates by locality.

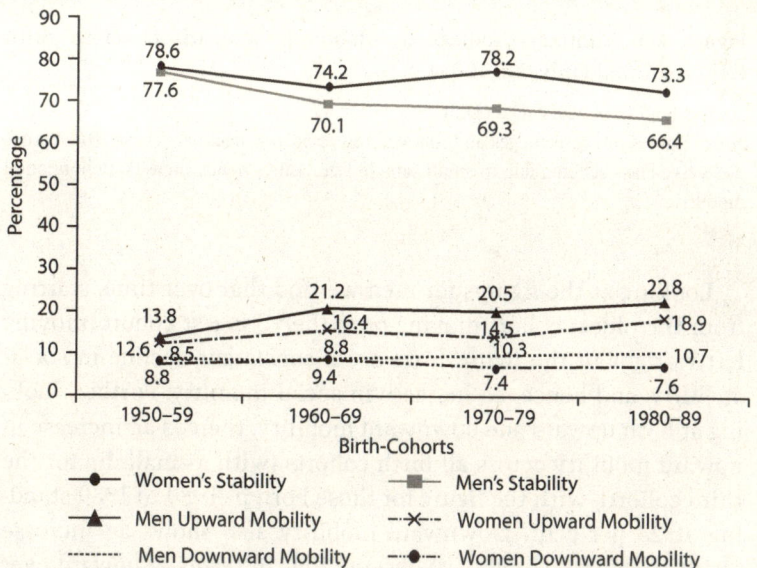

Figure 4.2 Summary Indices of Mobility, Comparison across Birth Cohorts, NES 2014

Source: NES 2014, CSDS Data Unit.

Note: Figures are percentages and rounded to the nearest decimal. These 2014 figures use a five-class schema due to small sample size issues, hence there is no horizontal mobility.

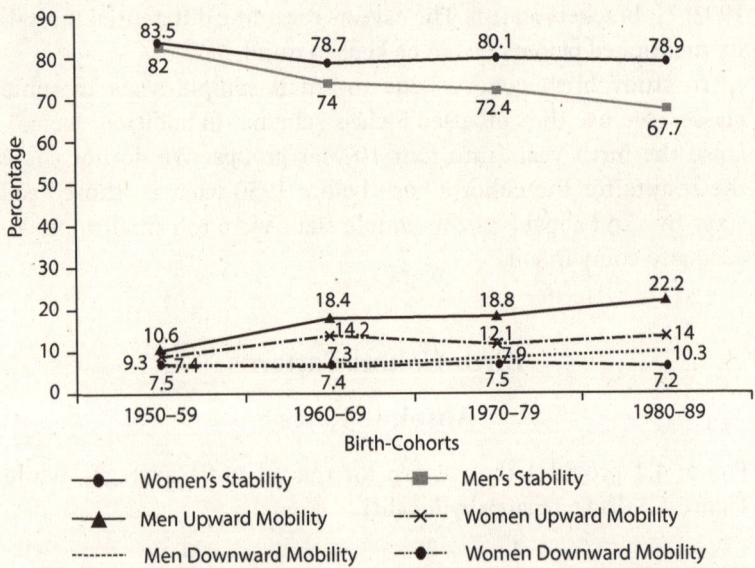

Figure 4.3 Summary Indices of Mobility, Comparison across Birth Cohorts, Rural Only; NES 2014

Source: NES 2014, CSDS Data Unit.

Note: Figures are percentages and rounded to the nearest decimal. These 2014 figures use a five-class schema due to small sample size issues, hence there is no horizontal mobility.

Looking at the figures for men we find that over time, starting from the oldest cohort moving onto the youngest cohort (moving left to right in the figures), we see a consistent decline in social stability, and hence, an increase in social mobility. Further, looking at both upward and downward mobility, there is an increase in upward mobility across all birth cohorts (with a small dip for the third cohort), with the figure for those born in 1980 to 1989 standing at 23 per cent. Downward mobility also shows an increase over time. Interestingly, we observe that in terms of upward over downward mobility, there is, across all cohorts, more upward than downward mobility. This is highest for those born in the 1960s and the lowest for those born in the 1950s.

Turning now to the figures for women, we have earlier seen that women are more stable intergenerationally than men and this seems to be consistent across cohorts (though the amount of stability for women as compared to men seems be higher for the younger cohorts). However, there is no distinctive pattern of stability when comparing across birth cohorts. In terms of upward mobility, the pattern varies as it does for downward mobility. However, across all cohorts there has been an excess of upward over downward mobility and this seems to be increasing over time.

For rural India (Figure 4.3), we find that the amount of stability is greater than the national average though the overall patterns are similar. Interestingly, for rural women the amount of stability is fairly high, close to 80 per cent across all cohorts.

It is in urban India where we see the greatest departure from the national and rural figures. The urban figures for stability are substantially lower than rural figures, indicating more mobility over time in urban India. For urban India, by birth cohort, we find that unlike in rural areas, there is no clearly distinctive pattern of social mobility for men. The amount of stability for men stands at approximately 60 per cent except for those born in the 1960s who are the most mobile. This was also the cohort that we saw experience the most upward over downward mobility for rural India. In terms of patterns of upward mobility, again, there is no distinctive pattern across cohort for women or for men. What is interesting in this table is that women are more mobile than men for both the oldest and the youngest cohort but not for those born in the middle two cohorts. A closer scrutiny of the figures seems to indicate that those newly entering the labour market and those already established while exhibiting high mobility do so driven by different factors. Those in the earliest cohort, who have been in the labour market the longest, are intergenerationally more downwardly mobile than later cohorts. On the contrary, new women entrants to the urban labour market in opposition to what is expected or seen for men are more likely to be largely upwardly mobile. This begs the question of what's driving urban women's social mobility, especially for those born in the youngest cohort, nearly 50 per cent of whom are socially mobile, that is, they move away from their father's occupation. Looking at the figures for upward over downward mobility it appears that for women, those born in the last two cohorts from 1970 to 1989 seem to have experienced

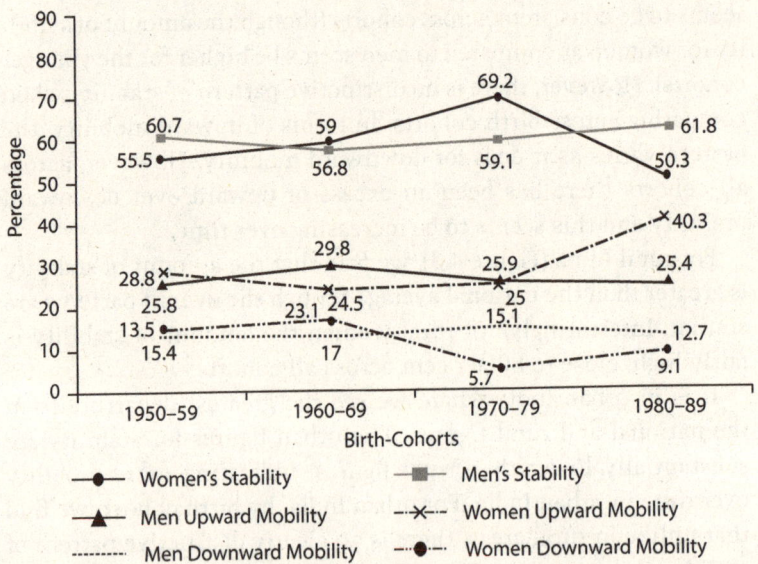

Figure 4.4 Summary Indices of Mobility, Comparison across Birth Cohorts, Urban Only, NES 2014

Source: NES 2014, CSDS Data Unit.
Note: Figures are percentages and rounded to the nearest decimal. These 2014 figures use a five-class schema due to small sample size issues, hence there is no horizontal mobility.

the most amount of upward over downward mobility. So opportunities seem to have improved quite substantially for working women in urban areas, not only when compared to their fathers, but also when compared to working men in urban areas. Chapter 6 will explore what the possible processual factors influencing this mobility are. However, unlike rural women who were born in the 1960s, urban women born in the 1960s display the least amount of upward over downward mobility.

Relative Rates

To test whether social fluidity or relative mobility has increased over time as would be expected under the modernization hypothesis, we now turn to exploring the model of constant social fluidity.

In Tables 4.11 and 4.12 (for men and women, respectively), instead of estimating the log-linear models across gender (as was previously done in the common social fluidity model for relative rates, Table 4.10), we fit the models over *time*. The key research question is whether social fluidity has remained constant over time or whether fluidity has increased as would be expected under the modernization thesis. The first two models of complete independence and conditional independence do not fit the data well for either men or women. The third model is the constant social fluidity model (CnSF) which postulates an association between origins and destinations, but it is presumed to be constant over

Table 4.11   Log-linear Models of Social Fluidity Trends, Men, NES 2014

	G^2	d.f.	P	Δ	Bic
Complete Independence O, D, C	6988.27	88	0.000	47.7	6224.58
Conditional independence OC, DC	6871.92	64	0.000	47.52	6316.51
Constant Social Fluidity OD	86.62	48	0.001	2.90	−329.94
Unidiff OD|C	75.73	45	0.003	2.60	−314.80

Source: NES 2014, CSDS Data Unit.
Note: N=5874; five-class schema; O=origins, D=destinations, C=Cohort (models in text)

Table 4.12   Log-linear Models of Social Fluidity Trends, Women, NES 2014

	G^2	d.f.	P	Δ	Bic
Complete Independence O, D, C	2716.42	88	0.000	49.9	2042.58
Conditional independence OC, DC	2655.71	64	0.000	49.5	2165.65
Constant Social Fluidity OD	65.03	48	0.051	3.45	−302.52
Unidiff OD|C	64.50	45	0.030	3.48	−280.071

Source: NES 2014, CSDS Data Unit.
Note: N=2116; five-class schema; O=origins, D=destinations, C=cohort (models in text)

time (Erikson and Goldthorpe 1992; Goldthorpe 1987). As can be seen from the tables below, the CnSF model fits the data well for both women and men (though by conventional criteria, it is a better fit for women than for men), hence suggesting that there are similar relative rates of mobility across cohorts. In other words, there has not been much change over time (especially for women). Therefore, this provides evidence against the hypothesis that with an increase in industrialization and modernization more change in relative mobility over time would be observed.

Next, we fit a Unidiff model to the data to test for the general strength of association between origins and destinations across the four cohorts, and whether this has weakened over time. According to Erikson and Goldthorpe, under the Unidiff model 'all odds ratios expected under the model for different cohorts will differ uniformly (though not by a constant amount) in moving together either towards or away from independence' (1992: 92). The goodness of fit measures of the Unidiff models are provided in the last row of both the tables (4.11 and 4.12) for men and women. The Unidiff model (only marginally for men, and not significantly for women) improve the fit of the CnSF model. Therefore, there does not appear to be any particular strengthening or weakening of the link between class origins and class destinations over time.

The parameters of the Unidiff model are graphed and displayed in Figure 4.5. For men we observe that the origin-destination association weakens for those born between 1960 and 1969 compared to those born in the 1950s fairly substantially, it then increases very marginally and then weakens again for the youngest birth cohort. For women, we see a weakening between the first and second birth cohorts and then an increase and a levelling off for the youngest cohort. The youngest cohort displays a pattern similar to those born in the 1950s, something we also observed in the absolute rates. What this table tells us is that over time the association between origins and destinations, that is, the amount of intergenerational inheritance has weakened for men fairly substantially between those born in the 1950s and those born in the 1960s, and then stabilized itself. For women too, we see a weakening between the first two decades but then an increase followed by a stabilization. We must emphasise here that these are overall figures and do

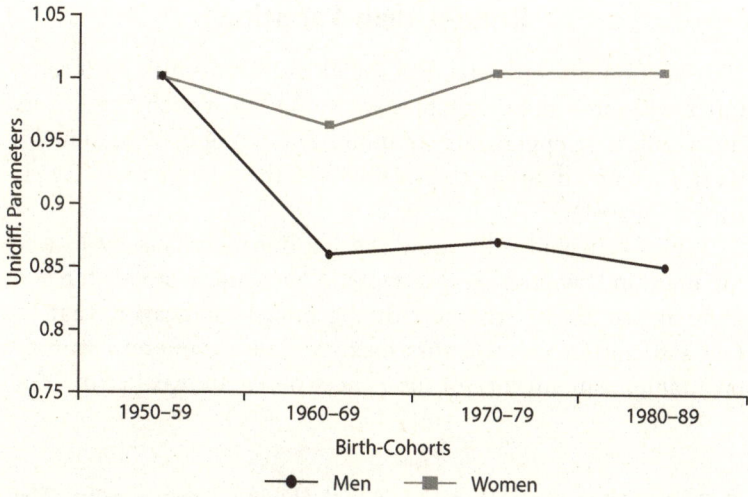

Figure 4.5 Unidiff Parameter Estimates across Birth Cohorts for Women and Men, NES 2014

Source: NES 2014, CSDS Data Unit.
Note: Figures are parameter estimates of Unidiff models in Tables 4.11 and 4.12.

not account for the big change we see for urban women in mobility rates, discussed in the next section.

Given the results of the Unidiff and the constant social fluidity models we find some support for the modernization hypothesis as our results show some overall weakening of the link between class origins and class destinations over birth cohorts. However, the figures for women also show some fluctuations. Our research thus seems to support the results of Erikson and Goldthorpe (1992) among others.[17] While highlighting the 'indeterminate' nature of the relation between economic development and change in social fluidity Breen (1997: 430) argues that 'contrary to earlier belief, and even within the terms of the liberal theory itself economic growth and the level of social mobility bear no necessary relationship to each other' (p. 431) and this seems to be true in the Indian context as well.

[17] While making this conclusion it is important to reiterate that we use a birth cohort approach using a cross-sectional dataset.

Rural–Urban Variation

This section disaggregates the social fluidity results by locality. In the absolute mobility tables we found lower mobility in rural India and more opportunity of mobility (including upward mobility) for women in urban areas. How does the relative mobility picture compare?

Tables 4.13 and 4.14 show the log-linear models by locality for men and women, respectively. The Unidiff model for both women and men is the best fitting model—indicating that the OD association varies across locality. The parameter estimates (available from author) for men and women are weaker in urban

Table 4.13 Log-linear Models of Social Fluidity across Locality, Men, NES 2014

	G^2	d.f.	p	Δ	Bic
Complete Independence O, D, R	9800.46	40	0.000	50.34	9445.67
Conditional independence OR, DR	7051.20	32	0.000	43.20	6767.36
CmSF OD	25.05	16	0.069	1.3	−116.87
Unidiff OD|R	22.43	15	0.097	1.2	−110.61

Source: NES 2014 , CSDS Data Unit.
Note: N=7115, five-class schema; O=origins, D=destinations, R=Locality (models in text).

Table 4.14 Log-linear Models of Social Fluidity across Locality, Women, NES 2014

	G^2	d.f.	P	Δ	Bic
Complete Independence O, D, R	3700.07	40	0.000	52.39	3386.16
Conditional independence OR, DR	2867.63	32	0.000	45.63	2616.50
CmSF OD	34.19	16	0.005	2.73	−91.36
Unidiff OD|R	31.20	15	0.008	2.46	−86.51

Source: NES 2014, CSDS Data Unit.
Note: N=2560; five-class schema; O=origins, D=destinations, R=Locality (models in text).

areas than in rural areas—for women these figures are substantially weaker—indicating more mobility and less OD association in urban India. This supports the absolute mobility results of the specificity of an urban location, and specifically, it's significance for women's experiences of social mobility.

* * *

This chapter had set out to answer a number of questions regarding patterns of intergenerational class mobility in India. Firstly, we find a slow pace of structural change in India. Though there has been a change in the shape of the class structure, there has only been a marginal increase in the size of the professional classes and a marginal decline in agrarian classes, especially for men; for women, while there has been a decrease in their proportion in the lower agricultural class as compared to their fathers, they are still more concentrated here than men are. For women, clearly opportunities for mobility lie more in the low professional class. These structural changes have important consequences on the patterns of mobility. The impact of this structural change has meant that both women and men display very high intergenerational stability rates. Also, men have a slightly higher surplus of upward over downward mobility than women and seem to have, in this sense at least, benefited from the economic changes to a greater extent. However, the locality disaggregated results highlight the opportunities available to urban women. Interestingly, while comparing Indian results with existing research on industrialized countries there appears to be a similar *direction* of mobility in India as well; that is, there is more upward over downward mobility (due possibly to more increasing 'room at the top') for women and men, though the surplus is not as large in India as in the developed countries (reflecting the lack of much change in the class structure). However, in India, women show more intergenerational stability than men, a finding quite the opposite of that observed in most Western countries, where the amount of mobility for women is much higher than that for men. This seems to be a reflection of the Indian occupational structure.

Secondly, looking at the social fluidity picture, the symmetrical odds ratios studied show high levels of *stickiness* in some class contrasts, particularly in the movement between the various agrarian classes as well as the movement between the manual and non-manual classes. However, it emerges that the relative rates of mobility are similar for women and men, a finding found to be consistent with studies in the West. This is a surprising result, as with the large prevailing gender inequalities and the enormous differences in absolute and relative rates of mobility when compared to developed countries, one did not expect to see this pattern. What this seems to show is that in India privileged families are preserving their privileges for both their sons *and* daughters. Hence, it can be concluded that, as observed by Erikson and Goldthorpe (1992: 252) it is from the unequal 'opportunity structures' facing women and men that differences in the absolute rates of mobility derive rather than due to the 'sex differences in fluidity patterns'. That is, it is the structural features of the labour market which amount to forms of direct and indirect discrimination against women (Erikson and Goldthorpe 1992: 253; see also Marshall, Roberts, Burgoyne, Swift, and Routh for a further discussion of this aspect, 1995: 2–3). We also observe that there is no strong evidence that the strength of association between origins and destinations is lower for one sex rather than the other (women have a marginally stronger OD association), that is, there does not seem to be substantially more fluidity for any one gender.

Thirdly, analysing the picture of mobility over time while keeping in mind the necessary caveats, we make two observations. On the one hand, it emerges that despite there being no obvious pattern there does seem to have been a steady increase in the absolute amount of mobility, particularly upward mobility. It is too soon to make any conclusion of a steady pattern with authority. On the other hand, in terms of relative rates of mobility we observe that social fluidity differs somewhat across cohorts for men (though there isn't a clear pattern for women). The picture is thus not so much about 'continuity rather than change' (Kumar, Heath, and Heath 2002b: 4096), but rather about 'continuity and change', as even though some increases in fluidity are seen they seem to be of a limited kind. This further supports Vaid and Heath's (2010) findings.

Finally, our locality-wise results seem to support the picture of a diverse country. Rural India unsurprisingly appears to be more intergenerationally stable with a higher level of inequality of opportunity; whereas urban India seems to display higher fluidity for both women and men in line with what would be expected under the modernization thesis and this increased opportunity in urban India is much more apparent for women.

On the basis of these results, we can conclude that while there has been some impact of modernization and industrialization, the overall effect on mobility has been a bit weak. Urban India is clearly distinct and the overall mobility patterns may be driven by the rural experience which may be the result of the vast size of the agricultural sector and slow rate of change. However, the slow pace of change seen may also be a function of the time span used to study mobility and we might need to wait longer to be able to gauge the true impact of economic change in India, especially of policies such as the MGNREGA.

Appendix A4.1

While small samples sizes make it difficult to analyse mother to daughter mobility, we did conduct a simple analysis on the 2014 NES. Table A4.1.1 displays the class profiles for mothers and daughters. Substantially, more women compared to their mothers are in high professional classes in urban India. In terms of absolute mobility rates (Table A4.1.2) we find that urban women compared to their mothers are not only more mobile, but they are more upwardly mobile than rural women. Interestingly, the amount of social stability that women experience when compared to their mothers is much higher than the social stability they experience compared to their fathers. However, we also find that across both rural and urban India, the amount of upward mobility over downward mobility is more for women when compared to their mothers, thus indicating more opportunities available to the *daughters*. These results would require a more detailed analysis with a larger sample size.

Table A4.1.1 Class Profiles of the Origin (Mother's class) and Destinations of Women and Men across Locality, NES 2014

	Overall 2014			Rural 2014			Urban 2014		
	Mother's class	Daughter's class	O-D diff.	Mother's class	Daughter's class	O-D diff.	Mother's class	Daughter's class	O-D diff.
High Professional	1.1	1.6	−0.5	1.1	1.2	−0.1	1.0	4.0	−3.0
Large Business	1.5	1.7	−0.3	1.3	1.5	−0.1	2.5	3.5	−1.0
Large Farmer	6.9	6.7	0.2	7.3	7.2	0.1	4.0	3.5	0.5
Low Professional	1.3	2.8	−1.5	0.8	2.2	−1.4	5.1	7.1	−2.0
RNM Clerical	0.7	1.0	−0.3	0.2	0.5	−0.3	4.0	4.5	−0.5
Petty Business	1.5	1.4	0.1	0.7	0.8	−0.1	7.6	5.6	2.0
Skilled	4.1	5.3	−1.2	2.1	3.2	−1.1	17.7	19.7	−2.0
Small Farmer	17.6	17.0	0.6	19.3	18.9	0.4	5.6	4.0	1.5
RNM Service	2.6	3.2	−0.6	1.8	2.3	−0.4	8.1	9.6	−1.5
Semi-unskilled	7.6	8.0	−0.4	7.3	7.8	−0.4	9.6	9.6	0.0
Low Agriculturalist	55.0	51.2	3.8	57.9	54.4	3.5	34.8	28.8	6.1
N	1560	1560		1362	1362		198	198	
Index of Dissimilarity	4.7			4.1			10.1		

Source: NES 2014, CSDS Data Unit.

Table A4.1.2 Mother-Daughter Social Mobility Rates; NES 2014

	Stability	Upward Mob.	Downward Mob.	U/D
2014 (N=1560)	89.2	7.8	3.0	2.6
Rural (N=1362)	89.7	7.3	2.9	2.5
Urban (N=198)	84.9	12.0	3.0	4.0

Source: NES 2014, CSDS Data Unit.

Note: Figures are percentages and rounded to the nearest decimal; this table uses the five-class schema and hence there is no horizontal mobility.

Appendix A4.2

Table A4.2.1 Adjusted Residuals of the CmSF Model, Women, NES 2014

Class Father 11 categories	Class Respondent 11 categories										
	High Prof.	Business	Large Farm	Low Prof.	RNM Clerical	Petty Business	Skilled	Small Farm	RNM Service	Semi-Unskilled	Lower Agric.
High Prof.	**2.352**	−.719	−.092	−.650	.779	−.533	1.355	**−1.958**	−1.859	−.316	−1.530
Business	−1.087	−.356	.000	1.245	−.176	−.224	.886	−1.546	.929	−.505	−.603
Large Farmers	−1.105	.929	−1.579	−.667	−.682	−.816	1.306	1.250	1.728	−1.511	1.543
Low Prof.	−.344	−.570	.958	1.080	−1.557	−.767	1.323	−1.485	−.671	−1.142	1.326
RNM Clerical	.424	−.035	.061	1.144	−.056	.394	−1.802	.850	−.357	−1.015	−.086
Petty Business	.111	1.815	.000	1.154	.755	−1.835	−1.000	−.155	1.339	.093	−.892
Skilled	−1.477	1.428	−.805	−.946	.112	**2.865**	−.827	−1.097	.802	.372	.837
Small Farmers	.161	.097	**2.282**	−.516	−1.211	.541	.939	.941	**−2.488**	1.251	−1.278
RNM Service	−.903	.825	.000	.488	**2.967**	.131	−.895	−.899	.094	−1.518	−.861
Semi-Unskilled	−1.431	−.182	−.729	1.370	−.888	.139	**−1.982**	.224	1.012	1.408	−.552
Low Agric.	.643	−1.362	.190	**−2.689**	.710	.199	1.821	−.267	.082	−.805	1.029

Source: NES 2014, CSDS Data Unit.

Note: Statistically significant residuals are in bold.

5

Cutting Through

Caste and Class Mobility

Social mobility in India has been studied either in terms of group mobility through caste (for example, Silverberg 1968) or through individual level social class mobility. In this chapter, we look at the impact caste has on individual intergenerational class mobility chances.[1,2] Are certain groups advantaged or disadvantaged when it comes to occupational mobility opportunities? As previously discussed in chapter 2, certain castes or jatis have been historically associated with particular occupations[3], but this association

[1] This chapter draws on previous work done using the 2004 NES dataset and published in Vaid (2012).

[2] This chapter focuses especially on *Hindu* castes, however, at the same time, we also present empirical results for minority religions, such as the Muslims, as it is of interest to see how these groups fare with regard to the Hindu castes. Hence, in the text we often discuss 'community' rather than caste results. Due to small sample size in urban areas, we are unable to disaggregate the results by locality in the cohort analysis. However, we do control for rural–urban differences in the regression models.

[3] With regard to this chapter, it is important to acknowledge that most of the literature on caste deals with the relation of jatis with *occupations* (that is, at the micro level), rather than with *class* (at the more aggregate level with the exception of literature on the manual and non-manual divide). Hence, any conclusions drawn should, by necessity of the data,

is believed by some to be eroding due to the processes associated with industrialization, economic liberalization, and the resultant urbanization as well as due to legislative changes and state and national level policies. Further, the importance of ascribed charac- teristics like caste, on individual's opportunities to gain access to scarce resources like jobs, is also expected to decline with indus- trialization and liberalization; or, what by some have been termed as the larger processes of modernization (see Gist 1954; Karanth 1996; and Panini 1996, among others). Some, such as Kolenda, have raised the question of whether in place of caste there is a class system emerging in India (1986: 108). While we argue that the existence of one form of stratification does not preclude another and caste and class are not on a 'continuum' (Kumar, Heath, and Heath 2002), this chapter aims to trace the relationship between caste, class, and social mobility in contemporary India.

Despite the 'centrality of caste' in Indian society (see Deshpande 2003) and debates on the relation between caste and class (Béteille 1996b) and on whether class rather than caste is critical in deter- mining social disadvantage[4] (as discussed in Chapter 2), few research studies have empirically analysed this relationship, par- ticularly at the national level (McMillan 2005; Kumar, Heath, and Heath 2002a; Vaid and Heath 2010; Vaid 2012; Deshpande and Palshikar 2008, are some exceptions). Most often the reluctance to study this relation has been due to the lack of adequate data to make such a study possible. This reluctance also stems from the wariness of sociologists (and social anthropologists) in using a national framework to study a concept as localized as jati (Kolenda 1986; Deshpande 1999). These arguments hold some weight and local ethnographic studies are invaluable to analyse this complex relationship. This should not, however, preclude national research that is able to study this caste–class relationship at a macro level, thus enabling a study of this relation and its evolution over time

---

be treated with caution. The drawbacks of this approach are discussed in more detail in this and the concluding chapter (see also Chapter 2 for a discussion).

[4] Here the context of social disadvantage relates to the opportunities of social mobility available, especially the lack of access to upward mobility.

allowing us to isolate certain periods of change. In the context of the enduring debates surrounding reservation policies, this is an important area for analysis in India.[5]

In light of this, we pose questions (in the next section) arising from the literature on the relation between caste and class and on the impact of caste on social mobility opportunities. Before that, we briefly discuss this literature.

Caste, Class, and Mobility

Since castes have been historically associated with particular caste occupations (for example, Gist 1954), any movement of a caste from its hereditary occupation to another is seen to be a form of social mobility within the caste structure (Silverberg 1968). Some authors have concluded that this type of mobility is quite restricted, for example, Weber (1958) stated:

> A caste may comprise people who follow very different pursuits; at least this is the case today, and for certain upper castes this has been the case since very early times. Yet as long as the caste has not lost it character, the kind of pursuits admissible without loss of caste are always, in some way, quite strictly limited. Even today 'caste' and 'way of living' are so firmly linked that often a change of occupation is correlated with a division of caste. (p. 31)

There are others who have maintained that 'absolute fixity of hereditary status is not and never has been maintained perfectly' in India (Davis 1949: 385). In even earlier research, Blunt (1931) gives examples of changes in status of a caste with a change in their occupation. More recently, contributions in Fuller (1996) and Srinivas (1996b) underlie the absence of exact concurrence between caste and occupation (see also Parry 1980).

---

[5] While the present analysis cannot focus on reservations directly, it provides a macro-view of the situation where there have been nearly seven decades of reservation policies for SCs and STs, and more than two decades for the OBCs. Only temporal changes will provide an indicator of how the relation between caste and occupational class stands presently.

More recent research suggests that economic changes, urbanization, and migration have brought about changes in the relation
between caste and class. It has been argued that the creation of
newer jobs as the economy opens up and develops will lead not
only to an increasing movement of people away from hereditary
occupations to 'non-caste' occupations, but also to occupations
that were originally the prerogative of the higher castes. As Panini
states and we quote at length:

> Economic liberalisation in the long run is likely to weaken the hold
> of caste over the economy. The free play of market forces implied in
> liberalisation is likely to dilute the importance of caste in economic
> calculations. As economic controls are lifted, the privileges enjoyed
> by groups because of their social connections are likely to disap-
> pear.... Further as liberalisation entails free flow of information as
> well as resources, caste monopolies that operate in the various intri-
> cacies of the economy will become ineffective. Since enhanced com-
> petition is likely to encourage professional management of firms to
> ensure enhanced productivity and profit, criteria stressing efficien-
> cy and skill will prove to be more important in recruitment than
> the caste of the worker and his loyalty to the firm. As competition
> opens up and productivity increases all round, the economic growth
> rate is likely to get accelerated, which in turn would multiply job
> opportunities to such an extent that workers do not have to ply their
> caste background to get jobs. (1996: 60)

This quote highlights a variant of the modernization theory specific to India. That is, with modernization it is expected that in
addition to the decline in ascribed characteristics like father's class
as is theorized for developed countries, in India there will also be a
decline in caste as an important factor influencing recruitment to
jobs. Srinivas (2003) seems to share Panini's view, but in an article
titled 'An Obituary on Caste as a System', he extends the argument
beyond economic liberalization to include various changes that are
occurring simultaneously, and leading to the decline in the relation
between jati and traditional occupations. According to him:

> ... the improvement of communication, the spread of education, a
> host of governmental policies favouring the weaker sections, politi-
> cal mobilisation of the people, and the many technological changes

... have all had the effect of greatly weakening the link between jati and traditional occupations. Even where it lingers in its attenuated form, monetisation, and market forces have combined to free economic relations from the baggage[6] which they have traditionally carried. (Srinivas 2003)

Panini's (and Srinivas') view of the changes that liberalization and modernization will bring to the caste system do not find universal support. Basile and Harriss-White, through their study of village *Arni* in Tamil Nadu, do not see any 'sign yet of the erosion foreseen by Panini'. They go on to state that:

On the contrary, caste is being selectively reworked to mean different things at different positions in the economic system of the town. Among Scheduled Castes and Other Backward Classes, caste remains a condition of hierarchy. Physical and ritual pollution still successfully repel higher ('backward') castes from low caste occupations. They also prevent all but a handful of those associated with this contamination from access to most 'clean' occupations, from private finance and from residence and worship in upper caste localities. (Basile and Harriss-White 2000: 41)

It has also been noted that the benefits of liberalization are not enjoyed equally by all castes, as is evidenced by the existence of the *creamy layer*; that is, the more advanced sections of the 'backward' castes that are able to take advantage of the preferential policies, whilst the most deprived sections are unable to do so (see Chapter 2).

The continued association of castes in particular occupations despite liberalization has been much debated. According to Jayaram (1996: 82) the 'conjugation of caste and class is no longer a sociological axiom', and Kumar, Heath, and Heath (2002a and b), for example, show considerable occupational variation within castes. However, regarding the disassociation of castes from traditional

---

[6] At this point Srinivas is talking predominantly of the breakdown of the 'traditional', often hereditary, patron–client relations between the dominant land-owning caste and the lower (agricultural labourer) castes, also called the 'jajmani' system.

occupations, Karanth (1996) differentiates between the higher and lower castes. According to him the members of the lower (particularly former 'untouchable') castes find it tougher to move from their traditional occupations than do the higher castes. This may be for many reasons, such as pressures (social, economic, and political) exerted by the upper castes to continue the traditional patron–client relations (see footnote 6) due to which lower castes may remain economically dependent on the upper castes. Thus, even if disassociation is taking place, it is more apparent for the higher rather than the lower castes, who might still be restricted by certain factors to perform their 'traditional' defiling jobs (this seems to support Basile and Harriss-White's [2000] conclusion. Similarly, Dube[7] (1996) theorizes that at the extremes of the caste system the overlap of caste and occupations persists. For example, a Brahmin still does a priest's job and scavengers and sweepers are the lowest castes. She asserts that it is in the middle where all the fluidity and mobility really occurs.

Panini (1996) too reviews literature spanning a wide time spectrum that looks at clustering of castes and more recent de-clustering in different occupations. These studies show how caste no longer inhibits individuals from taking to newer occupations, or what could be considered more caste 'non-traditional' occupations. But, having laid down the changes that have occurred for different castes, Panini demonstrates with numerous examples that castes continue to cluster in particular occupations. In addition to clustering in agriculture, Panini also shows the clustering of higher castes in higher levels of government services (p. 32);[8] managerial and professional occupations (p. 33); in the industrial milieu (p. 34); between the organized and unorganized sector (p. 35) as well as by skill level (see also Jodhka 2012; see Biswajit and Knight [1985] for more on caste based discrimination in the labour market).

[7] This argument seems to be similar to that of Weber (1958) mentioned previously.

[8] Quoting from the Mandal Commission report on the backward classes, Panini states that the non-OBC 'upper and middle castes form nearly 90 per cent of the Class 1 services although according to the Mandal Commission they constitute not more than 20 per cent of the total population of the country' (p. 33).

Summarizing the literature in this field of caste and occupational mobility Panini concludes (1996: 29) that 'evidence suggests accelerated occupational mobility which has broken down the caste based division of labour. Yet, such a change was not drastic enough to loosen the hold of caste over the economy. Caste continues to be a salient category in the social infrastructure of the economy'.[9] Vaid provides a more recent survey of the field and concludes that 'although caste cannot be directly associated with occupation, certain castes can use other resources at their disposal (such as economic, cultural or social capital and political leverage) and ensure that they control scarce resources such as jobs to the greatest extent possible' (Vaid 2014b: 406).

This literature, thus, while indicating the possibilities of change with liberalization and industrial changes, also underlines the congruence at certain levels between caste and class. To extend this argument further to test these propositions at the more macro level, in this chapter we provide an empirical test of whether there are indeed such 'privileges' (or leverages) that can be used by some castes to control access to social mobility and prevent the mobility of others. For the empirical analysis, this chapter poses the following three sets of questions:

First, we begin by asking whether there is an association, if any, between caste and class in contemporary India. Here we will test whether there is more congruence of castes and classes at the extremes of the caste system (Dube 1996; see also Karanth 1996 and others).

Next, we pose questions related to the argument of over time change due to economic liberalization and modernization (Panini 1996; Srinivas 2003).[10] First we ask, whether the congruence between caste and class origins has declined over time? Second, we ask whether the relation between caste and class destination has weakened over time (Kumar, Heath, and Heath 2002b)? These two questions provide a handle on contemporary India.

[9] See Dube (1996) for a discussion on caste and occupational continuity and the role played by women.

[10] As mentioned in Chapter 4, class origin refers to father's occupational class and class destinations to respondents own occupational class.

If these two questions are answered in the negative, we will be able to support Basile and Harris-White's (2000) conclusion from their ethnographic study that there has not been much change over time, or at least that the salience of caste has not declined appreciably.

Finally, we ask questions on caste and its impact on social class mobility. First, has there been a decline over time in the relative importance of caste, and an increase in the importance of class origins, on class destinations?[11] And, second, whether any particular group, such as the SCs, finds it harder to move up in social mobility terms compared to members of other castes and communities from the same social class origins (Karanth 1996)?

Analysing Caste and Class

Given the national-level nature of the study (with rural–urban differences flagged when possible), castes for us are categorized at the level of constitutionally recognized groups such as the SCs, STs, and OBCs. While historically the association between jati and occupation has been of interest, since sample size is an issue and since we have the information available, in this chapter we provide results on broader categories of 'community' (see Appendix A5.1). This allows us to look at religious minorities such as the Muslims as well.

The threefold task of studying the association between caste and class; the patterns of over time change, if any; and, the impact of caste on social mobility chances requires a specific coding of the information on caste/jati in the NES 2014 data. Appendix A5.1 of this chapter discusses the details of the NES dataset, a comparison of the data with Census and NSS figures, and it more significantly provides details of the caste/community categorization used in this book.

We now turn to the data analysis to answer the questions posed.

---

[11] This question enables us to go some way in answering Kolenda's (1986) question on whether a class system is emerging in India.

Caste and Class in Contemporary India

In the first question relating to the congruence between caste and class in contemporary India we analyse specifically whether there is greater congruence between the two at the extremes of the caste system. Since some occupations, and hence, the class composition under study can be location specific, we also observe rural–urban differences.

An answer to this question requires us to study a cross-tabulation of caste and class origins. However, while a cross-tabulation shows us the association between the two variables, it does not say anything about whether the distribution is as would be expected if there was no association, that is, under pure randomness. While we can use a chi-square test to establish whether the association between the two variables is significant, that test applies to the table in its entirety and does not indicate whether any particular cell of the table (that is, any particular relation between caste and class) is significant. In order to be able to look at individual associations or cells in a table, we look at the adjusted standardized residuals of the cross-tabulation of class origins and community (a method also used by Kumar, Heath, and Heath 2002a). A large adjusted residual (more than 1.96; or simply, anything greater or less than 2) shows that the particular cell in question has more, or less, if it is a negative residual, people in it than would be expected by chance alone (a similar analysis was conducted in Chapter 4). The results are shown separately for community and father's class by locality (Figures 5.1 and 5.2). Here we show the adjusted residuals for the eight category community variable.[12]

We find larger adjusted residuals in rural India. On studying the figures a relatively clear pattern is observed. If we consider the extremes of the caste system, with high castes at one end and the SCs on the other, we see a picture of congruence of high castes in the more secure 'white collar' occupations and so called lower

---

[12] The adjusted residuals are influenced by sample size. For the log-linear analysis, where small samples are a concern, we use a six-category community variable. For the adjusted residuals, cross-tabulation and the logistic regression we use the more detailed eight-category variable.

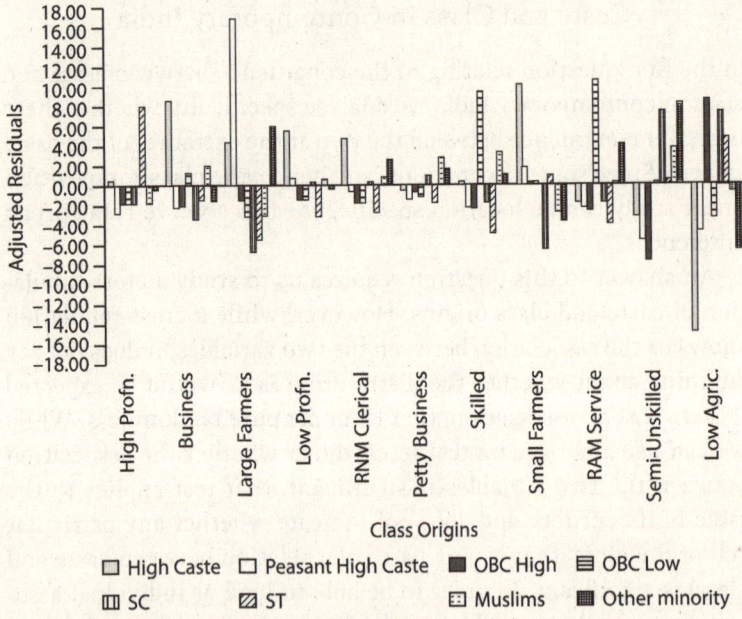

Figure 5.1 Adjusted Residuals of Caste/Community and Class Origins for Rural India, NES 2014 (N=7556)

Source: NES 2014, CSDS Data Unit.

castes in the insecure and temporary occupations. We make the following observations:

Firstly, in urban areas, high castes are over-represented in the high and low professional classes and the RNM Clerical class, as compared to the other Hindu castes and the Muslims. In rural India, they are over-represented in the two lower professions. The STs are over-represented in the low professional class (indicating some limited advantage to their position in terms of occupational access) in urban India. Conversely, in rural India given their proportion in the population they are over-represented in high and under-represented in low and RNM Clerical professions. The other minorities are over-represented in the RNM Clerical class, while the peasant high castes along with the upper OBCs are under-represented here. Muslims are under-represented in the low

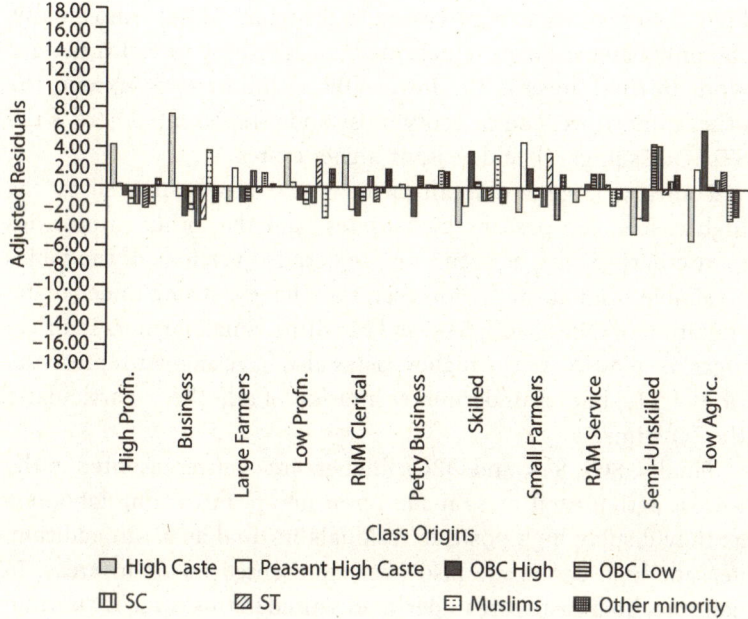

Figure 5.2 Adjusted Residuals of Caste/Community and Class Destination in Urban India, NES 2014 (N=1961)

Source: NES 2014, CSDS Data Unit.

professions, while no other results for Muslims are statistically significant.

Secondly, in the large business class it is the high castes in rural areas and high castes and Muslims in urban areas who have a high positive residual and are over-represented, whereas in the petty business class it is solely the Muslims in rural areas who are over-represented (as expected, see Kumar, Heath, and Heath 2002b). Castes such as the OBCs (especially higher OBCs), SCs, STs are under-represented in business generally.

Thirdly, in terms of manual work: OBCs and Muslims are over-represented in skilled work; and, high castes and peasant high castes and STs are under-represented here. SCs, Muslims (rural), and other minorities and lower OBCs (urban) are over-represented in semi and unskilled work; and interestingly, higher castes are under-represented in both rural and urban areas (including the high castes, peasant high castes, and higher OBCs). And finally, the only category over-represented substantially in RNM Service work in rural areas is the lower OBCs and, to some extent, the other minorities. The category most under-represented here is the STs, OBCs (higher), and peasant higher castes.

Fourthly, large and small farm owners are dominated by the high castes, the peasant high castes, and the 'other' minorities (particularly Sikhs) as seen in more detailed versions of the tables (available from author). However, they have a strong under-representation of OBCs, SCs, STs, and Muslims. Small farmers in urban areas, in addition to the higher castes also have an over-representation of STs, but an under-representation of all others, particularly the Muslims.

Finally, SCs, STs, and OBCs (higher) are over-represented in the lowest agricultural class made up of non-farm owning labourers as they display high positive residuals in rural areas. In addition, peasant high castes are also over-represented in urban areas. In contrast, high castes are under-represented in this category in rural and urban areas (and peasant high castes in rural areas) with a very high negative residual. The minority religions including Muslims are also under-represented in the low agricultural class, especially in urban India.

These patterns lead us to conclude that regardless of rural–urban differences the high castes are concentrated in the professions, clerical work, business (especially large business), and as farm owners (large and small). They are clearly under-represented in the lowest most unstable agricultural class and in semi and unskilled manual work (given their proportion in the population). Conversely, SCs are under-represented in big business and as farm owners, though over-represented in lower agricultural labour in rural areas, and semi and unskilled work in urban areas. Scheduled Tribes show an interesting pattern: they are over-represented in lower agricultural work, but on the other end, they are well represented in low professions in urban areas and high professions in rural areas.

Muslims as the largest religious minority show an interesting concentration given their rural–urban distribution. In rural

India, they are over-represented in petty business and in skilled and semi-unskilled work. They are distinctly under-represented as farm owners (large and small). In urban India, they are highly concentrated in big business and in skilled work and under-represented in the low professions and in the agrarian sector.

Other Backward Classes (especially the creamy layer) are over-represented in low agricultural labouring class and among small farmers, and in skilled work in urban areas. They tend not to engage in manual work, or in business. Lower OBCs are conversely engaged in skilled and RNM Service (in rural areas) and unskilled (in urban areas) work. They are under-represented in agrarian work in rural areas and in business in urban areas.

These graphs seem to indicate that there is quite a degree of marked clustering at the extremes. We see the high castes at one end over-represented in the more stable and prestigious 'white collar' or 'clean' work categories of the professional classes, and RNM classes as well as in farm-owning classes and large businesses. The SCs, on the other end, are not only under-represented in all these classes, they are moreover over-represented in the lower income, less stable, temporary employment, in the manual work categories, and in lower agriculture as labourers. Therefore, in answer to our question, we do find general support that there is clustering, in contemporary India, at the extremes of the caste system; and an indication of a strong caste based manual-non-manual barrier.

A rural–urban disaggregation of the association between caste and class underlines continued clustering which is further highlighted when we look at figures by gender. To do this, we look at class destination or both women and men's own class (we are unable to disaggregate these by locality due to small sample sizes for women). We find (tables available from author):

1. While high caste men and women are over-represented in the professions, this figure is much higher for higher case women in the lower professions as well as ST women in the high professions.
2. In terms of business, Muslim men and other minority women are over-represented in the self-employed category.

For petty business Muslims are the sole category that is over-represented for men.

3. In manual work, the patterns are somewhat similar for women and men, with minor differences. In the agrarian sector too we find broadly similar patterns.

Modernization and Change

We now move to the second set of questions addressed in this chapter which look at change over time. In order to observe whether modernization and economic change has indeed altered the relation between caste and class, we begin by asking whether any congruence between caste and class *origins* has weakened over time. We then ask whether the relation of caste/community and class *destinations* has weakened over time allowing us to look at fathers and sons/daughters.

In the first question, we use father's class rather than respondent's own class to study the relation with caste. This is because here we aim to look at the two 'ascribed' origin characteristics of caste and class, and also studying class of origin might help us in avoiding problems caused by contamination due to life cycle effects or career mobility. In the second question, we study caste and its relation with an individual's final class destination. These two questions allow us to study the relation of caste with both origins and destinations.

1. *Has the congruence between caste and class origins declined over time?*

To answer this question, we extend the previous analysis on the congruence of caste and class in contemporary India, but instead look at the over time perspective. Here we use the method of log-linear analysis which was introduced in Chapter 4.[13] In order to study whether the association between class origins and community has changed over time, we use the model of CnSF for both women and men (also called the constant association model by

---

[13] For the log-linear analysis in this chapter, the six category 'community' variable was used due to small sample sizes. See Appendix A5.1 for details.

Kumar, Heath, and Heath 2002b). The results for the study are shown in Table 5.1.[14]

If the CnSF model provides a good fit to the data (that is, a G^2 with a p-value of over 0.05), we cannot reject the null hypothesis that there has been no change over time and we must conclude that the association between class origins and community has not changed across birth cohorts, that is, it has instead remained constant. Our question would thus be answered in the negative.

In Table 5.1, in comparison to the model of complete independence (O, C, Y) and conditional independence (OY, CY) the CnSF fits the male data well by the conventional G^2 criterion and it misclassifies approximately 3 per cent of the cases. According to the *BIC*

Table 5.1 Log-linear Analysis for Class Origins, Community, and Cohort

		G^2	d.f	p	Δ	*BIC*
Men	Complete independence O, C, Y	705.91	107	0.000	13.54	−220.99
	Conditional Independence OY, CY	631.24	80	0.000	13.06	−61.78
	CnSF (OC)	63.20	60	0.364	3.20	−456.56
	Unidiff	59.92	57	0.370	3.08	−433.85
Women	Complete independence O, C, Y	354.27	107	0.000	14.90	−462.45
	Conditional independence OY, CY	297.92	80	0.000	13.61	−312.71
	CnSF (OC)	93.92	60	0.003	6.30	−364.05
	Unidiff	85.25	57	0.009	6.33	−349.82

Source: NES 2014, CSDS Data Unit.
Note: N Men = 5783; N Women = 2065; O = Origins (5 categories); C = Community (6); Y = Cohort (4).

[14] $CnSF \log_m = \lambda + \lambda_i^O + \lambda_j^C + \lambda_k^Y + \lambda_{ik}^{OY} + \lambda_{jk}^{CY} + \lambda_{ij}^{OC}$; O=Origin class; C=Community; Y=Cohort.

criterion as well it is the 'preferred' model. For women, however, none of the models quite fits the data very well. The CnSF has the least cases misclassified, but not a conventional fit according to the G^2 criterion.[15] Tentatively, we do find some support for the hypothesis that there has been over time stability in the association between caste and class origins in the case of men, but we are less confident of this conclusion in the case of women. In the second step, we fit a Unidiff model to see whether the pattern of association between class origins and community strengthens or weakens over time.

The Unidiff model provides a better fit than the CnSF according to the G^2 for men but not for women. The Unidiff parameters are shown in Figure 5.3. In the figure we see that the parameters for men are not following any consistent pattern. There is instead some 'trendless fluctuation' in terms of the relation between class origins and community. However, they display an overall decline from the oldest to the youngest cohort. The picture for women is similar—though it seems to show that the relationship between class origins and community is declining more sharply. But, as mentioned above, this model is not a conventionally fitting model for women and the results should be read in that light.

On observing our results we can say fairly conclusively, at least for men, that the association between origin class and caste has weakened over the longer term—though the overall pattern is of fluctuation (something that was only visible as a possible trend in the 2004 data is now more distinct). Thus, indicating that people perhaps have more opportunities (in class terms) to leave caste behind.

2. *Has the relation between community and class destinations weakened over time?*

Here we analyse whether people from certain communities are associated with particular class destinations; this brings out any changes that have occurred over time. That is, we ask, whether the link between community and class destination is weakening as we expect under liberalization and modernization (Kumar, Heath, and Heath 2002a).

---

[15] We studied the residuals of the CnSF model to see where the model does not fit adequately. But no clear pattern seems to emerge.

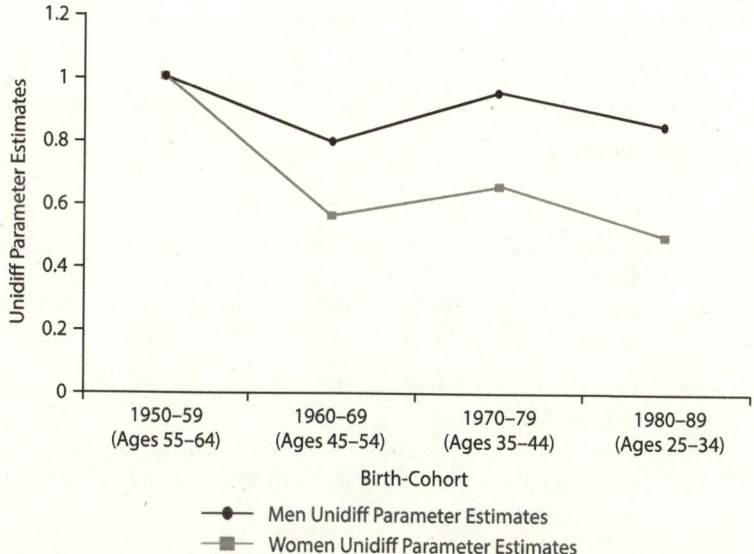

Figure 5.3 Unidiff Parameter Estimates of Class Origin and Community for Women and Men across Birth Cohorts, NES 2014

Source: NES 2014, CSDS Data Unit.

We use log-linear analysis similar to that used to answer the previous question, but instead of class origins we observe the relation of community with class destinations. Table 5.2 shows the results of fitting these log-linear models for men and women. According to conventional criteria the model fits the data remarkably well (as the p-value of the G^2 is over 0.05) for both women and men. As the CnSF provides a good fit, it leads one to conclude that the relation between community and class destinations has not changed appreciably over the birth cohorts. Thus, even though the class distribution in the country has changed following modernization, the 'underlying association' between community and class destination has not changed much.[16]

---

[16] As the model misclassifies approximately 3 and 5 per cent of the cases (for men and women), we studied the adjusted residuals of these models to see if there was any pattern in the deviance. But no certain pattern emerged.

Table 5.2   Log-linear Analysis (Class Destination, Community, Cohort)

		G^2	d.f	p	Δ	BIC
Men	Complete independence D, C, Y	735.05	107	0.000	14.12	−191.85
	Conditional independence DY, CY	597.13	80	0.000	12.73	−95.88
	CmSF (DC)	54.50	60	0.676	3.27	−465.26
	Unidiff	51.05	57	0.697	3.10	−442.73
Women	Complete independence D, C, Y	410.97	107	0.000	16.42	−405.75
	Conditional independence DY, CY	335.34	80	0.000	14.59	−275.29
	CmSF (DC)	71.58	60	0.145	6.10	−386.39
	Unidiff	59.98	57	0.368	5.57	−375.10

Source: NES 2014, CSDS Data Unit.
Note: N Men=5783; N Women=2065; D=Destinations (5 categories); C=Community (6); Y=Cohort (4).

However, since the Unidiff model to study the strength of the association between community and destination class over time fits the data better than the CnSF for men and women we map the parameters. On mapping the parameters in the graph (Figure 5.4), a fairly clear pattern is seen. For both men and women the association between community and destination class seems to decline for the second cohort; it increases and then declines again for the youngest cohort. While there is fluctuation, in the over time scheme we can see a pattern of the weakening of the relation between class destination and community over birth cohorts. This seems stronger for women. We should not overemphasize the stability in the relationship. Rather, this seems to change over-time. This supports the results that looked at class origins and community—that is, there is indeed change, but it is accompanied by fluctuations over cohorts.

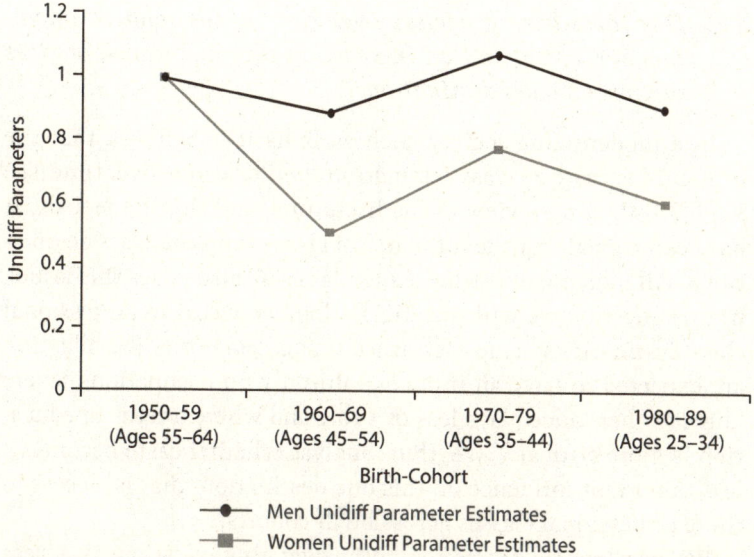

Figure 5.4   Unidiff Parameters for Caste and Destination Class for Men and Women across Cohorts, NES 2014

Source: NES 2014, CSDS Data Unit.

Caste and Social Mobility

The previous section allows us to map the possible changing association between caste and class over time; however, we are interested in studying the impact of caste on social mobility chances. As modernization is expected to have an initial influence on gaining access to professional occupations, where 'direct' inheritance might play less of a role, we first ask whether there has been a change in the relative importance of the two origin effects (caste and class) on access to one class destination—the professional class.

We follow this by asking whether any groups in particular, when compared to other castes from similar low class origins, are less or more able to take advantage of upward class mobility opportunities, that is, with regard to this question we are particularly interested in observing an interaction effect.

1. *Has there been a decline over time in the relative impor-tance of caste, and an increase in the importance of class origins, on class destinations?*

In a modernizing society such as India it is believed that the influence of caste on class destination should decline over time (see Vaid [2014b] for a review of the literature), and simultaneously, it has been argued that the influence of class origins on class destina-tions will increase over time (Kolenda [1986] also raises this issue). In this question we will specifically look at access to professional class destinations, as modernization and economic liberalization are expected to have an influence initially on occupations where 'direct' inheritance plays less of a role and where 'merit' or educa-tion is more critical.[17] We, thus, analyse whether caste becomes a less important influence on this one destination, that is, access to these professional classes across birth cohorts.

We use logistic regression to answer this question as access to professional class destinations is dichotomous (the profes-sional class includes within it high and low professionals and RNM Clerical). We use the collapsed five-class schema intro-duced earlier to avoid small sample sizes. In the logistic regres-sion we include class origins and the more detailed variables on communities/castes as independent variables; with access to the professional classes as the dependent variable. We use deviation contrasts (similar to Kumar, Heath, and Heath 2002a) to arrive at the parameter estimates which can be 'interpreted as fitted log odds ratios' (Kumar, Heath, and Heath 2002a: 2987). In this regression 'deviation contrasts compare each group other than the excluded group to the un-weighted average of all groups' (Nichols 1997). Put another way, all parameters above 0 show that for the

---

[17] Basile and Harriss-White (2000: 178) have argued that caste networks are still important for *recruitment* purposes in the informal sectors of the economy. Here we maintain that though this might be the case for the informal sectors, we would expect there to be a declining influence of caste on the expanding professional sectors where 'merit' may have a greater role to play. However, work by Jodhka and Newman (2007) questions this expectation since they find that 'merit' itself is deeply loaded with connotations of family background and is, hence, not a value neutral term.

origin class or caste in question there are better chances than average of gaining access to the professional class and avoiding any
other class; and anything below 0 (negative parameters) shows
lower than average chances of getting to the professional class (see
also Kumar, Heath, and Heath 2002a). The two Tables 5.3 and 5.4
(for men and women) show us the results of this study.

In the tables we focus primarily on the trend or change in the
parameter estimates (represented by B in the models, along with
the standard errors).[18] Some of the main highlights of the tables
are as follows:

1. For both women and men the parameter estimates for class
   origin display 'trendless fluctuation' with some indication of
   a slight increase in these estimates from the oldest to the
   youngest cohort. For instance, the professional class origin
   parameter-estimates for men over the birth cohorts are 1.5,
   2.2, 1.9, and 1.9. Similarly, for men from low agricultural origins the parameter has remained negative and statistically
   significant in all birth cohorts (for women as well a similar
   pattern is seen). Coming from manual work for both men
   and women seems to have a statistically significant negative
   effect on gaining access to professional classes while farming
   class origins do not have a significant effect on the oldest
   cohorts; for the younger cohorts it seems to indicate a significant and negative impact on professional class destination.
2. In terms of caste the parameter-estimates show an interesting pattern that varies by gender. For men in the two oldest
   birth cohorts belonging to high caste Hindu category has a
   positive and significant effect on professional class access.
   However, this effect seems to disappear for the youngest
   cohorts indicating that men from these origins area not especially privileged in the labour market where access to professional class destinations is concerned. None of the other
   caste parameters are significant for men, with the exception
   of Muslims in the youngest cohort experiencing a negative

---

[18] The results of the oldest cohort for women may be unreliable given
the very large standard errors due to small sample sizes.

impact and SCs from the oldest cohort actually seeming to benefit where arriving at professional class destination is concerned. This, latter, is an interesting finding, discussed in detail later. For women, however, we see a much stronger and consistent impact (positive) for those from high castes; and, other minority women from the two youngest cohorts seem to have an advantage as well (not much difference is seen between the high and low OBCs).

We control for locality in our regressions—which underlines the disadvantage faced by those from rural areas in getting access to professional occupations—since all the parameters across cohort for men (and the youngest two cohorts for women) are negative and statistically significant. We do not see any clear trend in the decline of the influence of caste on class destination in the logistic regression. However, we do note that class origins rather than caste background have a stronger parameter and seem to influence access to professional classes to a greater extent.[19] A major result of this analysis is that contrary to expectation father's class rather than caste has, over all birth cohorts, been the stronger determining factor for access to professional class destinations; thus, highlighting that India seems to display a picture similar to developed societies even before 'modernization' is believed to have truly set in (Vaid and Heath [2010] show a similar result with 2004 NES data).

One caveat regarding our results needs to be mentioned: these results are specific to a particular way of categorizing caste and class. Thus, the comparison of the parameter estimates made here is specific to the particular measure and aggregation of caste and class used. If we used more detailed classifications, such as information on individual jatis, for example, we might get a slightly stronger result for that particular jati, though, perhaps not for the others. However, having noted this, given the broad categorizations

---

[19] These logistic regressions, while highlighting the distinctiveness of high castes when compared to the lower castes, also indicate that the lower castes are quite similar to each other (this can be observed through the parameters for caste).

Table 5.3 Logistic Regression Parameters for Access to Professional Classes across Birth Cohort; Men Only

	Cohort 1 Born 1950–9		Cohort 2 Born 1960–9		Cohort 3 Born 1970–9		Cohort 4 Born 1980–9	
	B	SE	B	SE	B	SE	B	SE
Constant	−2.410*	0.202	−1.688*	0.118	−1.938*	0.108	−1.319*	0.077
Rural	−0.701*	0.172	−0.499*	0.114	−0.283*	0.103	−0.421*	0.080
Class of Father								
Professional	1.476*	0.306	2.206*	0.201	1.902*	0.160	1.846*	0.137
Business	−0.136	0.368	−0.067	0.239	0.252	0.199	0.033	0.157
Farm	0.294	0.266	−0.328	0.178	−0.323	0.172	−0.382*	0.127
Manual	−0.831*	0.411	−0.865*	0.246	−1.171*	0.271	−0.561*	0.146
Lower Agric.	−0.804*	0.345	−0.947*	0.206	−0.659*	0.181	−0.937*	0.139
Caste								
Higher caste Hindu	0.626*	0.309	0.409*	0.204	0.237	0.190	0.158	0.160
Peasant High Caste	−0.361	0.568	0.305	0.325	−0.216	0.336	0.444	0.244
OBC High	0.377	0.312	0.252	0.206	0.080	0.178	0.062	0.138
OBC Low	−0.737	0.557	−0.152	0.324	−0.120	0.255	0.109	0.193
SC	0.706*	0.352	0.015	0.257	−0.181	0.215	−0.047	0.161
ST	−0.546	0.672	0.191	0.326	−0.003	0.283	0.012	0.204
Muslim	−0.081	0.502	−0.531	0.314	−0.110	0.265	−0.466*	0.196
Other Minorities	0.018	0.589	−0.489	0.384	0.314	0.297	−0.272	0.264

(Cont'd)

Table 5.3 *(Cont'd)*

	Cohort 1 Born 1950–9		Cohort 2 Born 1960–9		Cohort 3 Born 1970–9		Cohort 4 Born 1980–9	
	B	SE	B	SE	B	SE	B	SE
Goodness of Fit								
Nagelkerke R2		0.211		0.293		0.231		0.247
Model Chi-Square/d.f. (sig.)	71.856/12 d.f. (0.000)		214.465/12 d.f. (0.000)		210.030/12 d.f. (0.000)		331.641/12 d.f. (0.000)	
Total/N		759		1243		1665		2116

Source: NES 2014, CSDS Data Unit.

Note: significant parameters (*) are more than twice their standard error (SE). Main effect model only.

Table 5.4 Logistic Regression Parameters for Access to Professional Classes across Birth Cohort; Women Only

	Cohort 1 Born 1950–9		Cohort 2 Born 1960–9		Cohort 3 Born 1970–9		Cohort 4 Born 1980–9	
	B	SE	B	SE	B	SE	B	SE
Constant	-4.127	SE	-1.995*	0.280	-1.312*	0.190	-0.665*	0.159
Rural	-.120	0.324	0.040	0.223	-0.619*	0.187	-0.699*	0.154
Class of Father								
Professional	1.512*	0.528	3.038*	0.460	2.744*	0.324	2.934*	0.334
Business	2.235*	0.683	-0.559	0.636	0.287	0.386	0.332	0.273
Farm	-1.118	0.605	-0.322	0.344	-0.573*	0.290	-0.888*	0.264
Manual	.171	0.571	-0.709	0.415	-1.143*	0.349	-0.757*	0.267
Lower Agric.	-2.800*	0.872	-1.447*	0.394	-1.315*	0.288	-1.621*	0.254
Caste								
Higher caste Hindu	2.521	SE	0.987*	0.417	1.032*	0.358	1.282*	0.342
Peasant High Caste	3.166	SE	0.743	0.625	0.091	0.549	-0.577	0.524
OBC High	2.356	SE	0.291	0.398	-0.650	0.340	-0.063	0.267
OBC Low	1.156	SE	-0.220	0.676	-0.504	0.519	-0.022	0.377
SC	2.116	SE	-1.613*	0.664	-0.260	0.364	-0.455	0.313
ST	1.443	SE	0.548	0.495	-0.051	0.382	-0.593	0.344
Muslim	-17.069	SE	-1.548	1.077	-0.766	0.718	-0.969*	0.475
Other Minorities	4.310	SE	0.813	0.556	1.109*	0.449	1.398*	0.487

(Cont'd)

Table 5.4 (Cont'd)

	Cohort 1 Born 1950–9		Cohort 2 Born 1960–9		Cohort 3 Born 1970–9		Cohort 4 Born 1980–9	
	B	SE	B	SE	B	SE	B	SE
Goodness of Fit								
Nagelkerke R2		0.535		0.417		0.440		0.534
Model Chi-Square/d.f. (sig.)	79.406/12 d.f. (0.000)		106.071/12 d.f. (0.000)		176.241/12 d.f. (0.000)		289.461/12 d.f. (0.000)	
Total/N		256		426		675		708

Source: NES 2014, CSDS Data Unit.

Note: Significant parameters (*) are more than twice their standard error (SE); SE signifies a very high standard error. Main effect model only.

used here (due to sample size issues), we can conclude that class is indeed an important influence on gaining access to professional destinations.

In the last question we ask:

> 2. *Whether certain castes find it harder to move up than members of other castes from the same lower class origins?*

To answer this question we look specifically at whether certain castes, when compared to other caste groups from similar origin classes, are unable to take advantage of opportunities of upward class mobility; and conversely, whether high castes are protected from being downwardly mobile (Karanth 1996). Here we intend to extend the results from the previous logistic regression to focus on the relevant interaction effects.

We begin by analysing men and women's CmSF and Unidiff models to test whether the relation between class origins and class destinations across the various communities is common or whether it varies (this analysis can also be done by observing logistic regression parameters, but the interpretation is more coherent using log-linear analysis). That is, we are interested specifically in looking at an interaction effect. Through the Unidiff model we study whether the strength of association between origins and destinations is weaker for any particular caste group or groups. If we are indeed able to show that some communities have a stronger association between class origins and destinations, then we can conclude that they have less chances of mobility.[20]

According to the conventional criteria both the CmSF models for women and men have a G^2 with a p-value less than 0.05, and hence, these models do not fit the data adequately (see Table 5.5). But on observing the other statistical calculations like the *BIC* and Δ, the CmSF is the *preferred* model. This seems to indicate that there are similar relative rates of mobility for all castes, that is, the

---

[20] The notation for the model of common social fluidity is displayed below:

$$\log_m = \lambda + \lambda_i^O + \lambda_j^D + \lambda_k^C + \lambda_{ik}^{OC} + \lambda_{jk}^{DC} + \lambda_{ij}^{OD}$$

Where O=origins; D=destinations and C=community.

association between class origins and class destinations does not vary much by community.

Even though the CmSF provides a weak fit according to the G^2 criterion and it misclassifies 3 and 4 per cent of the cases for men and women respectively, in order to observe where the model does not fit well, we studied the adjusted residuals of these CmSF models (available from author). On analysing the adjusted residuals we would expect, if the higher castes were indeed protected from downward mobility, to find more negative residuals above the diagonal in the high caste table. This would indicate less downward class mobility for this caste than expected.

On observing our data, this is not the case. Also, in terms of intergenerational stability (cells along the diagonal) fewer high castes are stable in professional and manual and low agricultural classes than would be expected on the basis of the model.

Table 5.5   Log-linear Analysis (Class Origin, Class Destination, Community)

		G^2	d.f	P	Δ	BIC
Men	Complete independence O, D, C	8911.99	136	0.000	47.99	7707.64
	Conditional independence OC, DC	7558.55	96	0.000	45.12	6708.42
	CmSF (OD)	111.46	80	0.012	3.15	−596.98
	Unidiff	105.79	75	0.011	3.0	−558.38
Women	Complete independence O, D, C	3600.11	136	0.000	51.67	2535.82
	Conditional independence OC, DC	3045.99	96	0.000	47.53	2294.73
	CmSF (OD)	122.66	80	0.002	4.47	−503.40
	Unidiff	113.64	75	0.003	4.13	−473.28

Source: NES 2014, CSDS Data Unit.
Note: N Men = 7013; N Women 2504; O = Origins (5); D = Destinations (5); C = Community (6).

Furthermore, if it were true that the SCs were indeed less likely to be upwardly mobile we would expect to find more negative residuals below the diagonal in the SC table. Even though we do find this to be the case, none of the residuals are significant (except one for women). These tables quite generally do not display much of a pattern of the residuals for any of the caste/class origins combinations for both women and men.

To observe the strength of the association between origins and destinations for different communities, we then look at the Unidiff parameters, which are a similar fit to the CmSF (Table 5.5). Here (Figure 5.5) the parameter for high caste men and women is set to 1, anything greater than 1 indicates a stronger association, whereas anything less than 1 shows a weaker association. The Unidiff parameters show that the strength of the association between origins and destinations is marginally weaker for all community groups compared to high caste men, with an exception of the 'other' category. For women on the other hand, OBC, SC, and ST women display a stronger association between their origins and destinations than women from higher castes and 'other' groups.

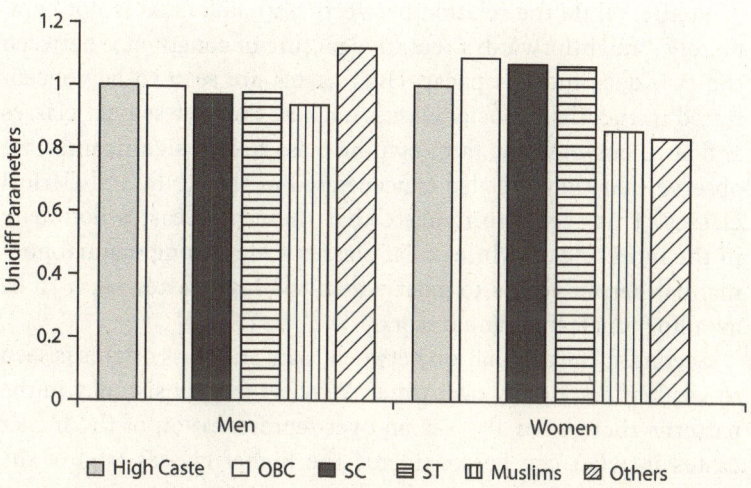

Figure 5.5 Unidiff Parameters for Origin Class, Destination Class, and Community, NES 2014

Source: NES 2014, CSDS Data Unit.

The main result of this analysis is that upper castes seem *not to be* protected from downward mobility (especially women), but there are hints that SC, OBC, and ST women may have difficulty in gaining mobility (both upward and downward) as we observe a stronger origin-destination association for these groups, which indicates that they have a harder time leaving their class origins behind. However, for men, it seems that OBC, SC, ST, and Muslim men have a weak association which would lead to chances of upward mobility, but also greater chances of downward mobility.

★ ★ ★

The *traditional* association between caste and certain occupations has often been discussed. In recent times there has been an increase in the literature proclaiming a breaking down of this congruence. In addition, sociologists have questioned whether the 'traditional' caste system is now giving way to a more class based society. In this chapter an attempt has been made to study the relation between caste and class systematically, and in particular, to highlight any changes that may have occurred over time.

Firstly, while the relation between caste and class is not completely straightforward, a tentative picture of congruence between the two does indeed appear. High castes are seen to be concentrated in the higher social classes such as the professional classes and large business and farm owning classes. But, significantly, we observe that they are also concentrated in the RNM and clerical classes. This seems to indicate that these high castes dominate in the more 'clean' white collar classes and a strong manual-non-manual barrier seems to exist where the high castes seem to be avoiding 'unclean' manual work.

Secondly, the association between caste and class origins is seen to weaken marginally over time. We observe a consistency in the patterns though we also see an over-representation of the higher castes in what can be considered the higher classes, and of the lower castes in the lower classes.[21]

---

[21] In the concluding chapter we discuss a possible reason for why the picture of congruence between caste and class is not entirely

Thirdly, when community and class origins are studied together, particularly with regard to access to a particular class, in this case the professional class, the effect of class origins is seen to be much stronger than the effect of community or caste. This pattern seems to hold consistently over the birth cohorts. However, the impact of caste does not disappear over time, though it is negligible for most castes except the high castes. We also conclude that other than being from a high caste background which seems to display a significant positive impact on access to the professions, the other lower castes seem not to be very distinct from each other in this regard. In answer to Kolenda's question of whether a class system is emerging in India (1986: 108) we can conclude that rather than a system 'emerging', class has instead been around for a long time in India.

Though we are unable to study the impact of reservations on SCs and STs directly, due to the lack of data in large enough numbers on government Class I and II jobs (where seats or places are specifically reserved for the SCs and STs), we have studied more generally how these groups perform as compared with the higher castes and the OBCs. The legacy of reservation does not seem to have benefited the SCs and STs as much as was expected (though we see SC men from the oldest cohort having some slight advantage), as despite these policies (for example, education policies) these groups seem to consistently lag behind the higher castes, in terms of access to the professional classes. The drivers of these patterns (education) are studied in the next chapter.

Fourthly, we observe that the relation between class destinations and community is weakening over time. Though, we also observe an enduring and pervasive effect of caste. This study seems to support Kumar, Heath, and Heath's conclusions about the story in India being one of 'continuity rather than change' (2002b: 4096).

Finally, we conclude that SCs do indeed seem to be experiencing difficulty in gaining upward class mobility though conversely

---

straightforward. This has to do with the more micro-level association between jatis and occupations rather than between castes and classes at the macro-level.

the high castes are not cushioned from the forces of downward class mobility. This result supports our previous conclusion on the access of the SCs and STs to the professional classes as seen by the 'main effect' of coming from an SC background. The experience of the Muslim respondents sets them apart. Not only are they more highly concentrated in self-employment, but the youngest cohort of Muslim men and women seem to be disadvantaged as compared to older cohorts, as well as other community groups, where access to professional work is concerned.

In sum, caste or community still has a relatively strong relationship with class. However, when both caste and class are studied together the influence of caste, at least as measured by our broad categorization, is weaker than that of class origins though it has not disappeared, and we see a pervasive effect of caste.[22] Perhaps the most important conclusion is that class origins, rather than caste, have long been the major factor in influencing one's class destinations. Where Kolenda and others might have been mistaken is in supposing that the effects of class origins are a new phenomenon.

In India, modernization has not had the expected effect as the influence of caste has not disappeared though in comparison to older NES data (2004) the effect of caste seems to be declining (see Vaid 2012).[23] However, we observe that the importance of class origins has so far been under-emphasized in the literature. In India the *family*, especially for members from the service or high manual classes, is an important source of resources to ensure that its members maintain their 'edge' in gaining access to scarce resources like jobs. But, significantly, the 'resources' that the

---

[22] A more microanalysis that studies individual jatis and occupations rather than castes and classes might give us more insight on the relationship between the two and their influence on occupational destinations.

[23] The results for 2014 seem to be consistent broadly with Vaid (2012) which used the 2004 NES data. However, quite critically, the most recent NES data seems to indicate that some of the caste-class effects are indeed weakening—so Vaid's tentative conclusion on possible weakening of the association seems to be borne out. Though, the caveat that the effect of caste has not disappeared holds.

family now employs extend beyond caste and include more specifically aspects of class such as wealth. Thus, in arenas where caste cannot be used to get access to these resources, these privileged families are able to use their wealth and class instead (see also Basile and Harriss-White 2000). This importance of the 'family' in India has also been highlighted by Béteille (1993) and is observed further in our next chapter which looks at the importance of education and the role that the family plays.

Appendix A5.1: NES Dataset and Information on Community

According to the 2011 Indian Census, Hindus make up just under 80 per cent of the Indian population followed by Muslims with 14 per cent of the population. The other large minority groups are the Christians (2 per cent) and Sikhs (under 2 per cent). Table A5.1.1 shows how the sampling in the NES dataset being used in this book compares to the Census figures. As can be seen, Hindus are represented fairly well in this dataset, while the Muslims are under-represented and other minority groups, in turn, marginally over-represented. The sample distributions overall are relatively close to the Census figures. The discrepancy in sampling is due to the procedure followed by the NES which uses a state-wise sampling frame.

The breakdown of figures by caste groups is shown in the Table A5.1.2 which compares the Census figures to the NES

Table A5.1.1 Religious Groups as a Proportion of the Total Population

	NES 2014	Census 2011
Hindu	79.3	79.80
Muslim	11.8	14.23
Christian	3.3	2.30
Sikh	3.3	1.72
Other Religions	2.3	1.96
Total	22,295	1210854977

Source: Census figures from http://www.censusindia.gov.in/2011census/C-01.html (accessed 18 May 2016).

Table A5.1.2   Caste Groups in the Census and the NES

	*NES 2014**	**Census 2011**
Other (High) castes	29.6	Not collected
Other Backward Classes (OBCs)	40.7	41**
Scheduled Castes (SCs)	20.0	16.63***
Scheduled Tribes (STs)	9.7	8.63***

Source: *NES 2014 figures are from the variable on caste group (not jatis).
** NSS (2006) figures (information not released by Census).
*** Census figures from: http://www.censusindia.gov.in/2011census/population_
enumeration.html (accessed 18 May 2016).

sample for caste groups. In the case of the OBCs (as discussed in
Chapter 2) the figures are from the NSS. The NES data seems to
represent the Census data fairly closely.

The 2014 NES has information on over 240 castes and tribes,
including information on castes found among other religious
groups like the Sikhs and Muslims. The information on community or caste was gathered from question Z5 in the survey: 'What is
your Caste/Jati-biradari/ Tribe name? And your sub caste?'

Responses to this question were coded into the master list of
the over 240 names, available from Lokniti, Centre for the Study
of Developing Societies (CSDS).[24] For this chapter we have recoded
this information to give a detailed eight-category, and a six-category collapsed list for analysis where small size is an issue, for
community and caste. The two terms 'caste' and 'community'
are used interchangeably: the author is aware of the simplification involved in using the term community rather than caste, but
given the interest in groups such as the Muslims and other minorities, for want of a better term, in the present context 'community'
seems appropriate.

[24] In the next question in the survey the respondents were also asked
for the name of their *caste group* (that is, they had to pick from a list of the
four major categories of 'Other, OBC, SC and ST'). This information was
only used to check on the figures obtained after recoding the first question
as it did not provide enough detail to be used in our more comprehensive
analysis.

Table A5.1.3 Eight Community Categorization, NES 2014

Cates/Communities	Per Cent
High Caste	16.2
Peasant High Caste	6.6
OBC High/creamy layer	24.2
OBC Low/non creamy layer	10.3
Scheduled Caste	17.8
Scheduled Tribe	8.9
Muslims	11.3
Other minorities	4.8
N	21967

Source: NES 2014, CSDS Data Unit.

The respondents who did not answer the question on their community affiliation were removed from the analysis. All the Muslims, Christians, Sikhs, and other smaller religious minorities that had information on their SC or OBC status, are excluded from the SC, OBC list, but included instead within their religious category. This enables us to treat caste as essentially Hindu, and compare these Hindu castes with the other community groups for the purpose of our analysis.

The detailed community categorization with eight-categories is shown in Table A5.1.3. This categorization makes it possible to separate the high castes from the peasant (higher) castes and to split the OBCs into two groups: the more 'forward' or 'higher' caste OBCs, often described as the 'creamy layer'; and the more 'backward' or 'lower caste' OBCs. By necessity, this categorization is rough since some jatis are listed as OBC in particular states but are absent from other state lists. We follow Vaid and and Heath (2010: 162) who tested the correct listing of jatis in the larger groups. The detailed category of community used here also separates the minority religious groups. Due to smaller sample sizes and given the use of log-linear analysis, we are unable to distinguish between the different categories within the Muslims.

As some of the groups in the data had very small sample sizes, for certain analyses this information was recoded to give six community categories that enable us to capture most of the major divisions, especially with regard to the legally and constitutionally enshrined caste groups. This categorization is similar in some ways to Kumar, Heath, and Heath's categories. The six groups are the high castes (made up of the high castes as well as high caste peasant proprietors); the OBCs (high and low together), the SCs, the STs, Muslims, and other minority groups (made up primarily of Christians and Sikhs). The recoded 'community' variable is shown in Table A5.1.4:

This collapsed community variable is used for all the log-linear analysis in this and the next chapter.

Table A5.1.4 Collapsed Six Category Community Group, NES 2014

		Column Per cent
1	High Caste	22.7
2	Other Backward Classes	34.5
3	Scheduled Caste	17.8
4	Scheduled Tribe	8.9
5	Muslim	11.3
6	Other minorities	4.8
	N	21967

Source: NES 2014, CSDS Data Unit.

6

Mobility Mechanisms*

The Role of Education

Education, especially formal education, has been viewed as a panacea for the ills facing society, particularly to overcome rampant inequalities due to inheritance which are known to magnify the advantages and disadvantages across generations. Does education in fact temper the barriers to mobility faced by particular groups, or does it further increase the advantages that other groups carry with them? This chapter takes forward the discussion on mobility patterns and expands it to include the role played by education as a driver of these patterns. The importance of education as a catalyst of social mobility opportunities is well established in sociological research (Breen and Luijkx 2007; Froerer 2011; Halsey, Heath, and Ridge 1980; Heath and Payne 2000; see also Ciotti 2006). India has had a long history of policies, especially education policies, aimed at alleviating inequalities suffered by socially and economically disadvantaged groups and encouraging their upward social mobility. In addition to policies at the primary education level, this also includes 'reservation' policies, or policies of affirmative action, that have been specifically directed at public higher education institutions and at jobs in the public sector (Galanter 1984; Weisskopf 2004; McMillan 2005). Despite the various policies, separate strands

* This chapter draws on previous research using the NES 2009 data published in Vaid (2016).

of research underline the persisting effect of factors such as caste, class of origin, and gender on the opportunities to gain access to education (Desai and Kulkarni 2008; Breen and Vaid 2008) or the effects of these factors on occupational positions (Kumar, Heath, and Heath 2002a and b; Vaid and Heath 2010; Vaid 2012; Borooah, Dubey, and Iyer 2007). However, we do not, as yet, have systematic research that provides a macro picture of the role, if any, that education plays with regard to social mobility in India. While building on existing research by exploring the role of education, this chapter also enquires into whether there are any persisting barriers to mobility faced by specific groups. Briefly, the chapter asks: whether education indeed mediates mobility; and, whether all individuals (irrespective of their social background) have benefitted from education in so far as opportunities open to occupational attainment and social mobility are concerned.

As discussed in Chapter 1, in the context of the OED triad, we have explored the patterns of social mobility or the OD, CD association in Chapter 4 (other studies include Nijhawan 1969, Kumar, Heath, and Heath 2002a; Vaid and Heath 2010); we have elsewhere studied the effect of origins on educational attainment, that is, the OE, CE association (Breen and Vaid 2008; see also Desai and Kulkarni 2008); and, finally, in Chapter 5 we have looked at the association between caste and class, that is, the OC link (see also Vaid 2012). However, we have limited research on the impact of education directly on social mobility and whether it mediates the effect of caste and class origins, that is, the ED association and the E-OD and E-CD associations. The present chapter explores these associations.

Education as a Mechanism of Mobility

The 'modernization' argument (Treiman 1970), postulates that over time we would expect social mobility to be on the rise; hence, we would expect there to be a decline in inheritance or the OD association as a country industrializes. Further, under the related 'efficiency' argument, we would expect education to have a greater impact on class destinations (the ED association) rather than social origins, as hiring someone due to their family background or other ascriptive criteria may not be the most efficient way to fill scarce positions in a competitive labour market (Heath 2003).

Breen and Vaid's (2008) study on the impact of caste and class origins (OE, CE association) on educational attainment, and the changes over time in India (using 2004 NES data) finds that the 'inequalities in educational attainment according to class origins have declined, starting with cohorts born in the 1960s, and that gender inequalities began to decline somewhat earlier; [while] inequalities by caste seem to have remained largely unchanged' (p. 1, brackets added).

In this context, we study whether education impacts social mobility by asking:

Question One: How do the patterns of social mobility vary across various levels of education?

Question Two: Does education act as a mediator for social mobility? In other words, do we see any effect of education on social mobility chances?

Question Three: Do we find any support for the 'meritocracy' argument?[1]

While being unable to study the impact of specific education or reservation policies directly, employing a 'birthcohort' approach allows the application of both a cross-sectional and a temporal perspective required to provide some answers to the main research questions.

The first part of this chapter studies intergenerational occupational change by level of education followed by an overview of patterns of absolute social mobility by education levels. The second part focuses on relative mobility patterns and the role of education. The third and final part extends the analysis conducted in Chapter 5 and asks whether the role of education or origin characteristics, such as father's class and caste, have an effect on the probability of women and men gaining access to professional

---

[1] Michael Young in his classic 'Rise of the Meritocracy' sets out a warning against the unsubstantiated conviction that education itself is a meritorious artefact (see Jodhka and Newman [2007] for an Indian study that underlines the tempered role of education).

occupations (expected to be more *meritocratic*), and whether this has changed over time.

The variable on education used here is derived from the NES survey question which delineates nine categories ranging from those who are non-literate to those who have professional degrees. Table 6.1 lists and provides the descriptives for the six-fold education variable used in this book.

In the Indian context, primary school includes grades one through five (children aged approximately six to eleven). Middle school includes grades six through eight; Matriculation is at grade ten, after which students either finish their schooling and get an intermediate certificate (grade twelve) or go to vocational 'no degree' colleges or to a degree college. Table 6.1 disaggregates the level of education in the NES 2014 by gender and locality. This disaggregation is significant, as the averages are hiding fairly wide rural–urban variations. Clearly, women in both rural and urban India predominate in the non-literate and primary school categories, though the urban figure is lower. Fewer women rather than men are in the middle education categories. Interestingly, however, the same proportion of urban women have college education as men underlying the specificities of the 'urban' for those women who are in the labour market.

In the context of the first question of interest in this chapter we look at the distributions of education by class destination across gender and locality, and we also study absolute rates of mobility by level of education. For the second question posed in this chapter on whether higher levels of education lead to more relative mobility, we adapt the models used in Chapters 4 and 5. We begin by fitting the complete independence model where Origins, Destinations, and Education are hypothesized to be independent of each other. In subsequent models we add various associations between OED to study which one provides the best fit. In particular, we focus on two models—the model of common association and the model of uniform difference. In the common association model (CmSF) we hypothesize that the class of Origin and class of Destination are associated (OD term); however, we also hypothesize that this association is similar across various levels of Education (E). If this model fits the data according to the usual goodness of fit statistics then we can conclude that while OD are associated, this

Table 6.1 Distribution of Respondent's Education by Gender in NES 2014[2]

Level of Education	Men Rural	Men Urban	Men Total	Women Rural	Women Urban	Women Total
College graduationand above (incl. professional degrees)	8.8	29.3	13.2	5.7	29.1	10.0
Intermediate schooling/ Non-degree college (including vocational courses)	12.7	18.7	14.0	7.0	10.4	7.6
School Matriculation	18.5	18.1	18.4	9.5	9.8	9.5
Middle school	17.2	13.9	16.5	11.5	12.0	11.6
Up to Primary school	22.3	13.0	20.3	22.6	21.3	22.4
Non-literate	20.6	7.1	17.7	43.7	17.4	38.9
Total	100.0	100.0	100.0	100.0	100.0	100.0
	(N=5554)	(N=1521)	(N=7075)	(N=2070)	(N=460)	(N=2530)

Source: NES 2014, CSDS Data Unit.

[2] These figures differ from the census as here these are figures for women and men who have or had an engagement with the labour market.

association is common across education levels; that is, education does not influence social mobility (OD term). If we find that the CmSF model does not fit the data adequately and hence that OD varies across Education, then we fit the Unidiff which allows us to establish exactly how the strength of OD association (or relative mobility) varies across levels of education.

The final analysis in this chapter expands the logistic regression models discussed in Chapter 5 to analyse the impact of education along with the 'origin' variables of class and caste on one outcome—professional class destination. As professional class destination is a dichotomous variable, logistic regression is the most appropriate technique. The deviation contrasts in the models give us 'parameter estimates which can be interpreted as fitted log odds ratios' or as 'measures of extent of inequality of opportunity' (Vaid and Heath 2010: 153; Kumar, Heath, and Heath 2002a; see also Nichols 1997). We also provide an over time analysis of the logistic regression models. The control for locality in these regression models allows us to focus on the difference between rural and urban India.

Empirical Analysis on the Role of Education

Question One: How do the patterns of intergenerational social mobility in India vary across levels of education?

This question requires that we study absolute rates of social mobility. Before that we provide some descriptives. While Chapter 4 described patterns of change in occupational distributions over a generation, Figures 6.1 and 6.2 help us visualize the concentration in specific occupations according to different levels of education. For men (Figure 6.1), we observe that those with college education are most likely to be engaged in low professional, high professional, and RNM Clerical white-collar work, as well as in business. However, as one moves down the education ladder (especially those who have not matriculated), the proportion engaged in white-collar (especially high professional) occupations (and as business owners) declines substantially, while the proportion engaged in low agriculture and manual work rises; we see that nearly 50 per cent of the non-literate male sample is in low

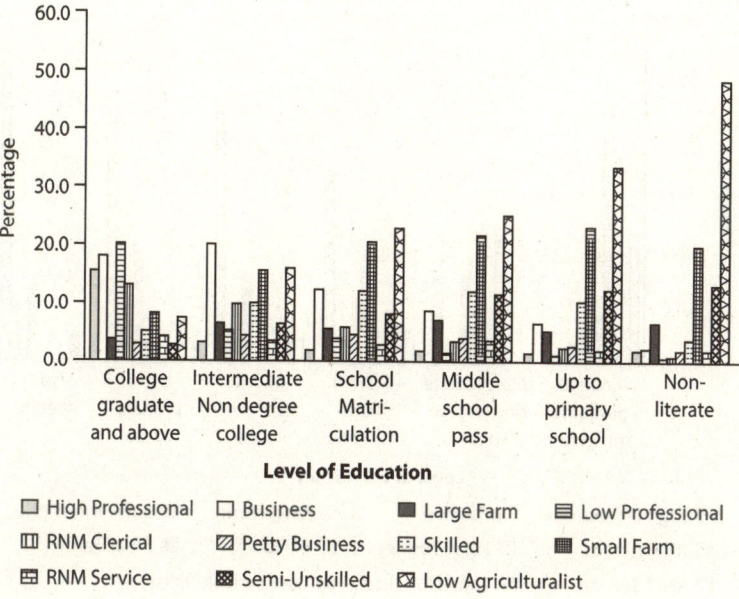

Figure 6.1 Distribution of Class Destination by Level of Education for Men, NES 2014 (N=7075)

Source: NES 2014, CSDS Data Unit.

agriculture). For women (Figure 6.2), there is a higher concentration of women with college degrees in the lower professional class (45 per cent compared to 20 per cent for men) followed by the high professionals (which begins to decline substantially for women who have less than intermediate or non-degree college education). For women, lower agriculture followed by small farming shows the highest concentration of employed women across all levels of education (with college graduates as an exception).

One of the interesting distinctions between women and men is in the professional classes, especially in the low professional class and in RNM Clerical work. Women with intermediate/non-degree college education and those who are school matriculates seem to be fairly well represented in these professions—especially in low professional work. For men, however, it is only the college graduates who work in large numbers in all three professions. This gender difference in the professions is further underlined by

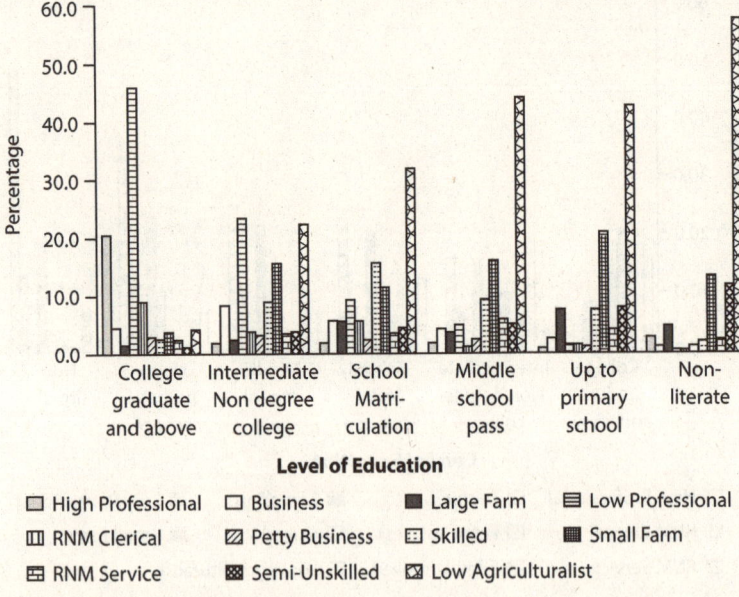

Figure 6.2 Distribution of Class Destination by Level of Education for Women, NES 2014 (N=2530)

Source: NES 2014, CSDS Data Unit.

the locality-wise difference as well (Table 6.2). As expected, more people are engaged in the professions in urban India. However, a fairly large number of college educated women (16 per cent and 41 per cent) in rural India are in the high and low professions, respectively. While the proportions are much higher in urban India, we find that RNM Clerical work is fairly distinctive—where generally more men rather than women are engaged—the opposite of the other two professional classes for college educated people. Urban intermediate schooling and non-degree college educated women are clearly predominant in the low professions.

A deeper analysis by locality (Table 6.2) indicates: first, non-literates have a similar concentration across gender in rural and urban areas in low agricultural work, (though the figures are much lower in urban areas) followed by semi-unskilled in urban and small farm work in rural. The only difference is the higher concentration in RNM Service for non-literate women and in business

Table 6.2 Distribution of Respondent's Class across Levels of Education, By Gender and Locality, NES 2014

Rural	College graduate		Intermediate		Matriculation		Middle School Pass		Up to Primary		Non-Literate	
	Men	Women	Men	Women	Men	Women	Men	Women	Men	Women	Men	Women
High Profsn.	8.6	16.1	2.7	2.8	1.7	1.5	1.8	2.5	1.5	1.3	1.8	3.2
Business	12.7	4.2	14.9	6.9	8.6	4.6	6.4	2.5	4.6	1.9	1.8	1.1
Large Farm	6.4	3.4	8.7	3.5	6.3	5.6	8.0	3.8	6.0	8.3	6.9	5.4
Low Profsn.	20.9	40.7	4.6	16.7	3.1	8.2	1.4	5.9	0.7	1.7	0.4	0.7
RNM Clerical	10.2	7.6	7.5	3.5	5.5	5.1	2.1	0.4	1.8	0.4	0.6	0.3
Petty Business	3.1	0.8	3.4	2.8	3.7	3.1	3.3	0.8	1.9	1.3	1.4	0.7
Skilled	4.5	5.9	7.4	8.3	9.2	14.3	9.2	7.9	7.9	3.6	2.9	1.5
Small Farm	14.1	7.6	20.5	20.8	25.2	13.8	25.4	18.0	25.9	24.1	20.8	14.5
RNM Service	3.9	3.4	3.0	0.7	2.2	3.1	3.0	2.5	1.6	2.8	1.5	2.2
Semi-Unskilled	3.3	2.5	6.8	5.6	7.9	5.1	11.2	5.4	11.6	7.7	11.5	10.9
Low Agric.	12.3	7.6	20.5	28.5	26.7	35.7	28.3	50.2	36.5	46.8	50.5	59.4
N	488	118	703	144	1027	196	958	239	1236	468	1142	905

(Cont'd)

Table 6.2 (Cont'd)

Urban	College graduate		Intermediate		Matriculation		Middle School Pass		Up to Primary		Non-Literate	
	Men	Women	Men	Women	Men	Women	Men	Women	Men	Women	Men	Women
High Profsn.	23.1	24.6	3.2	0	1.8	4.4	0.9	1.8	0	1.0	0	0
Business	23.6	5.2	32.4	12.5	25.4	11.1	18.5	12.7	17.3	5.1	4.6	6.3
Large Farm	0.7	0	0.4	0	1.1	6.7	1.9	3.6	1.0	4.1	1.9	1.3
Low Profsn.	19.3	50.0	7.0	43.8	6.9	15.6	0.9	1.8	3.0	3.1	0.9	0
RNM Clerical	16.2	10.4	16.2	6.3	7.6	8.9	9.0	1.8	6.6	9.2	2.8	1.3
Petty Business	2.5	4.5	6.7	6.3	7.6	2.2	6.2	10.9	7.1	2.0	6.5	8.8
Skilled	5.6	0	16.2	12.5	23.2	22.2	25.6	16.4	24.4	26.5	11.1	12.5
Small Farm	1.3	0.7	3.5	0	2.9	2.2	4.7	7.3	5.1	5.1	9.3	6.3
RNM Service	4.0	2.2	4.6	14.6	5.1	8.9	5.7	21.8	4.6	12.2	7.4	7.5
Semi-Unskilled	1.8	0	5.6	0	9.4	2.2	15.2	5.5	16.2	10.2	28.7	25.0
Low Agric.	1.8	2.2	4.2	4.2	9.1	15.6	11.4	16.4	14.7	21.4	26.9	31.3
N	445	134	284	48	276	45	211	55	197	98	108	80

Source: NES 2014, CSDS Data Unit.

for non-literate men. Second, men in urban India (with a middle school certificate and above) transition out of low agriculture into skilled work and business; whereas women who matriculate move out of low agriculture. Finally, college educated women and men are more likely to be in low professional work followed by business for men and high professional for urban and rural women.

These descriptives give us a sense of how education may be a pathway to certain occupations—and the absence of it a barrier to others. To answer the question posed in this section, we now turn to the mobility analysis. Table 6.3 disaggregates absolute rates of mobility by education. We find that men and women with college degrees are more likely to be intergenerationally mobile, especially upwardly mobile—more so for women than men. With each lower level of education, we observe subsequently lower amounts of mobility, with non-literates displaying the least mobility of all. Critically, the amount of upward over downward mobility (displayed by the U/D column in the table) indicates that while

Table 6.3 Social Mobility by Level of Education for Women and Men, NES 2014

Level of Education	Mobility	Stability	Upward	Downward	U/D
Men					
College (N=933)	48.0	51.6	37.8	10.2	3.7
Intermediate (N=987)	38.5	61.3	27.8	10.7	2.6
Matriculate (N=1303)	33.6	66.8	21.8	11.8	1.8
Middle school (N=1169)	31.9	68.1	20.1	11.8	1.7
Primary School (N=1433)	24.5	75.5	15.3	9.2	1.7
Non-Literate (N=1250)	15.3	85.0	9.3	6.0	1.6
Women					
College (N=252)	52.1	48.1	46.9	5.2	9.0
Intermediate(N=192)	40.5	59.4	30.7	9.8	3.1
Matriculate(N=241)	34.2	65.5	23.1	11.1	2.1
Middle School(N=294)	31.2	68.7	18.3	12.9	1.4
Primary School(N=566)	19.4	80.8	12.0	7.4	1.6
Non-Literate (N=985)	12.1	87.7	6.3	5.8	1.1

Source: NES 2014, CSDS Data Unit.

Note: Class = Five-class schema; for women all the chi-squares have less than 5 expected count in more than 20 per cent of cells, and hence, should be read as an indicator only.

women and men are both experiencing more upward than downward mobility, the proportion of upward over downward mobility declines at each lower level of education. This indicates that education has a significant impact on social mobility chances—at least with regard to absolute rates of mobility.

Rural–urban figures complicate these patterns (Table 6.4)[3] —while the overall pattern may look similar, women with a college degree in rural India display as much mobility as women in urban India and also as much as men in rural India. College educated women experience more upward mobility than college educated men—clearly this indicates that while fewer women are in college education, the ones who do enter it experience better chances of mobility than men do (and, this is much sharper for urban women). This is also indicated by the rate of upward over downward mobility (the U/D column).

Education is, thus, clearly a marker of difference, and women in both rural and urban areas who are able to acquire education are able to take advantage of professional occupations whereas men who matriculate enter into RNM Clerical work, as seen in the earlier discussion. While those women who are able to stay on in education (admittedly fewer than men) are able to experience similar opportunities as men; certain differences still remain—skilled work and business classes are some examples. While the discussion in this section indicates some broad changes, for our second question we are interested in seeing whether education leads to a weakening of stability or inheritance; or, in other words a weakening of the O-D association. Hence, does higher education lead to increased social mobility across a range of occupations (controlling for structural change)?

Question Two: Does education act as a mediator for social mobility? In other words, do we see any effect of education on social mobility chances once structural changes are accounted for?

To answer this question, we need to look at the relative rates of mobility and test whether the OD association is weaker for higher

---

[3] Due to small sample sizes in certain cells, especially for women, these results are simply an indicator and should be read with caution.

Table 6.4 Locality-wise Social Mobility Rates for Selected Levels of Education, NES 2014

Education Level	Mobility		Stability		Up		Down		U/D	
	Rural	Urban	Rural	Urban	Rural	Urban	Rural	Urban	Rural	Urban
Men										
College[Rural=488; Urban=445*]	50.9	45.2	49.1	54.7	41.2	33.8	9.7	11.4	4.2	3.0
Matriculate[Rural=1027; Urban=276*]	32.2	37.7	67.9	62.3	21.2	23.6	11.0	14.1	1.9	1.7
Non-Literate[Rural=1142*; Urban=108*]	14.4	25.8	85.9	74.0	8.7	16.6	5.7	9.2	1.5	1.8
Women	Rural	Urban	Rural	Urban	Rural	Urban	Rural	Urban	Rural	Urban
College[Rural= 118*; Urban=134*]	51.5	52.0	48.3	47.7	44.0	49.1	7.5	2.9	5.9	16.9
Matriculate[Rural=196*; Urban=45*]	30.0	53.3	69.9	46.7	19.9	37.8	10.1	15.5	2.0	2.4
Non-Literate[Rural=905*; Urban=80*]	11.1	23.5	88.8	76.1	5.6	13.6	5.5	9.9	1.0	1.4

Source: NES 2014, CSDS Data Unit.

Note: Class = Five-class schema; *the chi-squares have less than 5 expected count in more than 20 per cent of cells.

levels of education as would be expected under the meritocracy
and modernization argument. We fit a series of log-linear models
to the NES 2014 data as discussed in Chapters 4 and 5.

The first model of complete independence states that origins
(O), Destinations (D), and Education (E) are independent of each
other. The second model of conditional independence supposes
that O and E; and, D and E are associated. Neither of the two models fits the data. From the *BIC* statistics in Table 6.5, it emerges
that the marginally better fitting model for both women and men
is the common association or CmSF model. This indicates that
the association between O and D is, to an extent, common across
various levels of education. However, as the Unidiff model fits
the data marginally better we are able to model how much the
OD association does vary across Education levels; that is, we can
observe whether there is more intergenerational class stability for
certain education levels compared to others. Following the discussion of the *modernization/industrialization* thesis, the hypothesis

Table 6.5 Log-linear Models for Social Mobility by Education, NES 2014

	G^2	d.f.	p	Δ	*BIC*
Men (N=7075)					
Complete Independence 8775.594 (O,D,E)	9981.14	136	0.000	49.73	
Conditional independence (OE, DE)	7310.85	96	0.000	43.71	6459.876
Cmsf (OD)	122.87	80	0.001	3.15	−586.280
Unidiff OD|E	107.76	75	0.008	2.91	−557.068
Women (N=2530)					
Complete Independence (O,D,E)	4145.03	136	0.000	54.15	3079.340
Conditional independence (OE, DE)	2810.41	96	0.000	44.06	2058.154
Cmsf (OD)	118.85	80	0.003	5.14	−508.029
Unidiff OD|E	84.62	75	0.209	3.84	−503.075

Source: NES 2014, CSDS Data Unit.

Note: Five-class schema; O = origins, D = destinations, E = education (models in text).

here is that at higher education levels, the OD association weakens as education rather than class of origin becomes an important factor for determining certain class destinations and also due to the choices people make.[4]

In order to study what these mobility patterns (OD association) are in relative mobility terms across various levels of education, we graph the Unidiff parameter estimates (Figure 6.3). In this graph,

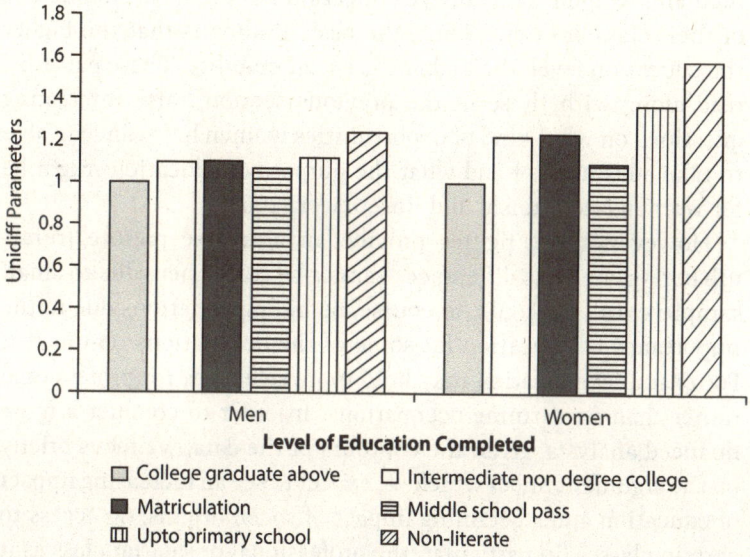

Figure 6.3 Unidiff Parameter Estimates of OD Association across Levels of Education, Men and Women, NES 2014

Source: NES 2014, CSDS Data Unit.

---

[4] In addition, we also are able to study whether the ED association is stronger for any particular class of origin (O). The hypothesis is that those who come from lower social origins display a stronger link between education and destination, that is, education has a stronger role to play for these social classes in gaining access to particular class destinations. Results of this analysis, available from the author, suggest that the ED association is strongest for those from manual class origins, followed by the two agrarian classes and the business class. The ED association is weakest for those from professional class origins. This supports our hypothesis.

'college degree' is set to one and any parameter greater than one implies a stronger origin-destination association for people with that education level, and hence, lower fluidity (relative mobility), and a parameter less than one implies a weaker association, and hence, higher fluidity. We see that at education levels lower than 'college degree' the OD association is stronger for both women and men (and this is much stronger for women)—that is, with an increase in education level we see increased mobility. We see that men and women with college education are the most mobile out of their class of origin. Thus, the basic finding is that the higher the education level, the higher the social mobility. These patterns, read along with those in the previous section, raise interesting questions on what kind of opportunities women have, and are able to take advantage of and what the purpose of education might be for women (see Munshi and Rosenzweig 2006).

However, these figures provide an aggregate picture (rural–urban or caste-wise differences cannot be traced here due to small sample sizes) and could, of course, be hiding variations due to the importance of education for some of the occupations on our list. For example, education may hold more relevance for professional rather than for farming occupations. In order to conduct a more nuanced analysis, given the contours of the data, we focus briefly on the argument under which we expect to see an increasing impact of education and a declining impact of social origins, on access to certain classes (in particular, the professional or salariat class as it is here where arguments of the role of qualifications or 'merit' are often made). To do this we move on to our final question.

Question Three: Do we find any support for the 'meritocracy' argument? That is, is the influence of social origin characteristics, including caste and class, on occupational attainment declining over time, while the influence of education increases?

We expand on this work to study whether the caste and origin effect can be explained by educational differences. Additionally, we also test for the possible interaction effects and the variations by locality. Hence, we are interested in seeing whether controlling for caste and class, education has an effect on gaining access to the professional class. As professional class access is a dichotomous variable (that is, one can either have or not have a professional occupation which includes the high and low professions and the RNM Clerical classes), we fit a series of logistic regression models, by birth cohort (Table 6.6 for men and Table 6.7 for women). This allows us to observe changes over time, if any.

Some of the highlights of the table are:

First: unsurprisingly, belonging to rural localities has a negative and significant effect on gaining access to professional class destination. Over time we find this to hold in the oldest and youngest cohort for men; and in the youngest cohort for women.

Second: class origin (especially coming from a professional class family) has a positive and significant effect over all birth cohorts for men, and for the three youngest cohorts for women. Belonging to all other classes has a negative effect (though the significance levels vary). The strongest negative effects are for those from lower agriculture (men and women) and manual class origins (men). Coming from farm origin has a negative impact for the youngest men and women. This seems to indicate that over time, the disadvantage of belonging to farm origin have increased, the disadvantage of low agriculture remains similar, and the advantage of professional class origin is consistent.

Third: the caste effect observed earlier interestingly seems to disappear over time, especially for the general caste Hindus once education is controlled for (except for the youngest women). We find no effect (either positive or negative) for OBCs. For STs we find a positive effect for the two cohorts to enter professional occupations for men. There is no additional negative caste effect of belonging to the SC category over time; rather, for men—the oldest cohort, even when controlling for education, has a positive effect on professional class occupation (however, for women one cohort shows a negative effect). Indicating that SC men born in the 1950s were able to take advantage of the opportunities available (such as reservations perhaps) and were able to enter into the professions (we are unable to split the professions into high and low here). However, younger cohorts of the SCs do not have any additional class advantage or indeed disadvantage in the case of men.

Table 6.6 Logistic Regression Models for Access to Professional Occupations Over Birth Cohort; Men Only, NES 2014

	Cohort 1 Born 1950–9		Cohort 2 Born 1960–9		Cohort 3 Born 1970–9		Cohort 4 Born 1980–9	
	B	SE	B	SE	B	SE	B	SE
Constant	−2.492*	.220	−1.930*	.143	−2.252*	.131	−1.872	.110
Rural	−0.490*	.183	−0.218	.125	−0.092	.113	−0.250*	.088
Class of Father								
Professional	1.029*	.329	1.950*	.226	1.626*	.173	1.672*	.152
Business	−0.394	.385	−0.333	.264	−0.025	.212	−0.310	.174
Farm	0.330	.273	−0.239	.190	−0.325	.178	−0.364*	.136
Manual	−0.516	.428	−0.586*	.265	−0.860*	.277	−0.332*	.155
Lower Agric.	−0.449	.361	−0.791*	.222	−0.415*	.189	−0.666*	.149
Caste								
High caste Hindu	0.537	.323	0.156	.224	−0.006	.203	−0.128	.172
Peasant Proprietor	−0.597	.579	−0.160	.359	−0.418	.361	0.141	.279
OBC High	0.413	.324	0.240	.222	0.075	.188	−0.087	.149
OBC Low	−0.825	.568	−0.170	.359	−0.108	.271	0.034	.208
SC	0.807*	.366	0.245	.285	0.026	.225	0.090	.174
ST	−0.470	.709	0.698*	.341	0.252	.293	0.445*	.216
Muslim	0.217	.515	−0.428	.336	−0.073	.280	−0.201	.210
Other religions	−0.082	.605	−0.581	.405	0.251	.313	−0.294	.292

Education								
Graduate and above	1.245*	.329	2.138*	.226	1.696*	.183	1.808*	.141
Intermediate/Non degree	0.524	.379	0.883*	.225	0.420*	.199	0.566*	.157
Matriculation	0.408	.292	0.071	.210	0.245	.186	−0.053	.175
Middle School	−0.580	.458	−0.837*	.298	−0.519*	.249	−0.485*	.201
Up to Primary	−0.479	.336	−0.850*	.271	−0.725*	.263	−0.997*	.256
Non Literate	−1.119*	.423	−1.405*	.369	−1.116*	.364	−0.839*	.322
Goodness of Fit								
Nagelkerke R2	0.272		0.434		0.326		0.372	
Model Chi-Square/d.f. (sig.)	93.654/17 d.f. (0.000)		332.105/17 d.f. (0.000)		302.664/17 d.f. (0.000)		519.352/17 d.f. (0.000)	
Hosmer and Lemeshow [Chi-square/d.f. (sig.)]	7.181/8 d.f. (0.517)		7.832/8 d.f. (0.450)		9.410/8 d.f. (0.309)		14.370/8 d.f. (0.073)	
Total/N	754		1240		1653		2105	

Source: NES 2014, CSDS Data Unit.

Note: Significant parameters (*) are more than twice their standard error (SE). Main effect model only.

Table 6.7 Logistic Regression Models for Access to Professional Occupations Over Birth Cohort; Women Only, NES 2014

	Cohort 1 Born 1950–9		Cohort 2 Born 1960–9		Cohort 3 Born 1970–9		Cohort 4 Born 1980–9	
	B	SE	B	SE	B	SE	B	SE
Constant	-0.715	SE	-1.808*	.374	-1.349*	.234	-1.009*	.192
Rural	-0.253	.618	0.492	.291	-0.217	.243	-0.447*	.176
Class of Father								
Professional	1.454	.929	2.688*	.529	2.965*	.400	2.882*	.369
Business	2.952	1.164	-0.718	.713	-0.514	.495	-0.116	.317
Farm	-1.174	1.369	-0.310	.398	-0.889*	.356	-0.679*	.292
Manual	-0.768	1.255	-0.399	.479	-0.750	.405	-0.934*	.311
Lower Agric.	-2.464	1.293	-1.261*	.424	-0.812*	.327	-1.153*	.273
Caste								
High caste Hindu	2.481	SE	0.454	.523	0.505	.461	1.013*	.390
Peasant Proprietor	4.684	SE	0.570	.777	-0.800	.666	-0.964	.603
OBC High	5.751	SE	0.431	.475	-0.695	.388	-0.049	.288
OBC Low	-13.868	SE	0.003	.695	-0.163	.564	0.041	.409
SC	7.159	SE	-1.473*	.711	0.006	.417	-0.450	.358
ST	4.135	SE	1.133*	.542	0.319	.410	-0.088	.365
Muslim	-17.865	SE	-1.809	1.336	0.057	.740	-0.902	.515
Other religions	7.523	SE	0.690	.659	0.773	.554	1.398*	.576

Education

Graduate and above	30.639	SE	2.310*	.544	2.977*	.452	1.964*	.302
Intermediate/Non degree	-4.121	SE	0.053	.879	0.910*	.376	0.522	.312
Matriculation	-2.567	SE	0.988	.538	0.020	.438	-0.097	.322
Middle School	-6.294	SE	-0.388	.485	-1.358*	.509	-0.206	.369
Up to Primary	-7.864	SE	-1.608*	.504	-1.062*	.393	-0.798*	.343
Non Literate	-9.793	SE	-1.355*	.448	-1.487*	.367	-1.385*	.416

Goodness of Fit

Nagelkerke R2	0.846		0.550		0.589		0.616	
Model Chi-Square/d.f. (sig.)	139.217/17 d.f. (0.000)		145.092/17 d.f. (0.000)		247.012/17 d.f. (0.000)		345.537/17 d.f. (0.000)	
Hosmer and Lemeshow [Chi-square/d.f. (sig.)]	6.622/8 d.f. (0.578)		3.740/7 d.f. (0.809)		3.492/8 d.f. (0.900)		9.471/8 d. (0.304)	
Total/N	251		420		666		703	

Source: NES 2014, CSDS Data Unit.

Note: Significant parameters (*) are more than twice their standard error (SE); SE in model implies a very large standard error. Main effect model only.

Finally, the effect of education seems to be consistent over time. Even controlling for background or family characteristics, having higher levels of education has a positive effect on reaching professional occupations, while middle school and lower education has strong negative effects. It appears that for younger cohorts holding an intermediate certificate is a minimum requirement for gaining access to professional occupations underlying the increased competition over time.

★ ★ ★

The role of education in an individual's life goes beyond the socialization that education provides. Rather, education is often essential in getting jobs and keeping them. However, education is often not the only factor that influences access to jobs—social capital including networks and family background are also key (Béteille 1991 and 1993; Fuller and Narasimhan 2008). Given this role of education, in this chapter, an attempt has been made to describe education's influence on social mobility and on gaining access to particular occupations.

First, we find, for women especially, that urban areas provide some avenue for education and also for professional class access. However, we also know that women's access to the urban is itself constrained and men may transition to urban areas earlier. Hence, accessing education is critical for women's mobility chances and this underscores the need for a gender analysis of opportunities and experiences women have both within families and in the labour market. We also find that higher levels of education, especially college education, are associated with higher rates of mobility (in absolute terms), especially upward mobility.

Second, the results of the relative mobility analysis support these findings as we see that higher levels of education are associated with higher social fluidity or increased mobility opportunities for women and men (this seems to be sharper for women).

Finally, access to professional jobs where qualifications play a key role is clearly influenced by the level of education. Higher education attainment helps in gaining access to these occupations

(though the results also suggest that one requires at least intermediate education for the advantage of education to translate into the
labour market and this is changing over time). So far, the findings
confirm our suspicions regarding the role of education which has
previously not formally been investigated.

However, the subsequent results with regard to the role of 'family background'—loosely construed to include caste and class of
origin throw up more nuanced results (this takes our analysis from
Chapter 5 further). For instance, the role of class of origin is clearly
significant for an individual's opportunities for gaining access to
professional class destinations. This importance of father's class
remains even when we control for the role of education, thus,
constraining those who do not have this social or cultural capital. However, the findings on caste indicate that while caste is
significant for gaining access to professional destinations, as soon
as education is controlled for, the effect of caste weakens, and in
some cases, disappears. An interesting observation regarding SC
men born in the 1950s, who would have entered the labour market
in the 1970s and 1980s, is that they seem to have had an advantage in entering the professional class even when controlling for
education effects. This advantage disappears over birth cohorts.
This presents an interesting line of enquiry for the future. Another
instance of this role of caste and education can be seen when the
positive advantage of belonging to a general caste category disappears once we also factor education in. These results indicate
that caste effects might work through education—in other words,
rather than the direct influence of caste on occupation—the influence of caste or the disadvantage suffered by certain castes seems
to be at the level of educational attainment itself (Breen and Vaid
2008). In other words, levels of education are themselves influenced by family background—caste and class origins, and hence,
the role of the family in terms of social reproduction should not be
downplayed (Béteille 1991, 1993). Once we control for caste level
differences in education, we find that caste effects on occupational
attainment are weaker. Interestingly, the role of class of origin
remains statistically significant even when education is controlled
for further supporting the conclusion in Chapter 5 that so far the
role of class has been underplayed in the literature.

7

Conclusions

Uneven Odds

Patterns of class mobility and fluidity are an indication of the level of openness and inequality in a society. It has long been believed that the more mobile and fluid a society is, the more equal it is in terms of opportunity 'to gain access to scarce resources' (Vaid and Heath 2010: 130). In this book, we have analysed patterns of intergenerational class mobility of women and men in India. As a developing country with a large agricultural sector and a concurrent rapidly expanding services sector, India provides an unusual case study for mobility. Moreover, ethnographic literature has highlighted the resilient nature of the caste system and its association with 'traditional' occupations (however, changes over time have been underlined), and in particular, the lack of mobility for certain caste groups.

Given this background, it was crucial to explore whether there is any indication of increasing mobility over time in India. Moreover, in the context of the industrialization process, which began soon after Independence and the rapid growth in the economy in the post-liberalization period of the early 1990s, is contemporary Indian society a more 'modern' society with signs of a weaker association between origins and destinations? Furthermore, what impact have these changes had on the mobility opportunities of women?

To confirm whether the forces of what has been termed 'modern-ization' (as discussed in Chapter 1) are indeed apparent in contem-porary India, we analysed three related substantive aspects of class mobility: firstly, the patterns of mobility through own employ-ment; secondly, the association between class and caste, especially whether caste disadvantage translates into class mobility disadvan-tage; and finally, the role played by education which is considered to be a driver of mobility opportunities. In the Appendix B to this book we also briefly look at marriage as a possible avenue of mobility.

In this chapter we bring together the major results of this research. The chapter is divided into three main sections: the first provides a summary of the significant findings; the second discusses possible limitations of this research project with the directions for future research; and the final section provides a dis-cussion of the results in light of the 'modernization theory'.

Major Findings

These three major aspects of class mobility were introduced in Chapter 1, and analysed in the empirical chapters (Chapters 4 through 6). This section summarizes the results of the analysis keeping in mind the research questions laid out in the introduc-tory chapter. Before we discuss the first research aspect concerning patterns of class mobility and fluidity, we briefly review the social and economic context of the analysis.

Through figures from the NSS and the Census in terms of eco-nomic participation and structural change, we observe that rather little change has taken place in India in the last four decades, though the last decade has seen more occupational change than previous decades. We see little dramatic decline of the workforce participa-tion in agriculture, neither do we see a rapid increase in the non-manual occupations as expected to be found in an industrializing economy. We do see some evidence of the marginalization of the female workforce with more women engaged in the lower-level seasonal agricultural occupations. But, as the Census and NSS data do not adequately cover the informal sector of the economy, we do not have conclusive evidence of this. However, it is clear that there has been a decline in overall labour force participation of women. In terms of caste, we still observe more SC and ST women in employment as compared to the higher castes. This supports results from ethnographic research that women from these castes need to work for economic reasons, whereas high caste women can be withdrawn from work once economic needs have been met to ensure their family's social standing (see Chapter 2 for a discussion). We turn now to a discussion of the major results of the three research areas.

In terms of class mobility patterns analysed in Chapter 4 we draw the following conclusions:

1. The impact of slow structural change has meant that we observe a distinctive pattern of intergenerational class stability in India, and this is more pronounced for women than it is for men. This pattern of stability is influenced by the shape of the Indian occupational structure, where women are engaged in the lower agrarian and manual occupations as men tend to leave these to take on jobs in the expanding sectors. In terms of mobility as well, women do not appear to have benefited from economic development to the same extent as men, as the surplus of upward mobility over downward mobility is smaller for them. However, a distinct rural–urban divide is seen. Rural India is even more intergenerationally stable, while urban areas have higher absolute mobility which is even more marked for women. This leads us to conclude that opportunities in urban areas provide women a greater chance to leave class origins behind. In terms of class profiles we see more women in low professional occupations in urban areas thus indicating possible opportunities of change. But, this is not solely in terms of upward mobility chances; rather, they are liable to be more downwardly mobile as well.

2. We find a slight increase in absolute mobility across birth cohorts brought about by structural changes in occupations with more upward over downward mobility over cohorts. Social fluidity has increased significantly for men especially for those born in the 1960s compared to those born in the 1950s (though this is not so clear for women). Overall, we do seem to observe a slight weakening of the association

between class origins and class destinations in the younger birth cohorts for men though these results are not conclusive for women. Urban India displays distinct patterns with not only more mobility over time than in rural India, but also more upward mobility for the youngest women in the urban labour market.

3. In addition to high levels of class stability we also observe very high levels of 'stickiness' between most class contrasts. That is, we observe very little movement between manual and non-manual classes, as well as little movement out of agriculture, especially lower agriculture. As the amount of fluidity observed in the country is very low, we can conclude that the equality of opportunity or level of 'openness' in the country is also quite low. But, surprisingly, we do not find any gender differences in the relative rates of fluidity as well as in the strength of association between class origins and class destinations. That is, the pattern and amount of fluidity seems to be similar for women and men, and no additional gender inequality in terms of opportunity is being observed.

4. As discussed above, locality-wise differences in mobility patterns come to light. With regard to fluidity, the urban areas are fairly distinct as expected under the era of liberalization and economic development. This is particularly the case for women who are experiencing more mobility in urban India.

The second research aspect concerned the association between caste and class and, in particular, the impact of caste on class mobility. In Chapter 5, we explored the relation between community, defined to include Hindu castes and minority religions, and class in India. We also analysed the differences in patterns of mobility of these different communities. It is found that:

1. The relation between caste and class is not entirely straightforward, though there does appear to be some congruence between the two. We observed an over-representation of the higher castes in what might be considered to be the higher classes and of the lower castes in the lower classes. More importantly, we found that higher castes are associated more

generally with white collar or 'clean' work and lower castes, especially the SCs, predominate in the manual work and low agricultural classes. With regard to Muslims, we see a concentration in self-employment and an absence from professional positions, which has an important impact on the limited mobility we find for this group.

2. The congruence of class origins and community seems weaker across birth cohorts, thus leading us to conclude that some change has indeed occurred. However, we still find an over-representation of higher castes in higher classes and lower castes in lower classes—thus, some amount of 'continuity' still persists. We also find a weakening of the association between community and class destination (with some fluctuations). That is, for the respondents in the study, over a period of time the association of caste with the class that they are in is weakening.

3. The effect of class origins is seen to be much stronger than the effect of community or caste with regard to access to particular class destinations, for example, the professional classes. This pattern seems to hold across birth cohorts. That is, father's class seems to have a continuing salience where access to class destinations are concerned. Moreover, the salience of being from the higher castes is observed to be weaker than that of coming from professional class origins. This too seems to be relatively constant over time, though the effect might be declining. Hence, we conclude that class origins rather than caste have long since been a major factor influencing class reproduction in India and apart from high caste, not much sets apart the other castes from each other.

4. We find some indication that SCs find it harder to take advantage of upward mobility chances but conversely we cannot conclusively say that high castes are prevented from downward mobility (supporting the 2004 data findings reported by Vaid [2012]).

We thus conclude that while caste effects (as measured through our categorization) have not disappeared, families are using 'class' along with caste to protect their children from downward mobility—while they are not always successful in this, it is clear that higher castes experience some persisting advantages.

The third research area looked at processes or drivers of mobility, focusing on the 'merit' argument under which it is expected that those who have attained a certain level of education would have a decided advantage in the labour market and, in turn, in terms of opportunities of mobility open to them. Whether this is seen in India, and further, whether all communities across gender and locality benefit due to higher education was examined in Chapter 6. We find:

1. Higher levels of education are clearly related to higher levels of absolute social mobility as well as greater relative mobility or social fluidity. This is more distinct for women from urban India. The opportunities for education and, in turn, for occupational mobility are much greater for urban women. However, as access to the urban areas is itself constrained for women (through distinct migration patterns and lower rates of migration), these opportunities are being used by fewer women than men.

2. Access to the professional class destination, which we observed in Chapter 5, and which is expected to be the class where most opportunities would be available (and where origins—caste and class—would have the least impact) is clearly influenced by educational attainment. This is seen to hold over time. However, most significantly, the impact of origins has not disappeared, especially not for those from rural areas. While father's class remains an important influence on professional class attainment, the influence of caste is seen to be weaker over time. For instance, any positive advantage of being from higher castes seems to have disappeared over time. We, thus, find that while caste effects are weaker they have not disappeared entirely—and that caste may be working indirectly influencing social mobility by in effect influencing access to education itself.

The fourth and final research aspect, discussed briefly in Appendix B of this book, concerned the patterns of marital mobility of women. While we only look at this area briefly, using NES 2009 data, this study of mobility in 'marriage markets' helps provide a more comprehensive account of class mobility in India, especially as employment of women is low and women face various socio-economic constraints in entering and staying in employment. We conclude that:

1. There is more intergenerational stability for women through marriage than for married men through their own employment. Thus marriage is not really an avenue for mobility as much as it is a mechanism to ensure that class positions are maintained.
2. We observe that there are similar relative mobility rates for women through marriage as for men through their own employment. Parents in India thus seem to be using different mechanisms to preserve their class privileges for both their sons and daughters.
3. With respect to caste we observe that in absolute mobility terms lower caste women are not as upwardly mobile as was expected in light of the hypergamy argument. But we do find that high caste parents are able to use marriages to *maintain* their daughter's class position to a greater extent than they are for their sons.

This summary of our main findings highlights the unique pattern of social stability in India and the slow rate of change. Large inequalities are manifested through low levels of fluidity for both women and men. Moreover, through our analysis we are able to conclude that class origins have, for long, been the more significant influence on class destinations for both sons and daughters; for sons through employment and for daughters through employment and marriage. Significantly, the impact of caste on class destinations is weaker than that of class origins on class destinations in terms of *both* own class mobility and mobility through marriage. We are able to conclude as Kumar, Heath, and Heath (2002a) did that 'even among people from the same caste or community, class origins still make a very substantial difference to their class destinations'. Most significantly, for the first time we are able to see how education is related to social mobility. And, while it provides opportunities to mobility, if access to education remains constrained by caste (see Breen and Vaid 2008), gender, or locality, we will not see a substantial equalization of opportunities in the country. The implications of this with regard to modernization theory are discussed in the concluding discussion of this chapter.

Alternative Possibilities

There are two aspects of this research that need to be addressed, especially with regard to their possible impact on our results. Firstly, we discuss the impact of using a birth cohort approach to analyse mobility trends, especially with respect to comparing the changing influence of caste and class origins on class destinations. And, secondly, we discuss the possible impact of using broad caste categories and macro-classes to analyse in particular the evolving relation between jati and traditional occupations.

1. Birth Cohort results

In Chapter 4 we have discussed in some detail the drawbacks of following a birth cohort approach to analyse trends in class mobility over a period of time, in particular due to drawbacks of differential mortality and recall bias (see Vaid and Heath 2010). As mentioned, due to the lack of repeated cross-sectional surveys and our reliance on a one time point dataset, our birth cohort results might not be entirely conclusive. This is especially important as we make some conclusions about modernization and its influence using this birth cohort approach. In order to substantiate our results we have relied on as many of the older NES surveys as had the requisite data and variables needed. Further, we are able to do some tentative work with the 1971 NES dataset in this section. Due to small sample sizes, especially in the sampling of women, we use the male sample from this survey. We focus in particular on one analysis: the differing impact of class origins and caste on class destinations.

Using the birth cohort approach, in Chapter 5, we found that the influence of coming from professional class origins on gaining access to professional class destinations has remained fairly stable, as has the effect of coming from the higher castes. But we also found that the influence of class origins appears stronger than that of caste. If, using the 1971 data, we find a similar pattern to the 2014 NES birth cohort results, we may be able to conclude more decisively that class origins along with caste have been important for a long time in India.

In order to test this, we use the 1971 data and conduct an analysis similar to that discussed in Chapter 5. We study the logistic regression (with deviation contrasts) for access to professional class destinations with caste and class origins as the independent variables. The results of this analysis are presented in Table 7.1. In the 1971 data we are unable to separate the peasant high castes from the non-peasant high castes, nor the high OBCs from the low

Table 7.1 Logistic Regression for Access to Professional Class—Men, NES 1971

	Parameter Estimates (Standard Error)
Father's Class	
Professional	1.9 (0.2)*
Business	0.3 (0.2)
Farmer	−0.5 (0.2)*
Manual	−0.8 (0.2)*
Low Agric.	−0.9 (0.1)*
Caste	
High Caste	0.7 (0.2)*
OBC	−0.3 (0.2)
SC	−0.5 (0.3)
ST	−1.3 (0.5)*
Muslims	0.3 (0.2)
Other Minority	0.6 (0.3)*
Constant	−1.9 (0.1)*
N	1809
Chi Sq.	281.32 (10 d.f.)

Source: NES 1971, CSDS Data Unit.

Note: Standard Errors in parenthesis. (*) parameter estimates are more than twice their standard error, and hence, statistically significant at the 5 per cent level.

OBCs as we did in the 2014 data analysis, but we are nonetheless able to look at the six major community groups.

The parameter estimates of the logistic regression depicted in Table 7.1 are remarkably similar to those seen in Table 5.3. In particular, the parameter estimate for professional class origins is very similar to the estimates observed in Table 5.3, where these estimates had remained fairly constant across birth cohorts. Furthermore, the parameter estimate for coming from low agricultural origins is also similar to that seen in Table 5.3.

In terms of caste, the parameter estimate for high caste is similar to that observed in the first two birth cohorts in Table 5.3. The main difference in terms of community seems to be the STs, who, in the 1971 data, are showing a very high negative parameter estimate for access to professional classes whereas this was not the case in any of the birth cohorts in the 2014 data. Also, the other minorities seem to have a positive impact on gaining access to professional destination in the 1971 data which is not seen in the 2014 data.

Through this analysis we can be rather more sure that the strong influence of class origins on class destinations that we observed in our previous birth cohort analysis is indeed a long-standing pattern. Thus, our understanding of the nature of Indian society may have been slightly incomplete as class origins have been of importance over a long time period, especially with regard to their influence on class destinations. This also provides support for Kumar, Heath, and Heath's research (2002a). Moreover, the importance of caste has been significant but slightly weaker than that of class, especially with regard to access to professional classes (which may be due to an interaction between the two and as we have seen that both caste and class may effect education attainment which in turn effects class attainment; see Breen and Vaid 2008). This conclusion also has support from ethnographic research, as caste networks may not be useful for members of the caste group in gaining access to professional classes where education and skills are of significant importance and which may be more closely related to social class. In contrast, in certain jobs like businesses or trade caste-networks may generally play a more important role than education or class (Harriss-White 2003).

2. Association between jati and occupations.

A possible limitation of our study concerns the use of broad categories of caste/community and class. One possible reason for why
the picture of the congruence between caste and class, as analysed
in Chapter 5, is neither entirely straightforward nor conclusive,
may be because the relationship that has been observed in the ethnographic literature is of jati with specific *occupations*, that is, at
a more disaggregated level rather than at the macro caste and class
level. And, it is possible that this association seems to disappear
as soon as occupations are coded into classes and jatis into big
castes.[1]

If we had detailed localized jati evidence, would we find a different pattern of association between jati and occupation? For example, ethnographic research tells us that custodial staff, referred to
as 'sweepers' in the NES surveys, are believed to come primarily
from the ex-'untouchable' or lowest SCs; and priests are traditionally Brahmins. It is not possible to study this congruence based
on an approach that uses macro classes and large caste groups. It
might, however, in a future project, be possible to conduct a more
detailed occupation-by-jati study to see if this caste and occupational clustering does indeed take place or whether it is apparent
only at the extremes of the caste system. It might be that anthropologists have tended to focus on extremes and may have lost
sight of the huge spread of people from different jatis in a range of
occupations in the middle.

Taking our example of 'priests' and 'sweepers', in light of ethnographic research, we would expect to find that all priests would
be Brahmins but all Brahmins need not be priests. We would thus
expect to find a spread of Brahmins in different occupations but
more significantly, no Brahmin would be a sweeper due to reasons
of ritual pollution. Conversely, all sweepers would be 'Bhangis'/
Balmikis (a caste term referring to 'traditional custodial communities' and included as is in the NES dataset), but not all 'Bhangis'
would be sweepers. Again, we might expect a wide spread of these
communities in varied occupations, but we would not expect to find

---

[1] See Gist (1954: 129) for another study that uses class rather than
occupations to study caste differentials in India.

any 'Bhangi' priest due to caste and ritual constraints. On similar lines, we may be able to analyse various traditional jati-occupation categories to see whether we do indeed observe a continued clustering on caste lines and whether this clustering takes on any specific pattern.

A preliminary result from a study using the NES 2004 observing only the two occupations and jatis mentioned here shows that in terms of the extremes of the caste system we do observe this clustering. For instance, regarding *sweepers* as an occupational group: of the fifty sweepers (not in government employment) in the sample, thirty-five are from the SC community with twenty-one of these from the 'Bhangi' community. More significantly, we see no members of this caste engaged as priests. The converse in terms of the Brahmins too holds true. However, a relatively large proportion (well over 90 per cent) of the 'Bhangi' community is in occupations other than its 'traditional' one. This example highlights the continued clustering at the extremes but with a wider variation in the middle. More importantly, this indicates that a more individual approach might be better suited for an in-depth study of the caste and class association.

We now discuss a potential area of research for the future.

A Way Forward

One of the ramifications of the dearth of mobility research on India is that there are a multitude of possibilities for future research. One possible avenue for future research concerns placing India in a comparative perspective and we discuss some preliminary comparative results next. At the end of this section we discuss some of the other possible avenues for future research.

Our research has shown that India is quite an immobile society with low levels of fluidity; to what extent then do the Indian patterns differ from those in other countries? We focus, albeit briefly, on the comparative perspective because as Deshpande (1999: 33) states 'a comparative approach has been conspicuous by its absence' in Indian sociology. He encourages a comparison of Indian society initially with neighbouring and other developing countries to have a better insight into Indian society. However, due to no previous mobility study in the South Asian region, in this chapter we compare the pattern of structural change and mobility in India to that of some selected industrialized countries of the West.[2] These countries have been selected primarily because there is extensive research on class mobility on them. Moreover, at some point in the past, these countries, for example France, Poland, and Ireland, had large agrarian sectors which declined quite rapidly. This is a brief overview and provides more of an indicator rather than a comprehensive cross-national account. Also due to the periods on which studies on these countries is available, we compare the result with the NES 2004 data.[3] When adequate data is available, it would be of importance to compare Indian patterns to those in less developed and developing countries.

Here, we conduct an analysis similar to that carried out in Chapter 4. We begin by observing the index of dissimilarity for these countries, then analyse some summary indices of mobility, and end with presenting selected symmetrical odds ratios.

In Table 7.2 both the origin-destination and the men-women dissimilarity indices are compared across countries. Observing the first two columns of the table, the origin to destination dissimilarity index is lower for women and men in India than in the other countries that have been studied. Also, as seen from the last two columns of the table, the men-women dissimilarity index for origin distributions is the highest for India, which underlines the specific nature of the Indian context and women's participation in the labour market. But, unlike the other countries, the dissimilarity index for destination distributions is substantially lower in India, showing a lower level of sex-segregation at least at the

---

[2] For more comprehensive accounts using a cross-national framework predominantly for Western industrialized countries see Breen 2004; Erikson and Goldthorpe 1992; Grusky and Hauser 1984; and Lipset and Bendix 1959 among others. We do not focus on the differences in relative rates of mobility for women and men at this stage, but leave it instead for a future study.

[3] For this comparison we use published research by various authors and compare those to the results that we discussed in Chapter 4 of this book.

Table 7.2 Cross-country Comparison of the Index of Dissimilarity

		Origin–Destination		Men–Women	
		Men	**Women**	**Origin**	**Destination**
India	2004	14	6	11	15
Britain	1973	10	45	1	45
	1992	14	39	2	34
France	1970	24	35	3	39
	1993	19	51	3	44
Poland	1972	31	27	5	29
	1994	22	40	3	34
Ireland	1994	20	–	–	–
		23	–	–	–

Source: Figures for India are from NES 2004, also see Table 4.2; figures for Britain are from Goldthorpe and Mills (2004: 196 Table 8.1); figures for France are from Vallet (2004: 122 Table 5.1); figures for Poland are from Mach (2004: 275 Table 11.1 and 11.2); and figures for Ireland are from Layte and Whelan (2004: 180 Table 7.2).

level of these broad classes. This distinctiveness of the Indian pattern is reflected in the results of the mobility analysis discussed in Chapter 4.

With regard to mobility rates, Table 7.3 attempts a cross-national comparison. It needs to be kept in mind that the percentages that one gets for upward, downward, or horizontal mobility are influenced by how one creates and orders the classes. For example, as seen in Table 7.3, for India the use of five levels rather than three levels to study mobility can give different results with the same dataset. In addition, the total amount of mobility or stability observed depends on how the classes were originally constructed. As Heath (1981: 56) states, 'we cannot possibly take a single figure as "the" rate of social mobility in a specific country. It would not be far-fetched to suggest that we can get almost any answer we want simply by fiddling with the categories'. Keeping this in mind there are two main results of this analysis. Firstly, there is more stability in India than for any of the other countries shown; and for women we observe more stability than for men. This finding is quite the opposite of the other countries shown in the lower

Table 7.3 Summary Indices of Mobility—Cross-country Comparison

	Total Mobility		Upward Mobility		Downward Mobility		Horizontal Mobility		U/D	
	M	W	M	W	M	W	M	W	M	W
India										
1996	33	–	19	–	7	–	7	–	2.7	–
2004	36	30	20	15	11	11	5	4	1.8	1.4
2004 (3 levels)[4]	36	29	13	12	8	6	15	11	1.6	2.0
Britain										
H & P	65	83	42	36	13	27	10	20	3.2	1.3
E & G	65	–	32	–	17	–	15	–	1.9	–
France										
1970	65	65	31	24	11	17	24	24	2.8	1.4
1993	67	74	36	32	14	20	17	21	2.6	1.6
Poland										
1972	59	53	35	30	8	8	16	15	4.4	3.8
1994	67	77	38	45	14	12	16	20	2.7	3.8
Ireland										
1973	59	–	22	–	20	–	17	–	1.1	-
1994	67	–	30	–	16	–	21	–	1.9	-

Note: The figures for 1996, for India, are from Kumar, Heath, and Heath (2002a); for 2004 the figures are from the NES; see also Table 4.7; for discussion of the three class version, see footnote 5 of this chapter; For Britain 'H & P' is Heath and Payne's paper (2000: Tables 7.6 and 7.9 for the youngest cohort born 1950–9); 'E & G' is Erikson and Goldthorpe (1992: 195; Table 6.3); figures for France are from Vallet (2004: 127; Table 5.3); figures for Poland are from Mach (2004: 276; Tables 11.3 and 11.4); and figures for Ireland are from Layte and Whelan (2004: 182; Table 7.4). Kumar, Heath, and Heath differentiate seven classes to study mobility; Heath and Payne use six classes, but collapse them into three to calculate upward or downward mobility; Erikson and Goldthorpe; Vallet; Mach; and Layte and Whelan use the seven class CASMIN schema, and group their classes into three levels to study upward or downward mobility.

[4] If out of the given classes only three levels to study upward and downward mobility are differentiated by collapsing certain classes to be at the same level (that is, rather than the five levels that we discussed in Chapter 4) one would observe more horizontal and less upward or downward mobility. This procedure of collapsing classes is followed by the CASMIN (Comparative Analysis of Social Mobility in Industrial Nations)

rows (except for Poland in 1972). We also present the results of grouping certain classes to form a three-class level similar to the Western CASMIN schema (rather than the five levels we used to study upward or downward mobility, as shown in Chapter 4, see also footnote 5 of this chapter). This makes an international comparison possible. These figures are shown in the last row for India.

Secondly, the *direction* of mobility of women is the same as that of men, that is, there is more upward over downward mobility (the last column in Table 7.3 shows this upward/downward ratio). This reflects the changes in the occupation structure. But the surplus in India is not as high as seen in some of the western countries as the professional and non-manual classes have not expanded and the agricultural classes have not contracted fast enough, thus indicating that structural change has been slower (see Chapter 4, Table 4.2). The overall figures for India are closer to those of Poland and Ireland, but still quite a far way off. As the comparison is made with these countries due to their historically large agricultural classes, analysing the selected countries enables us to observe the level of mobility (stability) at different stages of industrialization and modernization. For example, both Ireland and Poland showed more stability in the 1970s but there has been increasing mobility in these countries over the decades. This helps in putting the Indian case in context.

We now compare the amount of relative mobility or inequality of opportunity as measured by the 'stickiness' of certain classes

---

researchers and by Breen (2004) in their analyses where Goldthorpe classes I and II are for them considered to be at the same level, followed by classes III, IVa, b, c; V, and VI which are at one level, which leaves class VIIa and b at the lowest level (Breen 2004: 18). We do not follow this method of collapsing classes as reducing the class structure in the case of India into three levels, would be a rather gross simplification. But when we did collapse our categories into three classes similar to the CASMIN way, our results showed more horizontal movement and less upward and downward movement; though still more upward over downward movement that is, 13 per cent of men were upwardly mobile and 8 per cent were downwardly mobile, for women these figures were 12 per cent and 6 per cent, respectively. These figures are shown in Table 7.3 under the *three level* version of the 2004 dataset.

and present the results of one such comparison. As it is quite difficult to calculate equivalent symmetrical odds ratios for many countries since full mobility tables are not always included, in Table 7.4 we display an example of one such classic ratio that can be easily compared across countries.[5] The figures in Table 7.4 were calculated by studying mobility tables from different sources and making them as comparable as possible.

In Table 7.4 we see that the *Professional: Semi and Un-skilled Manual Work* odds ratio is much higher for both women and men in India than for any of the other countries, even when making a comparison with the odds ratios in these countries in the 1970s. For example, the odds of someone from semi-unskilled manual work origins making it to professional class destinations and

Table 7.4 Comparison of Symmetrical Odds Ratios for Professional Work: Semi-Unskilled Work

I + II: VIIa	Men (odds ratio)	ln (log odds)	Women (odds ratio)	Ln (log odds)
India (2004)	359:1	5.9	423:1	6.0
England (1997)	18:1	2.9	16:1	2.8
France (1970)	37:1	3.6	40:1	3.7
(1993)	23:1	3.0	29:1	3.4
Poland (1972)	8:1	2.1	11:1	2.4
(1988)	7:1	1.9	7:1	1.9
(1994)	8:1	2.1	8:1	2.1
Ireland (1974)	36:1	3.6	–	–

Note: Figures for India are from Vaid (2007) using NES 2004; for England the figures are from Heath and Payne (2000: Tables 7.4, 7.7); figures for France are calculated from Vallet (2004: 146; Table 5.A2.); figures for Poland are calculated from Mach (2004: 278/9; Tables 11.5 and 11.6); the odds ratio for Ireland is based on Ganzeboom, Luijkx, and Treiman's (1989) article rather than from Layte and Whelan (2004), as their paper does not show the different classes separately and merges classes that make a comparison difficult.

[5] It needs to be borne in mind at this point that our class I is not identical to Goldthorpe or CASMIN class I, but it is quite similar (refer to Table 4.1).

avoiding manual work are 359:1 for Indian men, and only 8:1 for Polish men.

India, thus, not only displays more stability rather than mobility in absolute terms when compared to these countries, it also displays a much more restricted movement of people from one class origin to a given class destination.

One of the drawbacks of comparing India with the industrialized West is that macro classes are not always easily comparable, for example, with regard to the large agricultural sector in India. In this case it would be more fruitful to take this preliminary research forward and compare India with countries at a similar stage of economic development (see Deshpande 1999: 33).

This cross-national comparison is but one possible idea for future research on Indian mobility. As the field of mobility analysis in India is very under-developed there are various other areas of interest that can be explored in future research. For example, one of these is the micro-class analytic approach as propagated by Grusky. Grusky and Weeden (2001, 2002) have argued in favour of using occupations rather than aggregate classes and ask 'whether barriers are more developed at the aggregate or disaggregate level' and whether it may be more useful to use occupation rather than class categories, as class may conceal changes at the occupational level (2002: 232). With regard to mobility analysis and the use of aggregate or disaggregated categories, they state that the use of what they call a 'full model' might lead to the finding that 'occupational reproduction is more pronounced than class reproduction, implying that decades of class analysts have been pursuing what amounts to minor class variation on an occupational theme' (Grusky and Weeden 2002: 232). For a critique of this 'micro-level' analysis see various papers in *Acta Sociologica* (2002: volume 45) in particular the papers by Goldthorpe and by Birkelund; for a reply to these criticisms see Grusky and Weeden (2002).

This book extends and adds to the existing research using a macro-class approach. It would be of interest in the future, if and when adequate data is available, to apply the micro-class approach as propagated by Grusky to see whether it provides greater insight into mobility in India, especially given the alleged importance of the jati/occupation link.

Discussion

> The industrial society is an open community encouraging occupa-
> tional and geographic mobility and social mobility. Industrialisation
> calls for flexibility and competition; it is against tradition and status
> based upon family, class, religion, race, or caste.
>
> (Kerr, Dunlop, Harbison and Myers, 1960: 26)

Under modernization theory, we expect to see three specific
implications for class mobility patterns and trends in India. Firstly,
if the thesis were to hold, we would expect to find high intergenerational mobility in absolute terms as well as high rates of
social fluidity. We would also expect to see an increasing trend in
these patterns and especially a weakening of the link between origins and destinations over time. Secondly, modernization would
also have an important role to play with regard to other ascribed
characteristics such as caste. Forces of modernization and resultant urbanization would break down the traditional association
between caste and occupations, and we would especially expect to
find increasing equality of opportunity for all caste groups. Finally,
achieved characteristics such as education would be expected to
become more salient for social mobility.

The results from our analysis do not conclusively support the
modernization hypothesis in the Indian context as also evidenced
by Vaid and Heath (2010). Since India has a distinct occupational
structure, as seen by the large agricultural sector, we would expect
to find less mobility and fluidity in India as compared to the West.
In this regard, it is particularly the lack of change over birth cohorts
that contradicts modernization. Thus, not only does India show
stability in absolute terms, it is also a society with high inequalities of opportunity in mobility chances. In our cross-national comparison this distinctiveness of the Indian pattern becomes even
more apparent. We do, however, see a pattern similar to the West
with regard to more upward mobility over downward mobility, as
was expected under the modernization thesis.

In terms of temporal change, we see some signs of an increase in
absolute mobility rates over time; however, while some sign of the
weakening of the origin-destination link is apparent, especially for
the younger birth cohorts, the patterns are not conclusive. This

seems to support Goldthorpe's conclusion for his research on Europe that 'contrary to liberal expectations that advancing industrialism should cause the association between individuals' class origins and their eventual class destinations to weaken steadily, this association has proved to be patterned in a remarkably stable way-once the effects of structural shifts are allowed for ...' (1992: 136; see also Breen and Whelan 1994).

With regard to caste, the influence of modernization is again not that evident. Despite industrialization, urbanization, and geographic mobility, the congruence between castes and classes seems to be apparent even now, especially at the extremes of the caste system. However, we do notice through our preliminary micro-level analysis that there is more mobility in the middle with most jatis entering a variety of occupations. With regard to the prediction that with modernization we would expect to find an increase in equality of opportunity for various caste groups, we see that SCs still seem to find it harder to leave their class origins behind and be upwardly mobile though there are no apparent signs that the higher castes are cushioned from downward mobility. Since our focus was primarily on caste, the results on religion require further and more disaggregated analysis. However, we find the mobility patterns of Muslims, especially women, are distinct particularly in urban areas. There is a much higher concentration of Muslims in self-employment, which has important implications where access to mobility opportunities are concerned, especially in the access to professional jobs. The specificity of the Muslim respondent's experience holds both for their experiences in the labour market, and for women in terms of marriage as well.

With regard to education we find, as expected, that education is critical to social mobility, especially upward mobility. However, education is clearly not replacing caste or class origins where social mobility opportunities are concerned. So, while urban women, for example, are clearly benefiting from increased educational opportunities, their social mobility is still to an extent constrained by their caste and class of origin. While we focus on one possible driver of mobility, i.e. education, there are other mechanisms that are also at play. For instance, Vaid and Heath (2010: 134) discuss the role of 'free-market competition' and the growth of the bureaucracy as possible reasons why merit would become more salient for mobility. In turn, the role of education, at least in terms of formal education, would become even more critical for equalizing opportunities and promoting social mobility. Further, formal education itself is not the only way to acquire knowledge that is useful in the labour market. Rather, skill acquisition can, and does, take place on the job. Clearly then, our use of formal education as a marker is simply one way to test whether theories of change have borne out.

More importantly, this study has underlined the need to study women along with men for a more comprehensive account of national patterns. Women clearly have differing experiences in the labour market, and critically women too are not a homogenous category. There are caste, religious, age and locality wise differences which set them apart from each other while also setting them apart from men. Urban women's experiences in terms of educational attainment, the role of education on social mobility and social mobility patterns broadly set them apart from rural women. Critically then, it is clear that studies that exclude women are not able to untangle the complexities of patterns and possible experiences in both the labour and marriage market.

The burgeoning size of the Indian youth has captured the imagination of policy makers, politicians, and writers alike. These young Indians are entering education institutions and the labour market in larger numbers. What expectations would they have where social mobility aspirations are concerned? The demand for public sector employment continues to be strong, despite the retrenchment of this sector and increased contractual work within it. The outcome has been an increase in demand for education since these public-sector jobs require a basic level of formal education or minimum qualifications. However, this increase of young people in education has not so easily translated into positions in the labour market as we have found in terms of patterns of mobility and this has important ramifications concerning future demands for education and access to mobility (Jeffrey 2010; Jeffrey, Jeffery, and Jeffery 2004). Since qualifications alone are not sufficient for job acquisition, other identities, such as caste or class, remain critical.

Discussing the Indian case as one of 'tradition' versus 'modernity' is perhaps counterproductive. What we see is that Indian society deals with both aspects of what have been considered as 'modern' and 'traditional' simultaneously (Vaid and Heath 2010). Perhaps in concurrence with Vaid and Heath we could argue that 'Western models of modernity and modernisation are not necessarily useful concepts for understanding contemporary India' (p. 159). What one needs is a more nuanced look at the experiences specific to a large diverse country undergoing economic change which may be benefitting some, but which is also leaving quite a few behind.

Social mobility is part of our everyday common sense and yet remains poorly understood. The desire for upward social mobility is a part of the everyday lexicon especially since the period of economic liberalization and the apparent increase of the middle class. But, we have seen that the patterning of social mobility is complex. While it may not be surprising that gender or caste matter where mobility opportunities are concerned, what we observe are the myriad ways in which these identities continue to pervade opportunities across locality and temper the expectations. It has significant ramifications for how mobility is really experienced.

Appendix A

Data and Class Validation

This appendix discusses the NES datasets used in the book, and also provides an initial validation of the Kumar and Heath class schema (Kumar, Heath, and Heath 2002a). This scheme is referred to as the Kumar and Heath schema, since the conceptualization of the schema draws on Anthony Heath's own work on mobility following his landmark text 'Social Mobility' (1981). This, in turn, draws on the Hope-Goldthorpe and subsequent Goldthorpe classifications (Heath 1981). We test the subsequent reformulation of the schema (Vaid and Heath 2010) for the present study with comprehensive occupational information.

Data

The data for the book comes primarily from the 2014 (May) round of the NES conducted by the Lokniti Program of the CSDS, Delhi. The book provides an overtime comparison of NES datasets from 2004–14. For the validation exercise, this Appendix uses the 2004 round of the NES data (as that provides a base year for the mobility analysis), as well as the 1996 round as this was the primary data source used by Kumar, Heath, and Heath when they derived their class schema.

The CSDS has been conducting NES surveys since the late 1960s. Earlier rounds of the NES surveys have been used by researchers to study mobility of men (Nijhawan uses the 1967 round, Kumar,

Heath, and Heath use the 1971 and the male sample of the 1996 round, as does McMillan; though he uses a combined male and female sample). Unfortunately, since none of the older rounds of the data collected the necessary information on women nor included an adequate representative sample of women, we only use the (1996 and) 2004 and later rounds, which did collect this information. In the concluding Chapter of this book we also use the male-only sample of the 1971 data to substantiate some results from the 2014 dataset.

The NES data collected by a nationally representative, stratified random sample of over 9,600 respondents in 1996, over 27,000 respondents in 2004, 36,500 in 2009, and nearly 22,300 respondents in 2014, from the electoral rolls[1] contains roughly the same number of men and women in each survey year. The use of 2004 as the base year for analysis is preferred over 1996 to study class mobility, not only because it is more recent but also because it includes a larger sample, and has a more detailed categorization of occupations. The class scheme is then replicated using the 2009 and 2014 datasets.

The 1996 survey covered 108 Lok Sabha (lower house/parliamentary) constituencies with 432 sampling points (this survey excluded the state of Jammu and Kashmir) and had a response rate of 64 per cent. The 2004 survey, covered all 28 states and four (of seven) Union Territories, and was conducted in 420 (of 543) Lok Sabha constituencies with 2,380 sampling points and had a 77 per

---

[1] As the electoral registration rates in India are high, and the onus of registration rests with the state, any selection bias in this dataset should be minimal (though this cannot preclude any mismanagement on the state officials' behalf). For a discussion of the 1996 dataset, how the sample was selected, and the variables included, see Appendix 1 of Mitra and Singh (1999). Kumar, Heath, and Heath (2002a) also briefly discuss the dataset.

For a discussion and history of NES practices, the methodology of the Election Studies, and an in-depth discussion of the 2004 NES dataset see the special issue of the Economic and Political Weekly (EPW, 18 December 2004) which has various articles on the dataset as well as alternative research areas where this data has been utilized. For the 2009 and 2014 datasets see special issues of the EPW from 26 September 2009 and 27 September 2014.

cent response rate. The 2009 survey, covered 536 Lok Sabha constituencies (covering all Indian states) with a response rate of 60.6 per cent. Finally, the 2014 survey covered 26 states with 306 Lok Sabha constituencies and a response rate of 60.2 per cent. While this might seem like a low response rate, it at par with previous NES studies, except the 2004 survey which allowed for substitution of respondents who could not be contacted from the sampling frame with others sharing similar demographics. However, after some discussion, based on the possible implications of this substitution, the NES has since then not allowed for any substitution. See Kailash (2012) for more on the implications of low responses for social and political issues in the NES survey, especially with regard to 'no opinion', 'don't know' and missing data. Details of the 2014 NES dataset with regard to information on marriage, communities and castes, and regions are provided in the relevant chapters of this book. The 2004 survey was the only one in which substitution of respondents was allowed which lead to the higher response rate.

These data are unique as the NES surveys ask all respondents (both women and men) about their occupation as well as their father's (and mother's, and except in 2014, their spouses') occupation. For the study of mobility, the use of the NES data over other national data sources is preferred for many reasons. Firstly, most other large national level datasets (for example the NSS and the NFHS) conduct household surveys in which the head of the household provides the information on the other members in the household. This makes it difficult to study women's *own* class mobility, especially as in these household surveys, due to various cultural reasons, the head of the household is more often considered to be a male member, even if he is not the primary earning member, and hence, women's economic participation can be under-reported. Another disadvantage of using household questionnaires such as the NSS and NFHS is that information is collected only for people currently living in the household which excludes men and women who leave their parental home. If women do not live with their parents, no information is collected on their occupational participation alongside their parents', thus, precluding any study of intergenerational mobility. Secondly, from the point of view of a study of intergenerational mobility the other national surveys do not include enough information on women's *own* occupation along with their father's and spouse's occupation. For example, though the NFHS does collect detailed information on women's work-force participation, including the seasonal and temporary nature of their work, it does not, however, collect requisite information on their parent's occupation, thus making it an inadequate source for our mobility analysis. And finally, the information on caste and community in these alternative national surveys is not as detailed as that available in the NES, especially where information on the non-SCs and STs is concerned.

While the NES data clearly has an advantage for the study of mobility, it is also important to mention the possible drawbacks of this data since it has not been collected specifically for the study of social mobility. Firstly, the definition of occupations is often quite broad and could include people performing the same jobs or holding the same job title but working under differing circumstances and with differing outcomes. For example, an accountant for a big firm and a bookkeeper for a small petty business are both included within the occupation of 'accountant'. Secondly, it is not possible to check the accuracy of the occupation information specified by the respondents and this is more apparent in the case of father's occupation. Furthermore, as Breen and Jonsson (1997) have noted in their review of class mobility measures, the reliability of the information on class origins given by the respondents was lower for the older respondents. This may have an implication for us, as a bias may be introduced in our data as well, especially for the older birth cohorts. Thirdly, these NES surveys do not collect information on the temporary or seasonal nature of the occupations nor do they emphasize the distinction between the informal and formal sectors of the Indian economy. This, as we observe through our discussion of the Indian context in Chapter 2, is a significant drawback due to the 'informal' and more fluid nature of work in India. However, as the dataset does contain more detailed occupational information than other data sources we are able to get a relatively clear picture of Indian occupations and classes. Fourthly, unlike data in the Oxford mobility study and subsequent research in Britain and in Europe, the NES data does not include occupational information for parents when the respondent was a child (for example, at age fourteen). This could mean that parental information on older respondents may more likely include parents who have retired or at the end of their careers (a very different moment in their lifecycle), thus making a comparison with younger respondents difficult since there may be differential mortality by class. This issue is discussed in the context of birth cohorts in Chapter 4. And finally, as the occupational categories of the NES have changed from one survey to another and as women have not always been included in these surveys, it is not possible to create a combined dataset to study changes in mobility over time. This issue is important especially in light of Breen and Jonsson's (1997) conclusion and is discussed in Chapter 4.

The limitations of the NES as they relate to individual aspects of this book have been highlighted and dealt with throughout the book, wherever relevant. However, we maintain that these limitations of the NES are not sufficient to ignore the vast untapped potential of this data source. Thus, again in brief, the major advantages of the NES are that:

1. It includes a National sampling frame which is quite rare for India
2. The NES have a long history dating back from the 1960s. Over this time period the data collection methods have improved. Also, the data is collected by a team of trained investigators.
3. This is one of the only data sources for India that includes individual level information on occupations of the respondents, of their fathers, and of their spouse, as well as detailed caste/community and locality information.
4. Most importantly, the NES, especially the 2004–14 rounds, collect the same information for male and female respondents allowing for a comparative study.

Along with the NES data, the Census and NSS (a quinquennial survey collecting employment and unemployment information) figures have been cited in detail in Chapter 2 to analyse patterns of economic participation of women and men in the country and economic participation by caste. We have used secondary data sources, published papers, and in-house statistical papers from both the Census and the NSS to analyse this workforce participation.

Class Validation

The strength of a class schema lies in its ability to stand up to tests of validity (Evans 1992, 1998). This implies that tests need to be conducted to check if the measuring instrument indeed measures what it is supposed to measure (Heath and Martin 1997). As no standardized class schema has been used for mobility research on India, this section of the Appendix tests the existing Kumar and Heath schema for its validity. This schema, as discussed in Chapter 3, is the closest to our conceptualization of class. As the data at hand is unable to provide the kind of information that would make possible a thorough and rigorous test of the validity of the schema, a more modest test of the predictive validity of the schema is attempted and any errors or omissions are discussed.

The validity exercise begins by using the 1996 NES dataset to validate Kumar and Heath's schema as that was their primary data source, and this validated schema then forms the basis for the class categorization used in this book. That is, the validated schema is used as a guideline to construct a class schema using the more detailed 2004 NES dataset. In the final section of the appendix the placement of occupations into classes for this new schema is tested. As the datasets after 2004 collect similar occupation information, a more consistent class schema can be arrived at. This Appendix concludes by presenting the final schema using the 2004 data, while Chapter 4 shows the final scheme using the 2014 data.

The NES 1996 Data

The NES 1996, unlike the 2004 and later surveys, did not collect detailed occupational data. Instead, the data on occupations is collected using an interviewer-coded schedule, where interviewers

Table A.1 Gender and Occupations in NES 1996, Column Percentages[2]

Occupations in NES 1996	Male	Female	Total
Executives	2.1	0.3	1.2
Professionals	3.1	1.3	2.2
White-collar	4.2	0.6	2.4
Class IV employees	2.9	0.4	1.7
Skilled workers	3.5	0.4	2.0
Craftsmen Grade-I	4.2	1.2	2.7
Semi-skilled workers	4.4	0.7	2.6
Craftsman Grade-II	1.6	0.6	1.1
Unskilled workers	11.2	7.9	9.5
Domestic workers	0.2	0.8	0.5
Petty business	5.0	1.2	3.2
Small scale business	5.4	0.6	3.1
Large scale business	0.9	0.0	0.4
Above 5 acres land	11.0	3.1	7.1
1 to 4.99 acres land	12.6	4.0	8.4
Less than 1 acre land	1.8	0.6	1.2
Sharecropper	0.7	0.1	0.4
Agricultural labourers	5.4	4.4	4.9
Landless labour	8.0	8.5	8.2
Tea plantation workers	0.3	0.3	0.3
Poultry and dairy farming	0.2	0.1	0.2
Fishermen	0.5	0.1	0.3
Shepherd	0.3	0.1	0.2
Unemployed/non worker	3.3	2.0	2.6
Student	3.9	2.0	3.0
Housewife	0.6	56.4	28.2
Any other occupation	1.7	0.7	1.2
N.A.	1.0	1.3	1.1
N	4865	4749	9614

Source: CSDS Data Unit.

[2] Most of these occupational titles are self-explanatory but some may need further clarification:

Class IV is a government classification for public sector employees engaged primarily as service workers, for example as sweepers.

In the NES 1996, manual workers are categorized on the basis of skill level ranging from the skilled labourers to craftsmen and the unskilled manual labourers.

assign jobs to twenty-three broad categories. Table A.1 lists these occupational categories by gender.

In Table A.2 these occupations are coded into classes on the basis of Kumar and Heath's class schema. There are some classes with women in a small minority, for example, the lower salariat and the business category, while in the others (as expected) they seem to be quite well represented, for example, in the unskilled manual labourer category and agricultural labourer category.

Table A.2 Gender and Respondent's Class in Kumar and Heath's Schema, NES 1996

Class of Respondent	Men	Women	Total
Higher Salariat	455	105	560
	(10.4)	(5.9)	(9.1)
Lower Salariat	143	20	163
	(3.3)	(1.1)	(2.7)
Business	306	31	337
	(7.0)	(1.7)	(5.5)
Petty Business	244	59	303
	(5.6)	(3.3)	(4.9)
Skilled and Semi-skilled	664	142	806
	(15.2)	(8.0)	(13.1)
Unskilled	552	413	965
	(12.7)	(23.1)	(15.7)
Farmers	537	147	684
	(12.3)	(8.2)	(11.1)
Lower Agriculturalists	1455	869	2324
	(33.4)	(48.7)	(37.8)
N	4356	1786	6142

Source: NES 1996, CSDS Data Unit.
Note: Figures in brackets are column percentages.

The business categories are separated on the basis of family owned business with no employees, that is, petty business; and small and large businesses on the basis of the number of employees.

More detailed information on how a particular job has been coded under a specific occupational title is not available in the NES.

Validity Tests

Various validity tests are employed in the social sciences, but the most common are construct validity, criterion validity, and predictive validity.[3]

A test of Construct validity would require 'whether a measure of a concept predicts other variables in theoretically prescribed ways' (Evans 1996: 211). For example, if theory predicts that class is related to partisanship, then a test of construct validity would require 'examining the associations between measures of class and voting behaviour ...' (Evans 1996). However, for this a very strong theory is required. 'Tests of construct validity are dependent upon the presence of well-established theories about the relations between the construct being tested, the variables used to assess its validity, and the relationships between those variables and contaminating factors' (Evans 1996: 212).

For Evans, in order to test the validity of the schema (given the problems that might arise by using construct validity, especially due to the lack of well-developed theories linking class to other outcomes),[4] criterion validity is the preferred test. This requires that a 'concept is measured in alternative ways ... The minimum grounds for criterion related validity are the discovery of strong relationships between different measures' (Evans 1996: 212).

Predictive validity, on the other hand, is a notion related to criterion validity which involves 'assessments of the empirical linkage between measures of the same concept' (Evans 1998: 199). In predictive validity 'what is needed is a theory about the relationship

---

[3] There is often some confusion surrounding the terms used to refer to these various validity measures. For a brief clarificatory note see Evans (1998: 199 footnote 2); Heath and Martin (1997).

[4] Evans and Mills (1998) in their paper attempt to deal with this weakness of construct validity and employ a modified procedure to test the construct validity of the Goldthorpe class schema. 'Instead of simply assessing whether or not the schema predicts various outcome measures', they 'compare its effects to those obtained using the alternative measure of class position and see if the schema predicts as effectively as does the criterion measure' (see p. 89).

between the unobservable concept and the observable behaviour' (Heath and Martin 1997: 81).[5]

Keeping the above in mind, and due to the lack of data that would make the test of construct or criterion validity possible, for the present purpose an elementary *predictive validity*[6] test was considered the best test for the schema.[7]

---

[5] For more on the different types of validity see Carmines and Zeller 1979; Heath and Martin 1997. For more detail on tests of criterion and construct validity in particular (as well as discussions on the various forms of validity especially the ones best suited to tests of class) see Evans 1992, 1996, 1998 and Evans and Mills 1998.

[6] This test may be considered to be more a test of the 'fruitfulness' rather than the validity of the schema (Evans 1996: 212), as the more rigorous construct or criterion related validity tests are not possible given the data restrictions. But, given the complete absence of any check on the existing Indian schema, we consider the present study a modest step in the right direction.

[7] In Britain, there have been rigorous tests to observe the validity of the Goldthorpe schema (Evans 1992, 1996, 1998 Evans and Mills 1998). For similar tests to be conducted on the Indian schema, more detailed information than that currently at hand will need to be available. To test for the relationship between the Kumar and Heath schema and the characteristics that are meant to underlie the schema (for example, the employment status and market and work situation) one would need information on these very characteristics. For example, more information is needed on job attributes such as security of the contract, career prospects, and so on. There might also be a problem in using the same criteria to study India as is used in the West, for example, legal employment contracts in India are not very common, probably because 83 per cent (according to Harriss-White 2003: 5) of the population works in the informal sector.

On the other hand, for tests of construct validity there is the need for variables that 'prior research has shown to have a clear pattern of association with social-class membership' (Evans and Mills 1998: 91). In India, due to the paucity of studies on class per se (that is, of studies not confounding it with caste), theories linking class with, for example, political participation cannot be taken to be robust. Though Sheth (1999) shows an association between class and voting, there is no theory why people from particular classes should vote for a particular party. Thus, even though we might be able to use information on vote or education to test the validity of the schema, the predictive validity method was found better suited to the current project.

In order to conduct a test of predictive validity one needs certain outcomes which can be used to estimate whether the class schema is a good predictor of the life chances that are shared by virtue of a common position in a particular class. In other words, the predictive validity test will use these outcomes to check if the different class categories are being clearly differentiated from each other with respect to a (limited) range of outcomes.

A detailed study of the NES questionnaire revealed two areas that could be a good measure of predictive validity of the schema. *Housing* and *Asset ownership* are seen to be two significant indicators of the life chances of an Indian.[8] Studies have shown a strong relation and clear association between class and housing, as well as ownership of other assets, and these were used to test the schema (Osella and Osella 2000; Chekki 1971; Breman 1989; Yadav, Mishra, and Srivastava 2003).

Prior to discussing the two areas of asset ownership and housing it is important to discuss the implication of 'ownership' of these assets and housing. In the NES data both assets and housing are 'family'- owned possessions, rather than owned by the individual respondents. With this in view, would it be correct to treat these assets as individual possessions for the purpose of the validity test as most of them are household or family-owned? Keeping in mind the patriarchal nature of ownership of assets and housing in India, these tests are probably a better indication of the validity of the class schema in the case of men than in the case of women. While this is a limitation of the dataset, this is not expected to have any major implication on our results, as in this book we are not interested in, for example, issues of household resource allocation where being able to measure women's own asset ownership would be of importance. As previously mentioned, due to restricted information at our disposal and, the method used, here is one method available to test the validity of the schema. The next section discusses the information on assets and housing in the NES.

---

[8] These are simply two possible outcomes, or aspects of life chances deriving from market situation, given the data at hand. Life chances in the Weberian sense refer to a broad range of outcomes (see Chapter 3). As the information in the data is limited, we are unable to look at a broader range of outcomes.

Asset Ownership

Question 13 of the Background Data section of the NES 1996 questionnaire deals with the asset ownership of the respondent:

Box A.1 NES 1996: Question 13: Do you or your Family
Own the Following:

a)	House/Flat	2. Yes	1. No
b)	Car/Jeep/Tractor	2. Yes	1. No
c)	Pumping set/Tube well	2. Yes	1. No
d)	Scooter/motor cycle	2. Yes	1. No
e)	Bicycle	2. Yes	1. No
f)	Television	2. Yes	1. No
g)	Radio/Transmitter	2. Yes	1. No
h)	Bullock-cart	2. Yes	1. No

An asset scale using the above question was constructed in order to study the asset ownership of the respondents. This scale is then used to test the validity of the class schema and the grouping of the occupational categories into classes.

For the construction of the scale it was considered prudent to weight the different items according to their monetary value (this was also the procedure followed by McMillan and the CSDS team for the construction of their class schema based on income and wealth[9]). Yadav, Mishra, and Srivastava (2003, see especially pp. 125–6) employ a similar technique to arrive at their socio-economic scale. But they give a weight to each item 'based on its importance in deciding the socio-economic developmental level of a household'. We, however, weighted them according to their monetary value rather than on any arbitrary criteria of importance in the household (as what might be essential for one need not be

---

[9] Personal correspondence with Alistair McMillan and with Dhananjai Joshi and Sanjay Kumar at the CSDS (the scale employed by them has more variables as it is based on the more detailed 2004 data); they also separately look at housing with the type of house and number of rooms (again information unavailable in the 1996 data).

for another). Monetary values and weights were assigned with reference to ownership of radios (the most widely owned communication medium in the country) which were assigned the value of 1.[10] The assets and the weights assigned are:

Radio = 1
Bike = 2
Pump = 4
Bullock cart = 5
TV = 15
Scooter = 20
Car = 25
House = 50

To be sure there is considerable variability in the value of assets such as houses, but following Lokniti protocol, it was felt that some weighting was preferable to a simple additive scale.

Housing

The second outcome considered was housing or accommodation. Breman (1989) in his study of urban labour markets and social classes (in the state of Gujarat) concluded that the '... favoured part of the labour force can also be recognised by its living standard. At the household level this is expressed in the type of house ...' (p. 272). For an anthropological look at housing differences see Osella and Osella (2000: especially page 29).

Box A.2   NES 1996: Question 15: Type of Residential Accommodation
  1. Pucca
  2. Pucca-kutcha (mixed housing)
  3. Kutcha
  4. Hut (Thatched house)

[10] The weights assigned were based on a similar asset variable included as a part of the NES (2004) dataset and created by Alistair McMillan. For the 1996 data a smaller range of assets were included in the questionnaire, and so the scale was modified accordingly.

For type of housing, Question 15 of the Background Data section of the NES questionnaire was used.

The distinction between pucca (cement houses) or kutcha (mud houses) is a significant one in India, where the pucca house could be a compelling indicator of the resources and life chances of the occupiers. Huts would be more predominant in villages (see Chekki 1971: especially page 372).

These housing categories were recoded and Pucca was treated as the reference category for the analysis. The categories were coded into binary variables, that is, pucca versus the rest, pucca–kutcha versus the rest and so on.

Discussion

In this discussion we first address some of the oversights in Kumar, Heath, and Heath's study, which we corrected for in the final schema. We will then analyse the results of the predictive validity analysis.

To begin with, a preliminary reading of Kumar, Heath, and Heath's paper shows that they fail to include domestic workers (an occupational category in the data) in their class schema. Even though the authors limit their study to that of men, of whom only a marginal number are domestic help (0.24 per cent of the total sample of employed men), this could, nevertheless, be a significant oversight more so if one needs to use the same schema for women, as a larger proportion of them are domestic workers (2.4 per cent of all employed women in the data). However, when we attempted to replicate their Table 1 (2002a) we found that this omission was only a theoretical one and in practice they had included these domestic workers, along with unskilled workers (though not mentioning this in either the table or the text). In Table A.3 when we conduct the validity test, we have included and shown domestic workers with the unskilled manual workers, as the authors did in their empirical analysis.

Similarly, the skilled and semi-skilled category seems quite large and heterogeneous. The authors club together occupations which, in reality, might have quite diverse life chances. For

Table A.3 Results of the OLS and Logistic Regressions: Parameter Estimates (Standard errors), NES 1996

Kumar, Heath, and Heath's class schema	Occupations NES 1996	Outcome 1 Asset Scale (OLS)		Outcome 2 Housing (Logistic Regression)			
		Men	Women	Men	Odds ratio	Women	Odds ratio
Higher Salariat	Executives	28.2 (2.5)	26.3 (5.8)	3.2 (0.3)	24.5	3.2 (0.6)	24.5
	Professionals	20.7 (2.1)	27.0 (3.0)	2.4 (0.2)	11.0	3.0 (0.3)	20.1
	White-collar	19.6 (1.9)	25.8 (4.2)	2.2 (0.2)	9.0	3.2 (0.4)	24.5
Lower Salariat[11]	Class IV employee	5.2 (2.1)	10.2 (5.0)	1.3 (0.2)	3.7	2.0 (0.5)	7.4
Business	Small business	23.7 (1.7)	22.0 (4.2)	2.1 (0.2)	8.2	2.2 (0.4)	9.0
	Large business	40.9 (3.7)	−35.8 (22.0)	3.7 (0.5)	40.4	−3.9 (22.2)	0.0
Petty Business	Petty business	6.7 (1.7)	7.1 (3.1)	1.1 (0.2)	3.0	1.4 (0.3)	4.0
Skilled and Semi.	Skilled workers	12.7 (2.0)	8.6 (5.0)	1.8 (0.2)	6.0	0.8 (0.6)	2.2
	Craftsmen Grade 1	10.9 (1.9)	7.8 (3.1)	0.6 (0.2)	1.8	0.4 (0.4)	1.5
	Semi-skilled work	7.8 (1.8)	8.0 (3.9)	1.2 (0.2)	3.3	1.0 (0.4)	2.7
	Craftsmen Grade 2	6.2 (2.8)	5.6 (4.3)	−0.2 (0.3)	0.8	−1.1 (1.0)	0.3

(Cont'd)

[11] Class IV employees include government employees in the lower grades including, among others, peons. The reason they have been placed in a distinct Lower Salariat category by Kumar, Heath, and Heath (despite lower parameters, in the table above, than say the skilled workers) is because of the nature of their employment which is considered to be more secure and stable by virtue of it being in the public sector, see the discussion on Conceptualization in Chapter 3.

		0	0	0		0	
Unskilled	Unskilled Manual						
	Domestic Workers	−7.9 (7.7)	−7.5 (3.7)	**1.3 (0.7)**	3.7	0.1 (0.5)	1.1
Farmers	Above 5 acres land	**17.6 (1.4)**	**17.0 (2.1)**	**0.7 (0.1)**	2.0	**1.2 (0.2)**	3.3
Lower Agric.	Between 1–4.99 acre	**8.6 (1.3)**	**14.6 (1.9)**	−0.1 (0.1)	0.9	**0.8 (0.2)**	2.2
	Less than 1 acre	−2.0 (2.6)	6.2 (4.2)	**−1.0 (0.4)**	0.4	0.1 (0.6)	1.1
	Sharecropper	−1.1 (4.1)	**−21.6 (9.9)**	−1.2 (0.7)	0.3	−3.9 (9.9)	9.0
	Agriculture labourer	**7.5 (1.7)**	**12.6 (1.9)**	−0.2 (0.2)	0.8	0.4 (0.3)	1.5
	Poultry, dairy farm	9.6 (6.7)	8.8 (9.9)	**0.8 (0.6)**	2.2	1.8 (0.9)	6.0
	Landless labour	−0.1 (1.1)	5.5 (1.6)	**−0.4 (0.2)**	0.7	0.0 (0.2)	1.0
	Tea plantation work	**−34.9 (6.2)**	**−31.1 (6.0)**	**2.1 (0.6)**	8.2	**3.1 (0.6)**	22.2
	Fishermen	**−12.9 (4.6)**	−8.6 (8.4)	−1.0 (0.7)	0.4	0.4 (1.1)	1.5
	Shepherd	−9.0 (6.0)	4.4 (9.9)	−0.4 (0.8)	0.7	−3.9 (9.9)	9.0
R^2		0.137	0.135	0.185		0.130	

Source: NES 1996, CSDS Data Unit.

Note: Men N = 4865; Women N = 4749. Standard errors are in parenthesis, parameter estimates in bold are statistically significant at the 5 per cent level; unskilled workers are the base category.

example, a rickshaw puller could have a very different standard of living and opportunities to that of a Grade 1 craftsman by virtue of the work they do, yet both have been put together under skilled and semi-skilled workers. It might be preferable to separate the skilled from the semi-skilled in the first instance (these could then be combined, if the schema needs to be collapsed). Similarly, the placement of different occupations within farmers and lower agriculturalists too raises questions, which are also discussed.

Analysis

The class schema created by Kumar and Heath uses the occupations of the respondents, which were included in the survey they used under the question: *What is your main job?* Given the seasonal and temporary nature of work in India, where individuals may have many different jobs, this question captures their *main* or primary occupation (see Kumar, Heath, and Heath [2002a] for a discussion on why this question is the best measure of the occupation/class of the respondent).[12]

To study the asset scale and the occupation of the respondent an OLS regression is used. For this purpose, all the occupations (twenty-three of them) were recoded as binary variables and the asset scale was regressed on the dummies. Separate analyses were conducted for men and women.

With the housing variable and the list of occupations, initially an ordinal regression was attempted. The results of this regression lead to very close thresholds for the different housing types, so it was decided that logistic regression would be a better technique instead (as the outcome is a binary variable) contrasting pucca housing against the other categories.

Finally, these OLS and logistic regression parameter estimates were cross-referenced with the occupational categories for both men and women, depicted in Table A.3 under the class headings used by Kumar and Heath.

---

[12] The 2014 survey has a change in question wording. The question now posed is: 'What is your occupation? If retired, try to ascertain his/her previous occupation. If student/housewife, then note down that as well.'

For the OLS regression the two columns for men and women display the parameter estimates and standard errors; for the logistic regression the first column for both women and men displays the log odds or parameter estimates of the regression, with the standard errors in parenthesis. The second column for both women and men displays the odds ratios to make them easier to grasp and compare.

Results

Observing the parameter estimates for the OLS and Logistic Regression, it appears that the Kumar and Heath class schema depicted in Table A.3 seems to work equally well for women and men, though in some cases, it works slightly better for men than it does for women.[13] For example, with regard to the asset scale, the parameter estimates for the occupations included under the higher salariat for men are relatively similar to each other, that is, 28.2, 20.7, and 19.6. The same is the case for women. But, the parameter estimate for the lower salariat for men (5.2) and women (10.2) are much lower than the ones for the higher salariat. This seems to justify the separation of these occupations into two classes. A similar pattern is observed for 'housing' parameter estimates. But since logistic regression is used and as it might be difficult to compare the log odds (that is, parameter estimates), we also depict the odds ratios which are easier to compare.[14] An odds ratio of 1 implies that the occupation has no effect on the outcome, which, in our case, is the respondent having 'pucca' housing. In terms of the higher salariat for men and women the odds of having pucca housing are 24.5 times higher for someone from

---

[13] But for women it seems to work especially well in some instances, for example, in the divide between the higher salariat and the lower salariat.

[14] Instead of the odds ratios, the probabilities as

$$\frac{Oddsratio}{1 + oddsratio}$$

can also be calculated.

an executive occupation rather than from the unskilled manual occupation (our base category). Observing the housing outcome, it can be concluded that indeed the higher and lower salariat are differentiated from each other; in other words, the boundary between these classes in Kumar and Heath's schema seems to be justified. In a similar vein the other occupational groupings under different class headings are being differentiated on the bases of the outcomes being analysed.

A look at the parameters for the business and petty business categories shows that men in both small and large business have parameters quite close to one another, rather than to the petty businessmen where both housing and assets are concerned. Hence, the boundary between business and petty business appears to be at the right place. In the case of women, the parameter of the large-scale business women is negative and insignificant, but this could be because there is only *one* respondent in this cell. Having said that, the difference between the small business and the petty business categories for women too is quite large, so the division into two business classes (business and petty business), at least at an initial stage, seems justified.

There does seem to be some difference between the various skilled and semi-skilled categories, though this is not as clear for women. A significant difference between the skilled–semi-skilled manual workers on one hand and the unskilled manual workers on the other is observed.[15]

Moving on to the agricultural divisions, the parameters for men show that farmers who own land less than 5 acres in size but larger than an acre are a category quite distinct from that of the lower agriculturalists, especially where asset ownership is concerned (for both women and men). Therefore, on this basis these larger

---

[15] Domestic workers seem to be somewhat of an anomaly, as they have a high parameter estimate on housing whereas they have a low parameter estimate on asset ownership. The reason for the high estimate on housing could well be due to their residence more often being with their employers. Thus, we consider it better to leave the domestic workers with the unskilled manual workers due to the nature of the work they perform and due to lack of asset ownership.

farm-owning occupations could be separated from the lower agriculturalists who do not own their own land.

An exception for lower agriculturalists seems to be tea plantation workers, especially where housing is concerned. At first glance this seems surprising as these workers do not seem to fit with any of the higher farming classes, as they do not own their own land, and are employed as labourers. But a study of the frequencies of the dataset reveals that there are not many of these labourers, and furthermore, they are quite a localized category. A similar problem seems to occur with fishermen and the asset scale. This discrepancy could thus be due to the small sample sizes.

Agricultural labourers (both men and women) as well as landless labourers (women) seem to be posing a bit of a problem as they seem to have parameters close to the middling farmers rather than to the lower agriculturalists in terms of asset ownership. But, in the case of housing they seem to have similar parameters to the lower agriculturalists. In order to confirm their place with the lower agriculturalists and not the higher category of farmers and to substantiate a more detailed rural classification, a further rural test was conducted.

Rural Checks

To conduct this rural test, the two variables of pump and bullock cart: assets restricted to the rural areas as revealed by a cross-tabulation were analysed; following which a logistic regression of all the farming occupations and these two assets was conducted, treating them as outcome variables (see Table A.4).

In Table A.4, small agriculturalists seem markedly better off in terms of both assets as compared to the lower agriculturalists, and this supports their placement in a separate category. Also, landless labourer women have parameters similar to the lower agriculturalists rather than the small or large farmers. Furthermore, these large farmers have substantially higher parameters as compared to the base category of the agricultural labourers. The three agricultural categories thus seem to be well differentiated.

Table A.4 Results of the Logistic Regressions for Rural Checks

Class schema	Occupations in NES 1996	Outcome 1 Pump		Outcome 2 Bullock-cart	
		Men	Women	Men	Women
Farmers	Above 5 acres	0.6* (0.2)	0.8* (0.3)	1.4* (0.2)	1.7* (0.2)
Small Agric.	Between 1–4.99 acre	0.1* (0.2)	0.0* (0.3)	0.2 (0.2)	0.8* (0.2)
Lower Agric.	Less than 1 acre	0.5 (0.5)	0.8 (1.0)	−1.2* (0.5)	−1.7 (1.0)
	Sharecropper	0.1 (0.6)	0.2 (1.1)	−0.4 (0.5)	−6.5 (27.1)
	Agric. Labourer			0	0
	Poultry, dairy farm	0.3 (1.1)	4.6 (16.4)	0.5 (0.7)	0.3 (1.1)
	Landless labour	1.7* (0.4)	1.8* (0.5)	−1.2* (0.3)	−1.3* (0.3)
	Tea plantation work	0.7* (1.0)	0.1* (1.1)	−5.6 (9.8)	−6.5 (16.1)
	Fishermen	1.1 (1.0)	4.6 (13.8)	-5.6 (7.2)	−6.3 (22.8)
	Shepherd	0.2 (0.8)	4.6 (16.4)	0.9 (0.6)	−6.3 (27.0)
Cox and Snell R2		0.138	0.160	0.122	0.159
N		865	4749	4865	4749

Source: NES 1996, CSDS Data Unit.
Note: Standard errors are in parenthesis, parameter estimates with a * are significant at the 5 per cent level; agricultural labourers are the reference category.[16]

[16] Odds Ratios similar to those studied in Table A.3 were also calculated, but are not displayed here.

As can be seen, tea plantation workers stand out, particularly with regard to ownership of pumps, but this could be due to the small sample size.

The results using the 1996 NES data by and large seem to support the class categories of the Kumar and Heath schema which are seen to be quite clearly differentiated from each other. The only changes made are with regard to breaking down the larger classes into smaller more homogenous ones. These classes can then be collapsed at a later stage, if the need arises. The refined version of the schema is as follows:

1. Higher Salariat
1a. Executives
1b. Professionals
1c. White-collar workers
2. Lower Salariat—Class 4 employees
3. Business
3a. Small Scale Business
3b. Large Scale Business
4. Petty Business
5. Skilled
5a. Skilled workers
5b. Craftsmen Grade 1
6. Semi-Skilled
6a. Semi-skilled workers
6b. Craftsmen Grade 2
7. Unskilled
7a. Unskilled manual workers
7b. Domestic workers
8. Large farmers with more than 5 acres of land
9. Small farmers with between 1 and 5 acres of land
10. Lower agriculturalists
10a. Less than 1 acre of land
10b. Sharecropper
10c. Agricultural labourer
10d. Poultry and dairy farming
10e. Landless labour
10f. Tea-plantation worker

10g. Fisherman
10h. Shepherd

The NES 2004 Data

Having validated the Kumar and Heath schema using their original dataset, the next task is to create a class schema on similar lines but using the more comprehensive 2004 NES dataset which is treated as the base year for the mobility analysis. As the NES has not maintained the same occupational categories from one survey year to the next, there are some significant changes between the 1996 and the 2004 dataset. Primarily, the 2004 data contains information on eighty-two rather than twenty-three occupational categories. Also, the categories have some implicit information on employment status that the 1996 data did not have. For example, sales executives are differentiated from sales persons and business categories are differentiated in more detail on the basis of the number of employees. This section tests whether the class schema created from occupational information in the 2004 dataset is capturing the major class divisions. Since the NES 2014 uses similar occupational information, it is easier to compare and update the 2004 schema.

The 2004 data requires that the occupations be coded into classes and then the final class categorization tested to see if it measures the class divisions. Table A.5 provides a starting point for this analysis and shows a rough class categorization derived from Kumar and Heath. The aim is to test whether the occupations included under the various class headings belong there.

To test this, as was done for the 1996 data, an asset scale was created and an OLS regression were conducted. As the new dataset divides the housing question by rural and urban areas, an analysis of housing is removed and instead the McMillan and CSDS created asset scale (provided in the data as the variable *assets2*) is used. The full list of items included in the asset scale (question 15 of the NES questionnaire) is shown in Box A.3. Unlike McMillan and others at the CSDS, the information on income is not used, as the question on income in the NES is quite suspect and as mentioned in the introductory chapter, it might be problematic to use income

Table A.5 Occupations in NES 2004 and Class Formulation Following Kumar and Heath

1	High Professionals: Scientist, Engineer, Doctor, Lawyer, Accountant, University lecturer, Writers, Artist, Other professional, Election Official High (Central level), Manager, Class I Officer
2	Low Professionals: Election Official Low (District), Technician, Computer technician, Alternative doctor, Medical technician, Teacher school, Teacher nursery, Art folk, Priest, Other low professional, Official class II, Superintendent, Sales Executive, Activist
3	Routine non-manual employees (Clerical): Class III, Clerks, Class IV (peons etc), Other administrators, Sales person, Shop assistant[17]
4	Routine Non-Manual employees (Service): Waiter, Dhobi, Barber, Domestic workers, Watchman, Sweeper, Other service
5	Business: Big business (with 7+ employees), Medium business (3–7 employees)
6	Petty Business: Petty shopkeepers, Hawker, Small business (1–2 employees), Rentiers
7	Farmers (Owners): More than 20 acres of land, between 10–20 acres, between 5–10 acres, between 1–5 acres, between 0–1 acre land
8	Tenant: Large tenant farmers (5+ acres land), Small tenant farmers (0–1 acre land)
9	Skilled manual workers: Mechanic, Electricians, Jewellers, Tailor, Weaver, Shoemakers, Blacksmith, Carpenter, Other skilled
10	Semi- and unskilled manual workers not in agriculture: Miner, Mason, Potters, Stone, Furniture, Rickshaw, Unskilled labour, Other manual
11	Lower Agriculturalists: Plantation worker, Other agricultural labour, Livestock farming, Dairy farming, Poultry farming, Shepherd, Forest gatherers, Hunters, Fisherman, Other Agricultural Labourers and Non-cultivators.

Note: The terms are as used in the NES handbook, CSDS Data Unit.

[17] Class I, II, III, IV here are the Indian government classifications for public sector employees.

information as not everyone declares or is aware of their accurate income. Hence, assets, which are a measure of wealth, are a better indicator and are used in this analysis.

From NES 2004 Questionnaire:

Box A.3   NES 2004: Question 15: Do you or your Family
Own the Following:

a)	Car/Jeep/Van	1. Yes	0. No
b)	Tractor	1. Yes	0. No
c)	Colour or B/W Television	2. Colour 1. B/W	0. No
d)	Cable Television	1. Yes	0. No
e)	Scooter/motor cycle	1. Yes	0. No
f)	Telephone	1. Yes	0. No
g)	Mobile Telephone	1. Yes	0. No
h)	Electric fan/cooler	1. Yes	0. No
i)	Bicycle	1. Yes	0. No
j)	Radio/Transistor	1. Yes	0. No
k)	Pumping set/Tube well	1. Yes	0. No
l)	Fridge	1. Yes	0. No
m)	Camera	1. Yes	0. No
n)	Goat/Sheep		Number
o)	Cow/Buffalo		Number

The occupations in this dataset are included under broader class categories largely on theoretical grounds, as well as on the basis of the 1996 validation exercise. There are indeed alternative methods to conduct such a study, and the present test is not the ideal test of validity. Rather, it is a way for us to test whether the amalgamation of occupations to create classes is indeed correct. This section does not attempt to introduce any new validity test, rather it is more concerned with whether we have allocated the occupations into classes correctly.

To do this, specific occupations that, on theoretical grounds, are suspect with regard to their placement in certain classes were observed. Their parameter estimates in the OLS regression were studied to see if the dilemma could be resolved on the basis of the outcome in question (Table A.6). That is, if the parameter

Table A.6 OLS for Asset Ownership and Occupations, NES 2004

Classes	Occupations in NES 2004	Outcome: Asset Ownership	
		Men	**Women**
1 High Professional	Scientist	**22.9 (10.1)**	21.7 (9.9)
	Engineer	**55.6 (4.2)**	79.6 (8.8)
	Doctor	**55.5 (5.9)**	64.9 (7.0)
	Lawyer	**60.5 (5.1)**	39.0 (8.8)
	Accountant	**43.9 (4.8)**	20.6 (5.8)
	University lecturer	**40.8 (4.2)**	35.0 (5.4)
	Writers	**38.9 (5.6)**	4.9 (8.8)
	Artist	**17.0 (7.6)**	7.7 (15.2)
	Other professional	**32.9 (4.8)**	27.4 (4.6)
	Election Official High	**35.9 (9.1)**	13.8 (9.3)
	Manager	**50.2 (4.5)**	54.2 (10.7)
	Class 1 officer	**55.4 (5.0)**	94.3 (11.7)
2 Low Professional	Election Official Low	**36.1 (10.1)**	207.0 (15.2)
	Technician	**26.1 (4.0)**	29.5 (7.6)
	Computer technician	**53.5 (4.9)**	52.3 (7.6)
	Alternative doctor	**41.3 (5.3)**	36.0 (15.2)
	Medical tech	**20.5 (5.5)**	45.9 (4.6)
	Teacher school	**37.9 (2.1)**	41.5 (2.4)
	Teacher nursery	**22.6 (3.0)**	23.6 (2.7)
	Art folk	**22.5 (8.8)**	28.8 (13.1)
	Priest	**20.8 (3.9)**	7.2 (9.3)
	Other low professional	**24.4 (4.6)**	18.5 (6.8)
	Official class II	**43.4 (3.9)**	40.3 (9.3)
	Superintendent	**40.4 (6.5)**	30.5 (13.1)
	Sales executive	**31.3 (4.1)**	40.8 (9.3)
	Activist	**29.5 (5.2)**	27.2 (7.0)
3 Routine Non-manual (clerical)	Class III	**31.9 (2.0)**	33.9 (3.3)
	Clerks	**23.4 (4.4)**	21.3 (9.3)
	Class IV	**13.1 (2.0)**	11.7 (3.0)
	Other admin	**27.1 (3.2)**	38.2 (5.5)
	Sales person	**18.2 (3.7)**	34.0 (9.3)
	Shop assistant	**17.5 (3.1)**	20.4 (5.6)
4 Business	Big business	**63.5 (3.9)**	40.3 (7.9)
	Medium business	**47.3 (1.8)**	50.0 (4.2)

(Cont'd)

Table A.6   (*Cont'd*)

Classes	Occupations in NES 2004	Outcome: Asset Ownership	
		Men	Women
5 Petty Business	Other business	30.0 (2.6)	26.5 (4.7)
	Petty Business	15.3 (1.9)	12.5 (2.8)
	Hawker	11.7 (3.9)	7.1 (5.0)
	Small business	23.4 (1.2)	20.8 (2.2)
	Rentiers	19.5 (2.9)	1.3 (5.8)
6 Skilled Manual Work	Mechanic	17.5 (1.8)	13.8 (4.9)
	Electricians	18.9 (3.3)	27.3 (18.6)
	Jewels	21.1 (5.0)	49.2 (9.3)
	Tailor	6.3 (2.8)	13.3 (3.1)
	Weaver	5.2 (3.5)	9.3 (2.4)
	Shoe	4.1 (4.7)	13.8 (6.6)
	Blacksmith	3.5 (5.9)	4.6 (10.7)
	Carpenter	6.6 (2.7)	5.4 (5.6)
	Other skilled	9.9 (2.3)	6.8 (3.3)
7 Semi-unskilled	Miner	8.0 (6.6)	22.7 (7.6)
	Mason	1.7 (4.0)	3.5 (9.3)
	Potters	1.9 (6.6)	2.7 (8.8)
	Stone Cuter	-1.0 (5.4)	2.9 (8.3)
	Furniture	5.1 (4.9)	-2.3 (7.6)
	Rickshaw	4.3 (3.9)	−4.0 (10.7)
	Unskilled labour	−1.4 (1.4)	−0.1 (1.7)
	Other manual	0.4 (2.1)	1.3 (2.4)
8 Routine Non-manual (service)	Waiter	4.6 (4.6)	7.4 (5.8)
	Dhobi/washer men	5.1 (4.6)	4.8 (7.6)
	Barber	4.3 (4.3)	19.5 (6.8)
	Domestic workers	33.9 (15.1)	4.4 (4.0)
	Watchman	6.9 (4.3)	3.5 (7.6)
	Sweeper	11.0 (5.2)	9.9 (6.8)
	Other service	16.5 (2.6)	12.2 (3.5)
9 Farm Owner	More than 20 acres	46.7 (1.8)	39.9 (3.5)
	10–20 acres	39.0 (1.8)	32.7 (2.6)
	5–10 acres	25.0 (1.4)	24.2 (1.8)
	1–5 acres	10.9 (1.1)	8.4 (1.2)
	0–1 acre	4.6 (1.4)	7.5 (1.6)

10	Tenant	Large tenant	**16.5 (3.1)**	**11.9 (5.0)**
		Small tenant	**8.1 (1.6)**	**6.6 (1.9)**
11	Low	Plantation worker	2.2 (4.2)	1.4 (3.8)
	Agriculturalists	Other agricultural labour	2.5 (1.6)	−0.1 (1.7)
		Livestock	**23.5 (5.9)**	**14.8 (5.5)**
		Dairy	**16.6 (4.5)**	**18.3 (6.8)**
		Poultry	3.0 (9.6)	6.0 (13.1)
		Shepherd	**17.1 (5.7)**	−4.2 (18.6)
		Forest	−0.6 (7.2)	−2.6 (7.6)
		Hunter	−1.5 (17.5)	−
		Fisher men	**8.7 (2.6)**	8.5 (4.8)
		Other	6.5 (5.3)	**42.7 (9.9)**
		(Constant)	12.2 (0.7)	10.0 (0.7)
	Adjusted R^2		0.194	0.219
	N		12940	5654

Source: NES 1996, CSDS Data Unit.
Note: Significant Parameters are twice their standard error and hence significant at the 5 per cent level, these are shown in bold.

estimates were similar for all our occupations within the class that they were placed in, they were left in that class. In the next stage of our analysis we picked out the few occupations that did not seem to fit with the larger class they were placed in. Each individual occupation that we were concerned about was then moved to another class to see whether the move improved the fit of the OLS regression, that is, of the R^2. If the R^2 did not improve in fit, we left the occupation in the original class.

As the basic schema in Table A.5 was grounded not only in theory but also on the validated Kumar and Heath schema, not many misplaced occupations were found. One of the occupations that was moved was the small business occupation, as its placement with the larger business classes or the petty business class was unclear. On moving this occupation, an improvement in fit of the OLS model was seen. In the final schema the small business are placed with the larger businesses.

Another example concerns sales executives and sales persons who were better placed with the other sales occupations in Routine-non manual IIIb (Service). In the agricultural occupations, as observed through the OLS, small tenants were placed with the lower agriculturalists rather than with the small farmers, and the dairy farmers were moved to the small farmers rather than placed with the lower agriculturalists. Even though the livestock farmers had parameters quite similar to the dairy farmers, when moved to the small farming class, the fit of model did not improve, so they were left with the lower agriculturalists.

Final Classes

The schema used in this book is derived and expanded from the Kumar and Heath schema, which, in turn, is similar to the Goldthorpe classification where the emphasis on studying the market and work situation of the occupations is concerned. Most critically, it is not our purpose to replicate the Goldthorpe schema for India; but, rather, to validate and expand the Kumar and Heath schema which has been developed for the Indian case. Hence, rather than reproduce the western schema entirely, the departures from the schema are of particular interest. The few noticeable differences in the final formulation are discussed further. The details of the occupations that are included in each class are provided at the end of this Appendix.

Table A.7 shows how our Indian classes compare with the Goldthorpe schema. There are a few major departures from Goldthorpe's work. For example, Goldthorpe Class V does not have an equivalent in our schema as no information was available on the lower or higher grade status of the technicians, nor is there information that can differentiate the supervisors of manual workers from those for non-manual ones; we, hence, did not create a separate class for them. Instead we introduced an additional Farming category, which separates the large from the small farmers based on their ownership of land (and also based on the results of the validation exercise). This, we believe, captures the variety in Indian agricultural occupations, as the amount of land owned can be expected to be a significant contributor to the life chances of the owners (Chaudhuri 1987; Nijhawan 1969; McMillan 2005 too place major emphasis on divisions in the agrarian classes).

Table A.7 Comparison of the Goldthorpe Schema and the Indian Schema

	Goldthorpe Classes (Reproduced from Breen 2004: 12)		Indian Classes used in this book
I	Higher Grade Professionals, administrators and officials; managers in large industrial establishments; large proprietors	I	**High Professionals:** higher professionals, administrators and officials; elected officials (Central/State level); managers
II	Lower Grade Professionals, administrators, and officials; higher grade technicians; managers in small industrial establishments; supervisors of non-manual employees	II	**Low Professionals:** lower professionals, administrators and officials; elected officials (District level); technicians, supervisors
IIIa	Routine Non-Manual employees, higher grade (administration and commerce)	III	**Routine Non-Manual Clerical:** High grade routine non-manual employees, other administrators, Class IV (peons etc), sales executives, sales persons, shop assistants, traditional clerks, Class III (clerical)
IIIb	Routine Non-Manual employees, lower grade (sales and services)	IV	**Routine Non-Manual Service:** Low grade routine non-manual employees, waiters, washer men, barbers, ayahs, other service etc.
IVa	Small proprietors artisans etc. with employees	V	**Business:** Big business (with 7+ employees), medium business (3–7 employees), small business (1–2 employees or family workers)

Table A.7 *(Cont'd)*

	Goldthorpe Classes (Reproduced from Breen 2004: 12)		Indian Classes used in this book
IVb	Small proprietors artisans etc. without employees	VI	**Petty Business:** Petty shopkeepers, rentiers
IVc	Farmers and Smallholders; other self employed workers in primary production	VI	**Large Farmers:** Farm owners with more than 5 acres of land
V	Lower grade technicians; supervisors of manual workers	VIII	**Small Farmers:** Farm owners with 0–5 acres of land; Tenant farmers (with 5+ acres of land)
VI	Skilled manual workers	IX	**Skilled Manual** workers
VIIa	Semi- and unskilled manual workers (not in agriculture etc.)	X	**Semi- and Unskilled Manual** workers (not in agriculture)
VIIb	Semi- and unskilled manual workers in agriculture	XI	**Low Agriculturalists** Agricultural Labourers and Non-cultivators; Small Tenants (with 0–5 acres of land)

Note: Detailed list of occupations included in the Indian classes is included at the end of this Appendix.

In addition, our class XI has more information on the lower agricultural classes (another differentiation important in the Indian context). Finally, in Class I, we do not include large proprietors as Goldthorpe does; we create a separate class for them and label it class V. These labels themselves are not so significant for the analysis conducted in this book.

This Appendix has highlighted the lacuna in the data that does not allow any detailed tests of the rigorous criterion validity of the schema. There is a possible criticism of placing 'classes' in any sort of hierarchy. For instance, how can we be certain that a lower grade professional is 'better of' than a large farmer for instance given their very distinct locations? Hence, following previous protocol, this schema is not treated as strictly hierarchical. This is discussed further in Chapter 3. However, despite possible limitations, it has been possible to conduct a more preliminary test of the schema using predictive validity. Though these tests are not watertight, we maintain that they do lend credence to the schema used in the current book. We take the validated 2004 NES data and update the same schema for the 2009 and 2014 datasets—thus providing a consistent schema for an over time study of mobility.

Detailed List of the occupations by class in the 2004 NES dataset (see NES Handbook)

High Professional
Scientists
Engineers
Doctors
Lawyers
Accountants
College/University teachers
Writers
Modern Artists
Other Higher professionals
Elected Officials (Centre)
Managers
Officials Class 1

Low Professionals
Science and Engineering technicians
Computer Operators
Alternative Doctors
Medical technicians
School Teachers
Nursery Teachers
Folk and Commercial artists
Priests
Other Lower Professionals
Officials Class II
Superintendents

Elected Officials (District)
Political Activists, Missionaries

Routine Non-Manual Clerical

Class III employee (Clerical)
Traditional Clerks
Class IV employee
Other administrative, managerial, clerical workers
Salespersons
Shop Assistants
Sales Executives

Routine-Non Manual Service

Waiters
Washermen
Barbers, beauticians—working at someone's shop
Domestic workers
Caretakers
Sweepers, scavengers
Other service workers

Business

Big business (all to have more than seven employees)
Medium (3–6 employees)
Small (1–2 employee or family workers)

Petty Business

Petty Shopkeeper - non-permanent or unauthorised structure,
    vegetable shop/stall, paan shop/stall
Hawkers, Vendors
Rentier—Rent from residential/commercial properties
Other Business

Skilled Manual workers

Mechanics, machine and tool operators, drivers
Electricians, plumbers
Jewellers
Tailors
Weavers

Shoemakers
Blacksmiths
Carpenter
Other skilled workers

Semi and Unskilled Manual Workers
Miners
Masons, bricklayers
Potters
Stonecutter and carvers
Furniture, basket, mat makers
Rikshaw puller—self owned (not more than one) or rented
Unskilled labourers
Other semi-skilled and unskilled workers

Farmers—Owners (Large/ Medium)
20+ acres
10–20 acres
5–10 acres

Farmers Small
1–5 acres
0–1 acres
Tenants 5+ acres
Dairy farming

Low Agriculturalists
Tenants 0–5
Plantation workers
Agricultural labourers
Other agricultural workers
Livestock farming
Poultry farming
Shepherds
Forest produce gatherers
Hunters and trappers
Fishermen
Other breeders and cattle rearers

Appendix B

Marriage and Mobility

The empirical analysis in this book as well as other mobility research has underlined the highly stable picture where intergenerational class mobility through own employment is concerned and this stability is especially apparent for employed women. But, as seen in Chapter 2, women's official employment is low in India (Chadha and Sahu 2002; McNay, Unni, and Cassen 2004). Focusing solely on their mobility in the labour market may not only provide us with an incomplete account of women's mobility opportunities, but it may well be depressing the degree of openness and the total amount of mobility that we observe for India per se.

Past research into class mobility in the countries of the Global North has highlighted the importance of analysing women's mobility through marriage, or marital mobility, in addition to their mobility through own employment to enable a more complete account of their social mobility (Glenn, Ross, and Tully 1974). Mobility through marriage, 'is an additional measure of the fluidity of the class structure—the extent of upward and downward mobility and the extent to which "privileged" fathers are able to secure the future of their daughters as well as their sons' (Abbott and Sapsford 1987: 54). However, others have argued that focusing solely on women's mobility through marriage and not on the mobility men may experience through marriage implies that women alone are associated with their father's class before marriage and their husband's after they are married (Payne and Abbott

1990). These critics argue that one must also study whether men use marriage as a pathway toward upward mobility opportunities.

Therefore, to enable a comprehensive account of class mobility in India and to analyse whether Indian society is indeed as stable, especially for women, as has been reported, in this Appendix we primarily explore patterns of women's mobility through marriage alongside men's own class mobility while also looking at men's marital mobility. As marriage is nearly universal in India (Bloom and Reddy 1986; Reddy 1998), studying women's marital mobility captures a larger proportion of the female population than class mobility through own employment does. Further, as caste, a hereditary form of stratification, plays a significant role in Indian society particularly where marriage is concerned, we discuss the patterns of mobility by caste.

In the sociological literature marital mobility is the mobility of women from their class of origin (parent's class) to their class of destination (husband's class). This stands in contrast to *own* class mobility where the class of destination is determined by an individual's own employment. The major questions posed in this Appendix are: Are Indian women more mobile through marriage than men are through employment, and what is the direction of their mobility? Does caste influence the patterns of mobility of women through marriage, as it has been shown to do for men through employment (Kumar, Heath, and Heath 2002a and b; McMillan 2005; Vaid 2007)? In other words, are parents from certain caste and class backgrounds indeed able to 'secure the future of their daughters as well as their sons' (Abbott and Sapsford 1987: 54)? In sum, is Indian society as rigid and intergenerationally stable as has been shown for employed women and men (Kumar, Heath, and Heath 2002a; Vaid 2007)? We use the 2009 National Election Study dataset, since the 2014 data does not have information on spouses' occupation. The 2009 data has relevant information on over 26000 married respondents (13563 men and 12875 women).

If we observe that women are indeed more mobile through marriage than men are through employment and that they display a weaker association between their father's class and their destination class (husband's class), we will be able to conclude that the intergenerational class stability through own employment that has previously been observed is only a partial account of the opportunities of mobility in Indian society.

Marital Mobility, Hypergamy, and the Indian Case

Despite the finding that women display a 'considerable' amount of mobility through marriage (Abbott and Sapsford [1987] provide a review of the literature), the notion that studying women's marital mobility would lead to the picture of a more mobile and fluid class society (Glenn, Ross, and Tully 1974; Heath 1981), has been disputed (Breen and Whelan 1996; Erikson and Goldthorpe 1992).

Numerous studies have argued that the overall patterns of marital mobility of women and occupational mobility of men are similar (Abbott and Sapsford 1987; Breen and Whelan 1996; Tyree and Treas 1974); but the exact form of these patterns is not entirely clear (Abbott and Sapsford 1987). For example, some have found that there is more downward mobility into manual classes of women through marriage than for men through their employment (Glenn, Ross, and Tully 1974), whereas others have found both greater upward *and* downward mobility for women (for example, Chase [1975] for the US; Heath [1981] for Britain). Furthermore, in terms of greater fluidity, while some researchers have found a weak association between father's class and husband's class for women (Chase 1975; Glenn, Ross, and Tully 1974; Heath 1981), others have not found conclusive support for this (Breen and Whelan 1996; Erikson and Goldthorpe 1992).

Hypergamy as an Explanation

One argument behind the hypothesis that women experience more mobility through marriage than men do through employment (a hypothesis tested by Breen and Whelan 1996, Chase 1975; Erikson and Goldthorpe 1992; Glenn, Ross, and Tully 1974; Heath 1981) is summarized by Erikson and Goldthorpe (1992: 254) who state that 'the processes of social selection that operate in marriage markets are different from those operating in labour markets, and tend moreover to be less restrictive'. Characteristics like personality and physical attractiveness are 'less closely associated with social origins than are those that chiefly influence men's achievements in their working lives' (Erikson and Goldthorpe 1992; see also Chase 1975: 503). Also, it has been noted that 'some occupations are virtually inherited by sons from their fathers—for example, a son can take over the family farm, his father's business .... the lack of a mechanism for the direct inheritance of an origin occupation would leave women freer to marry into statuses both above and below their origins' (Chase 1975: 504), hence resulting in more mobility of women through marriage.

Another related argument why women might be more upwardly mobile through marriage is connected to the notion of hypergamous marriages (Glenn, Ross, and Tully 1974). Here marriage is considered 'the primary source of females' status and thus of their vertical mobility; therefore, females are generally motivated to marry up. However, since the status of males does not usually depend on whom they marry, high-status males generally are not reluctant to marry low-origin females with desirable personal characteristics' (Glenn, Ross, and Tully 1974: 684). Hence, women are more likely to marry into classes different from or above their class of origin more often than men are to work in occupations divergent from their origin class.

In India, where arranged marriages are still the most common form of marriage and parents have more control over the choice of a partner for their children, we would expect this to have an influence on the castes and classes into which their daughters marry. Therefore, we might reasonably expect women to marry more often into their class of origin rather than outside it, thus displaying more intergenerational class stability. But, as we discuss in the next section on *marriage in India*, the picture is not as straightforward as the notion of hypergamous marriages for women has been 'institutionalised' not only within the caste system (Davis 1941; Pocock 1993) but is also apparent within classes as well (Basu 1998). Thus, even though the mechanisms that influence women's marriage into higher classes in India are expected to be different from those operating in the West, we might expect to see a similar end result in terms of patterns of mobility. That is, in India as well, we may expect women to be more mobile, especially upwardly, through marriage than men are through employment. Since there has been little research on marital mobility in India, this Appendix provides an initial look at this critical area of enquiry.

Marriage in India

The Role of Caste

Marriage is an essential institution for the perpetuation of the caste system (Ambedkar 1916). Even if, as has been argued, the centrality of caste in the transmission of hereditary occupations may be weaker than usually supposed (Vaid 2007), its importance regarding marriage is still considered highly relevant. 'Since a Hindu enters his caste by birth, and since marriage is the institutional machinery through which birth legitimately occurs, it is to be expected that caste distinctions in India can be maintained only through the proper regimentation of the marital bond, i.e., through the prohibition of intermarriage' between different castes (Davis 1941: 380). As marriage is also most often a family decision, and arranged marriages are still the most common form of marriage, though 'love' or non-arranged marriages are on the rise in urban areas, in most communities endogamy remains an essential feature of not only the 'orthodox Hindu caste system' (Davis 1941), but also for other community groups as well.

There is one important exception to the rule of endogamous marriage, and that is the notion of hypergamy. Hypergamy is a 'form of institutionalised intermarriage whereby the men of a higher caste group may marry women of a lower group, but not vice-versa' (Davis 1941: 381; see also Srinivas 1989; Uberoi 1993). According to Davis, hypergamy tends to occur more in 'closely related rather than widely separated ranks' (1941: 381), hence, marriages still occur within different levels or sub-castes of the same wider caste group.

Despite strict notions of endogamy within Hindu castes, hypergamy may occur due to many reasons. For the woman, marrying into a higher caste has benefits to her family, as they now have connections with the higher castes, as the wife 'acquires the rank of her husband at marriage' (Davis 1941: 385). For the man, the notion of hypergamy has advantages as their area of selection of a mate widens. Furthermore, men *profit* by marrying down in terms of caste, as families of lower caste women pay a higher price or dowry to have their daughters married into the higher castes.

Importantly, this practice of hypergamy is not only restricted to caste but also extends to wealth and class. Basu (1998) states that hypergamy with regard to caste

> is but *one* (and the most conventional) feature of such marital alliances. More and more the hierarchy is being defined by a variety of socially desirable characteristics such as wealth, social status, the professional qualifications of the groom, and so on. The general aim of a hypergamous marriage therefore is to marry one's daughter into a ritually or *otherwise* superior household, the expectation being that such an alliance also confers some superiority on the household of the bride-givers (Basu 1998: 91; emphasis mine; see also Srinivas 1989).

This practice of caste *and* class hypergamy is expected to have important implications for the amount of mobility a woman may experience through marriage as opposed to men's mobility through employment since parents might use marriage to maintain their daughter's status in ways in which they are unable to help maintain their son's status.

An Empirical View of Marital Mobility

The proposition that women are more mobile through marriage than men are through their own employment has been studied extensively by Chase (1975); Breen and Whelan (1996); Erikson and Goldthorpe (1992); Glenn, Ross, and Tully (1974); and Heath (1981). However, the Indian case may be expected to diverge from the research on industrialized countries due to the predominance of arranged marriages. In India we may expect to find more stability or upward mobility through marriage for women since in marriages that are arranged seldom would parents arrange for a marriage that would lead to downward mobility for their daughters. So, while sons may have the opportunity to directly inherit their father's class position due to the work that they do, daughters may also be 'inheriting' class positions through the arrangement of marriages. In addition, we would expect there to be more upward mobility due to the practice of hypergamous marriages. Subsequently, in industrialised countries women's `class fate' is found to be more loosely linked to their class of origin than a man's class fate (Heath 1981; tested by Breen and Whelan 1996; Erikson and Goldthorpe 1992). However, in India we may expect to see the opposite, or similar patterns for women through marriage as we would for men through employment.

In terms of caste, as caste and class are still closely associated (Chapter 5), there will be more upward mobility for lower caste women through marriage (due to hypergamy) than for lower caste men through employment, given that past research has shown that lower caste men are not especially upwardly mobile compared to high caste men (Kumar, Heath, and Heath 2002a, 2002b; Vaid 2007). Hence, the origin-destination association may be weaker for lower caste women through marriage than for lower caste men through employment as hypergamous marriage provides an avenue for upward mobility for lower caste women whereas lower caste men 'inherit' their lower caste positions. For high caste women and men we should observe no difference in the origin-destination association. We also observe rural-urban differences, if any.

The empirical analysis in this Appendix is conducted using the 2009 NES data. Only ever married respondents (including divorcees, widowers etc. who make up 2 percent of the sample) who have spousal information are included in the analysis. In the NES 92 percent of the female sample and 90 percent of the male sample has been married.

A look at the class distributions by marital status reveals that not only are single women distinct from married women where occupational positions are concerned; the fathers of married women are also distinct from those of unmarried ones. Single women's fathers are more predominantly distributed in the professions including clerical work, and in business and skilled work, and much less in agrarian and unskilled work when compared to married women's fathers. In turn, single women are also concentrated in similar classes to their fathers and show a distinctive class distribution when compared to married women who seem to be more concentrated in agrarian work. However, since only 8 percent of the female sample is never married we cannot disaggregate these figures by caste or locality.

To test the hypothesis that women are more mobile through marriage than men are through employment. Firstly, we observe the distribution of the data, the index of dissimilarity of the respective outflow rates, and the outflow mobility table and the summary indices of mobility.

The index of dissimilarity summarises the percentage of people who would have to change their positions to make the two mobility distributions, that is, for men and women, the same (see Table B.1). In other words, it summarises the differences in class mobility chances for women through marriage when compared to men through employment. We can look at these figures in two ways—once by comparing the full class distributions and second by comparing the outflow rates enabling to us to look at individual dissimilarity indices.

We find (in tables available from author) that spousal class distributions of women are closer to their fathers' classes, than men's class distributions are to their fathers. This implies that women seem to marry men similar to their fathers and in a way may be 'inheriting' their class of origin through marriage. This picture of marital stability further underlines the experience of stability that women face through their own employment as well.

The dissimilarity indices observed in Table B.1 are fairly large—the largest are for the high professional class, skilled workers and large business. Hence, for these classes the divergence between women and men is the largest. The only classes in which we see similar distributions of women through marriage and men through employment are the three agricultural classes, and to a lesser extent the manual working classes. This is nearly the opposite of what the Western studies have shown. For example, for Ireland according to Breen and Whelan (1996) it is the service class and the upper non-manual class where they observe a similarity in distributions.

Hence, we are unable to conclude, as Erikson and Goldthorpe did, that 'women's class mobility chances do not appear to diverge from those of men in any very systematic way' (1992: 255) as we

Table B.1 Index of Dissimilarity of Outflow Mobility Rates for Women through Marriage and Men through Employment

Class Origins	Δ
High Professionals	13
Big Business	10
Large Farmers	5
Low Professionals	8
Routine Non Manual Clerical	6
Petty Business	8
Skilled	11
Small Farmers	3
Routine Non-Manual Service	6
Semi and unskilled workers	4
Lower Agriculturalists	5

Note: Δ = Index of Dissimilarity.

find considerable divergence in certain classes at least. To analyse what is driving these divergences between men and women as seen through the dissimilarity indices, we study the outflow mobility tables in more detail. Table B.2 shows the outflow rates or row percentages of the mobility table for women and men. Here, the rows indicate class of father for the married respondents, and the columns indicate the spouses class for women, and their own class for men. Hence, if we read down the diagonal we find the respondents who are stable inter-generationally in terms of employment for men and through marriage for women.

Firstly, looking along the diagonal we see that daughters from high professional class origins seem to 'inherit' their father's class more through marriage than sons do through employment (for example, 38 per cent of high professional origin women remain in that class compared to 34 per cent of men). Men from the high professional class origins move into low professional, and RNM Clerical positions more than the women do through marriage. Regarding farming classes, more daughters surprisingly 'inherit' the large farm and low agrarian positions through marriages than do sons through their employment (about the same proportion of women and men inherit the small farm class). With regard to

Table B.2 Intergenerational Outflow Mobility Table for Women through Marriage and Men through Employment, NES 2009

Class Origins		High Profn.	Business	Large Farmers	Low Profn.	RNM Clerical	Petty Business	Skilled	Small Farmers	RNM Service	Semi-Unskilled	Low Agric.	N
													Class Destination
High Profn.	Women	38.2	16.0	0.7	13.2	6.9	3.5	6.3	4.9	2.8	2.8	4.9	144
	Men	34.3	9.9	2.3	14.5	15.1	1.7	5.8	4.1	3.5	3.5	5.2	172
Business	Women	5.5	56.2	0.4	8.0	9.0	3.3	6.5	1.7	2.8	2.8	3.9	825
	Men	5.1	65.9	.5	7.1	8.4	2.0	4.4	.7	2.7	1.5	1.7	957
Large Farmers	Women	2.1	5.7	68.1	4.3	3.5	1.8	3.9	3.2	0.9	2.1	4.5	774
	Men	1.9	6.1	65.6	5.5	4.9	1.8	3.0	4.2	1.4	2.5	3.2	969
Low Profn.	Women	13.7	10.8	0.8	33.6	16.1	3.5	5.4	4.8	2.2	3.2	5.9	372
	Men	16.8	9.0	2.1	35.3	12.2	4.6	5.1	5.5	1.6	2.5	5.3	434
RNM Clerical	Women	5.2	14.0	1.6	13.8	33.9	4.8	8.4	4.3	3.8	4.8	5.4	442
	Men	5.3	9.8	1.3	16.0	35.4	4.2	10.1	4.1	3.5	4.2	6.1	543
Petty Business	Women	3.0	10.8	0	5.3	8.9	48.8	11.9	1.7	2.2	4.7	2.8	361
	Men	3.4	11.7	.3	5.3	6.7	55.3	10.9	.8	1.1	3.1	1.4	358
Skilled	Women	2.4	9.9	0.6	5.0	6.9	4.2	54.6	1.1	4.3	5.0	6.1	625
	Men	1.7	6.5	.1	5.4	8.3	2.4	63.2	.6	3.0	5.2	3.5	707

Table B.2 (Cont'd)

Class Origins		High Profn.	Business	Large Farmers	Low Profn.	RNM Clerical	Petty Business	Skilled	Small Farmers	RNM Service	Semi-Unskilled	Low Agric.	N
							Class Destination						
Small Farmers	Women	0.9	6.1	2.2	4.7	4.9	2.7	4.2	64.8	1.6	3.7	4.2	2335
	Men	1.9	5.6	1.9	4.1	4.3	2.1	4.7	65.1	1.9	2.9	5.5	2464
RNM Service	Women	2.4	7.9	1.4	5.8	9.2	3.4	9.9	1.0	50.0	3.1	5.8	292
	Men	4.0	5.5	0	4.9	8.0	4.3	10.5	1.2	50.5	5.5	5.5	325
Semi-unskilled	Women	0.9	4.4	0.4	2.5	3.6	3.1	10.0	1.8	1.0	65.8	6.6	1007
	Men	1.6	4.9	.3	2.2	4.5	3.4	8.8	.7	1.9	66.5	5.3	1022
Low Agric.	Women	0.7	4.2	0.7	2.5	3.1	2.5	5.4	2.8	1.6	4.4	72.0	5698
	Men	1.5	4.7	1.4	3.7	3.9	2.3	5.9	2.7	1.9	5.0	66.9	5612
Total	Women	2.3	9.2	5.0	5.0	5.8	4.1	8.3	13.9	3.0	8.8	34.6	12875
	Men	3.0	10.0	5.8	5.8	6.5	3.9	9.0	13.8	3.2	8.7	30.3	13563

Source: NES 2009, CSDS Data Unit.

Note: Figures are row percentages; Class origins is father's class, Class destinations is spouse's class for women and employment for men.

the Business classes and skilled work, women are marrying less into the origin class as compared to men. For the other classes the amount of intergenerational inheritance is fairly similar for women and men.[1]

Next, we present the total mobility rates (calculated by observing the *table* percentages from Table B.2) in the top panel of Table B.3 for *all* respondents, which help us comment on the amount of mobility directly. We see that women are somewhat *less* mobile through marriage than married men are through employment (69 per cent of women are intergenerationally stable compared to 68 per cent of men), the opposite of what has been reported for most Western countries studied.

If we compare the marital mobility figures for women to their mobility through *own* employment, using the same 2009 NES data, we find that fewer women are intergenerationally stable through marriage (69 per cent) as they are through their own employment (74 per cent).

These results lead us to conclude that women in India are not substantially more mobile through marriage than men are through employment. Moreover, women are marginally more mobile through marriage as they are through their *own* employment. Finally, we can also infer that parents at both ends of the class structure, especially professional and agrarian ones, seem to be using marriage to maintain their daughters' class position.

We now move on to disaggregate these results by caste and locality.

Among women, Muslim women are the most mobile inter-generationally through marriage. They are also the only women who are more mobile than men are through their own employment. Muslim women also display less upward over downward mobility than other women or men. The least inter-generationally mobile

---

[1] We were interested to know whether men also 'inherit' positions through their own marriage. More men marry women similar to their class of origin belonging to the three farming classes and to the two skilled work classes, when this is compared to women and their husbands. Women marry men similar to their fathers in the professional class and business class.

Table B.3 Summary Indices of Mobility for Women through Marriage and Married Men through Employment, NES 2009

	Stable		Upward		Downward		Up/Down	
	Men	Women	Men	Women	Men	Women	Men	Women
All Respondents (Men=13563; Women=12875)	67.7	68.6	23.5	22.2	8.7	8.9	2.7	2.5
Community								
High Caste (Men=2876; Women=2671)	62.4	63.7	27.3	25.3	10.3	10.7	2.7	2.4
Other Backward Classes (Men=4504; Women=4134)	69.0	68.7	23.0	23.2	8.1	8.0	2.8	2.9
Scheduled Castes (Men=2104; Women=2062)	72.5	74.6	20.1	17.7	7.5	7.4	2.7	2.4
Scheduled Tribes (Men=1828; Women=1792)	71.0	74.8	20.7	18.1	8.3	7.1	2.5	2.5
Muslim (Men=1503; Women=1434)	64.3	61.2	25.9	25.5	9.7	13.1	2.7	1.9
Other Minority (Men=731; Women=768)	66.1	68.7	24.2	21.8	9.6	9.6	2.5	2.3
Locality								
Rural (Men=9889; Women=9458)	71.0	73.1	21.1	18.8	7.9	8.3	2.7	2.3
Urban (Men=3674; Women=3417)	58.5	56.5	30.3	32.1	11.2	11.4	2.7	2.8

Source: NES 2009, CSDS Data Unit.

Note: Figures are mobility table percentages for a 5 class schema; sample sizes in brackets.

are SC and ST women followed by the OBCs. In terms of direction of mobility, while all groups experience more upward over downward mobility, we find that men have an edge in terms of upward mobility through own employment. The only exception are the OBCs where their women are marginally more upwardly mobile through marriage than their men are through employment.

The rural–urban pattern is similar in a way to what we find in Chapter 4 through employment. Urban men and women are more mobile both through marriage and employment. Urban women are also more upwardly rather than downwardly mobile as compared to rural women and urban men. This again underlines the specificity of the 'urban' for women's experiences.

Relative Mobility through Marriage

To test whether women's 'class fate' is more or less loosely linked to their class origins than men's class fate, we need to go beyond the absolute mobility rates.

Given the picture of greater stability of women through marriage found while analysing the absolute mobility rates in the previous hypotheses, we might expect to find a stronger association between father's class and husband's class for women. To test this, we fit the Common Social Fluidity and Unidiff models similar to those used in Chapter 4 (see also Erikson and Goldthorpe 1992: 257) to arrive at a more definitive conclusion.

The results for these models (for *all* respondents) are summarized in the top panel of Table B.4 where we observe that the CmSF model does not fit the data according to the conventional G^2 criterion, but, on the basis of the other goodness of fit and model fit criteria (Δ and *BIC*), it provides a relatively good fit. This suggests that there are very similar relative rates of fluidity for women through marriage and men through employment. When Erikson and Goldthorpe (1992: 260) tested Heath's hypothesis about women's class fate being more loosely linked to class origins in their cross-national study, they concluded that this hypothesis may 'reflect the experience of women of certain class origins far more than that of others'. For them the daughters from service, petty bourgeoisie, and farm origins 'do not share in the same way as

Table B.4 Log-linear Models for Marital Mobility, NES 2009

	G^2	d.f	p	Δ	bic
All Respondents (N = 26438)					
O, D, S	36728.40	220	0.000	46.8	34488.2
CmSF (OD)	159.70	100	0.000	2.2	−858.6
Unidiff	158.67	99	0.000	2.1	−849.4
Community					
Other Hindu Castes (N=5547)					
O, D, S	5574.50	40	0.000	42.4	5229.7
CmSF (OD)	37.42	16	0.002	2.5	−100.5
Unidiff	36.20	15	0.002	2.4	−93.1
Other Backward Classes (N=8638)					
O, D, S	8898.65	40	0.000	43.8	8536.1
CmSF (OD)	34.76	16	0.004	1.7	−110.3
Unidiff	28.72	15	0.018	1.6	−107.2
Scheduled Castes (N=4166)					
O, D, S	4470.96	40	0.000	43.7	4137.6
CmSF (OD)	9.92	16	0.871	1.3	−123.4
Unidiff	9.86	15	0.813	1.2	−115.2
Scheduled Tribes (N=3620)					
O, D, S	3549.72	40	0.000	42.9	24094.7
CmSF (OD)	18.29	16	0.307	1.5	−112.8
Unidiff	17.25	15	0.304	1.2	−105.7
Muslim (N=2937)					
O, D, S	2606.35	40	0.000	40.7	2286.9
CmSF (OD)	29.07	16	0.024	3.4	−98.7
Unidiff	19.16	15	0.206	2.5	−100.6
Other Religious Minority (N=1499)*					
O, D, S	1766.78	40	0.000	46.5	1474.3
CmSF (OD)	13.59	16	0.629	2.3	−103.4
Unidiff	13.54	15	0.561	2.2	−96.2

(Cont'd)

Table B.4 *(Cont'd)*

	G^2	d.f	p	Δ	bic
Locality					
Rural=19347					
O, D, S	19653.53	40	0.000	43.4	19258.7
CmSF (OD)	43.45	16	0.000	1.1	−114.5
Unidiff	42.13	15	0.000	1.1	−105.9
Urban=7091					
O, D, S	5360.02	40	0.000	36.4	5005.4
CmSF (OD)	34.37	16	0.005	2.3	−107.5
Unidiff	30.33	15	0.011	2.0	−102.7

Source: NES 2009, CSDS Data Unit.
Note: O=Origins; D=Destinations; S=Gender; O, D, S is the complete independence model; CmSF (OD) is the Common Social Fluidity model; see text for model explanations. (*) The sample size is too small to draw conclusive results for the Other Minority group.

sons in the advantages that such class origins can confer'. They show that these daughters are 'exchanged' more readily than sons 'through their employment' (p. 259); that is, daughters from these class origins display more fluidity as sons here display more 'direct' inheritance.

In order to test if this pattern holds for India, we analyse the table of the adjusted residuals of the CmSF model (table available from author). We do not find much support for Erikson and Goldthorpe's conclusion; as we see a high inheritance effect through marriage for women in the high professional class, the RNM service class, in large farming and the low agricultural class.

Despite finding similar relative rates of fluidity of women and men, in order to test specifically whether the association between origins and destinations is weaker for women, we fit the Unidiff model. As seen by the parameters, the Unidiff does not substantially improve the CmSF model. A study of the Unidiff parameters (0.97 for women as compared to 1.00 for men) shows that the hypothesis does not hold for India, as the origin-destination association is relatively similar for women and men.

We can conclude that marriage does indeed seem to be an avenue for fathers to preserve their daughter's class, which supports our absolute mobility results. We cannot however conclude that only fathers from the elite classes are able to employ their privilege as in addition to the professional class and large farm owning fathers, women from the low agriculture and RNM Service too are more likely to inherit their class through marriage.

Caste

Expanding the discussion by caste, we ask whether the origin-destination association is weaker for lower caste women through marriage than for lower caste men through employment.

The middle panel of Table B.4 shows the Common social fluidity and Unidiff models by community. The CmSF as see through the G^2 provides a very good fit for the SCs, STs and other religious minorities. This shows similar rates of fluidity for women and men within these communities, rather than there being any difference between women and men. If we look at the other goodness of fit measures then we find this result could be expanded to all communities tentatively.

But, in order to particularly test whether the strength of the origin-destination association varies by gender and caste, we fit the Unidiff model. Only for Muslims, that too very marginally, does the Unidiff provide a better conventional fit than the CmSF according to the *BIC*, though for the other community groups, the Unidiff is a reasonably good fit according to other measures of model fit.

The Unidiff parameters for women are 1.04 (high caste), 0.94 (OBC), 0.99 (SC), 1.04 (ST), 0.87 (Muslims), and 0.98 (other minorities), while the parameters for men are set to 1. These parameters indicate that only for the high castes and the STs the origin-destination association is stronger for women than for men, though not by very large amounts. Hence, higher caste and ST women seem to have a stronger origin-destination association through marriage than the men through employment. Muslims on the other hand display a much weaker OD association for women, and the results are statistically significant, than for men. This when coupled with the absolute mobility results seem to show a distinctive picture for Muslim women.

On the basis of the CmSF we can conclude that there is little difference in fluidity between women and men within most communities. However, the tentative Unidiff results seem to support the proposition that lower caste women experience more fluidity through marriage than their men do through employment. Through the Unidiff model we find that high caste and ST parents specifically are able to use marriage as an avenue to preserve their class positions for their daughters as seen through the stronger origin-destination association for this group. In terms of locality, looking at the bottom panel of Table B.4, we find that the CmSF is not a fit by the conventional criteria—but, this model is, as expected, a better fit than the complete independence model. In terms of the unidiff, both rural and urban women show a weak OD association than men—but, the results are not particularly strong.

Summary

Analysing the results of both the absolute and the relative marital mobility hypotheses together, we find that:

1. Rather than there being more mobility for women through marriage than for men through employment as has been observed in the West, in India the situation is reversed. Hence, the 'direct inheritance' effect, seen to work for men from service class, petty business, and agricultural families, seems to work for women as well but not through the traditional channel of inheriting the occupation of the father, but indirectly by their marrying into a class similar to their father's.

2. In terms of caste, we see this effect to be strong for nearly all groups except the Muslims where they seem to be unable to maintain their 'privileges' more for their daughters than they are for their sons (Abbot and Sapsford 1987). We can also conclude that this marriage inheritance for women is not explained by caste.

3. Also, we see that marriage is being used by parents in both rural and urban India to preserve their daughters' class position.

We can conclude that including women's mobility through marriage does not lead to a picture of a more open and fluid Indian society, as parents are able to use different mechanisms to ensure that their daughters inherit their class of origin, even if they are unable to be upwardly mobile.

Discussion

The lack of research on the marital mobility of women and little research on women's mobility in India per se, has motivated this brief analysis.

One reason for the unusual pattern of stability seen in India and their departure from Western studies might stem from the continued existence and practice of arranged marriages in India. Marriages are still predominantly 'family' decisions rather than individual decisions (though there is some anecdotal evidence that the latter is on a rise), and arranged marriages are used as mechanisms through which women are married into similar classes and castes. In this regard it has also been noted that even if 'love' or non-arranged marriages are on a rise, they are more socially acceptable when they have the family's blessing which tends to be more so in the case of a couple with similar backgrounds (Goode 1970). As marriage is a family decision, it is more likely that parents' employ various measures to ensure that their daughters avoid 'unfavourable' marriages (Glenn, Ross, and Tully 1974: 685; see also Scott 1965). These means include the payment of high dowries. Research has shown that the level of dowry increases with the land ownership and level of education of the groom's father (Deolalikar and Rao 1998). This implies that in India, parents who have the resources are able to use them not only to help establish their sons in their careers, but also, to a greater extent, to establish their daughters favourably through marriage. Importantly, these arranged marriages are not purely a caste phenomenon; we can conclude that class origins play an important role as we observe significant class inheritance for women.

* * *

The high amount of intergenerational stability for women through marriage found in this Appendix substantiates the previous picture of a highly stable class structure. But, in contrast to men's employment stability, women's stability through marriage seems to suggest that the mechanisms that parents in India employ to ensure that their daughters are not 'maritally' downwardly mobile may well be different to their mechanisms for ensuring their sons' class inheritance. The end result is remarkably similar where mobility patterns are concerned.

Bibliography

Abbott, P. and G. Payne. 1990. 'Women's Social Mobility: The Conventional Wisdom Reconsidered', in G. Payne and P. Abbott (eds), *The Social Mobility of Women: Beyond Male Mobility Models*, pp. 12–24. London: Falmer.

Abbott, P. and R. Sapsford. 1987. *Women and Social Class*. London: Tavistock.

Acharya, S., R. Cassen, and K. McNay. 2004. 'The Economy—Past and Future', in T. Dyson, R. Cassen, and L. Visaria (eds), *Twenty-first Century India: Population, Economy, Human Development, and the Environment*, pp. 202–27. New Delhi, Oxford: Oxford University Press.

Acker, J. 1998. `Women and Social Stratification: A Case of Intellectual Sexism', in K. A. Myers, C. D. Anderson and B. J. Risman (eds), *Feminist Foundations: Towards Transforming Sociology*, pp. 21–30. Delhi: Sage.

———.1980. 'Women and Stratification: A Review of Recent Literature', *Contemporary Sociology* 9(1): 25–39.

Agnihotri, S.B. 2000. *Sex Ratio Patterns in the Indian Population: A Fresh Exploration*. New Delhi, London: Sage.

Ambedkar, B.R. 1916. 'Castes in India: Their Mechanism, Genesis and Development, Anthropology Seminar of Dr. A.A. Goldenweizer at The Columbia University, New York, U.S.A. on 9th May 1916', Source: Indian Antiquary, May 1917, Vol. XLI. Available online at http://www.ambedkar.org/ambcd/01.Caste%20in%20India.htm

Andres, L. A.; B. Dasgupta, G. Joseph, V. Abraham and M.C. Correia. 2017. 'Precarious drop : reassessing patterns of female labor force participation in India' (English). Policy Research working paper; no. WPS

8024. Washington, D.C. : World Bank Group. http://documents. worldbank.org/curated/en/559511491319990632/Precarious-drop-reassessing-patterns-of-female-labor-force-participation-in-India

Anker, R. and C. Hein. 1985. 'Why Third World Employers Usually Prefer Women', *International Labour Review* 124(1): 73–90.

———. 1986. *Sex Inequalities in Urban Employment in the Third World.* London: Macmillan.

Aschaffenburg, A. 1995. 'Rethinking Images of the Mobility Regime: Making a Case for Women's Mobility', *Research in Social Stratification and Mobility* 14: 201–35.

Bardhan, K. 1985. 'Women's Work, Welfare and Status: Forces of Tradition and Change in India', *Economic and Political Weekly* 20(50): 2207–20.

———. 1986. 'Stratification of Women's Work in Rural India: Determinants, Effects and Strategies', in D.K. Basu and R. Sisson (eds), *Social and Economic Development in India: A Reassessment*, pp. 88–105. New Delhi, Beverly Hills: Sage Publications.

Basile, E. and B. Harris-White. 2000. 'Corporative Capitalism: Civil Society and the Politics of Accumulation in Small Town India', *QEH Working Paper*, 38.

Basu, A.M. 1998. 'Anthropological Insights into the Links Between Women's Status and Demographic Behaviour, Illustrated with Notions of Hypergamy and Territorial Exogamy', in A.M. Basu and P. Aaby (eds), *The Methods and Uses of Anthropological Demography*, pp. 81–106. Oxford: Clarendon Press.

Basu, A., N.H. Chau and R. Kanbur. 2010. 'National Rural Employment Guarantee Act', in K. Basu and A. Maertens (eds) *The Concise Oxford Companion to Economics in India*, pp. 110–13. New Delhi: Oxford University Press.

Basu, S. 1999. *She Comes to Take Her Rights: Indian Women, Property, and Propriety.* Albany: SUNY Press.

Bendix, R. and S.M. Lipset. 1953. *Class, Status and Power: A Reader in Social Stratification.* Glencoe, Ill: Free Press.

Benei, V. 2010. 'To Fairly Tell: Social Mobility, Life Histories, and the Anthropologist', *Compare: A Journal of Comparative and International Education* 40(2): 199–212.

Béteille, A. 1965. *Caste, Class, and Power; Changing Patterns of Stratification in a Tanjore Village.* Berkeley: University of California Press.

———. 1969. *Castes: Old and New. Essays in Social Structure and Social Stratification.* Bombay, London: Asia Publishing House.

————. 1981. *The Backward Classes and the New Social Order*. Delhi: Oxford University Press.

————. 1991. 'The Reproduction of Inequality: Occupation, Caste and Family', *Contributions to Indian Sociology* 25: 3–28.

————. 1992. *The Backward Classes in Contemporary India*, pp. 435–51. Oxford: Oxford University Press.

————. 1993. 'The Family and the Reproduction of Inequality', in P. Uberoi (ed.) *Family, Kinship and Marriage in India*, pp. 435–51. Delhi: Oxford University Press.

————. 1996a. *Caste, Class and Power: Changing Patterns of Stratification in a Tanjore Village*. Delhi: Oxford University Press.

————. 1996b. 'The Mismatch Between Class and Status', *British Journal of Sociology* 47(3): 513–25.

Bhalla, S.S. and S. Jain. 8 May 2006. 'Right to Reserve-I', *Business Standard*. New Delhi.

Bhan, G. 2001. 'India Gender Profile: Report Commissioned for Sida; Report No. 62; Bridge Development-Gender', IDS University of Sussex, Brighton.

Bhengra, R., C.R. Bijoy, and S. Luithui. 1999. *The Adivasis of India*. London: Minority Rights Group International.

Billewicz, W.Z. 1955. 'Some Remarks on the Measurement of Social Mobility', *Population Studies* 9(1): 96–100.

Birkelund, G. 2002. 'A Class Analysis for the Future? Comment on Grusky and Weeden: "Decomposition without Death: A Research Agenda for a New Class Analysis"', *Acta Sociologica* 45: 217–21.

Biswajit, B. and J.B. Knight. 1985. 'Caste Discrimination in the Indian Urban Labour Market', *Journal of Development Economics* 17: 277–307.

Blau, P.M., O.D. Duncan, and A. Tyree. 1967. *The American Occupational Structure*. New York, London: Free Press; Collier Macmillan.

Bloom, D.E. and P.H. Reddy. 1986. 'Age Patterns of Women at Marriage, Cohabitation, and First Birth in India', *Demography* 23(4): 509–23.

Blunt, E. 1931. *The Caste System of Northern India: With Special Reference to the United Provinces of Agra and Oudh*. London: Oxford University Press.

Borooah, V.K., A. Dubey, and S. Iyer. 2007. 'The Effectiveness of Jobs Reservation: Caste, Religion and Economic Status in India', *Development and Change* 38(3): 423–45

Boserup, E. 1990. 'Economic Change and the Roles of Women', in I. Tinker (ed.), *Persistent Inequalities: Women and World Development*, pp. 14–24. New York, Oxford: Oxford University Press.

————. 1970. *Women's Role in Economic Development.* New York: St. Martin.

Breen, R. 1997. 'Inequality, Economic Growth and Social Mobility', *The British Journal of Sociology* 48(3): 429–49.

———— (ed.). 2004. *Social Mobility in Europe.* Oxford: Oxford University Press.

————. 2005. 'Foundations of Neo-Weberian Class Analysis', in E.O. Wright (ed.), *Approaches to Class Analysis*, pp. 31–50. Cambridge University Press.

Breen, R. and J. Jonsson. 1997. 'How Reliable are Studies of Social Mobility? An Investigation into Consequences of Unreliability in Measures of Social Class', *Research in Social Stratification and Mobility* 15: 91–112.

Breen, R. and R. Luijkx. 2007. 'Social Mobility and Education: A Comparative Analysis of Period and Cohort Trends in Britain and Germany', in S. Scherer, R. Pollak, G. Otte, and M. Gangl (eds), *From Origin to Destination: Trends and Mechanisms in Social Stratification Research*, pp. 102–24. Frankfurt: Campus

Breen, R. and D.B. Rottman. 1995. *Class Stratification: A Comparative Perspective.* New York, London: Harvester Wheatsheaf.

Breen, R. and D. Vaid. 2008. 'Inequality in Educational Attainment in India—A Birth-Cohort Approach', paper presented at the International Sociological Association's Research Committee on Social Stratification and Mobility's (RC 28) meeting, Stanford, California, August, unpublished manuscript.

Breen, R. and C.T. Whelan. 1994. 'Modelling Trends in Social Fluidity: The Core Model and A Measured-Variable Approach Compared', *European Sociological Review* 10(3): 259–72.

————. 1995. 'Gender and Class Mobility: Evidence from the Republic of Ireland', *Sociology* 29(1): 1–22

————. 1996. *Social Class and Social Mobility in the Republic of Ireland.* Dublin: Gill and Macmillan.

Breman, J. 1989. 'Particularism and Scarcity: Urban Labour Markets and Social Classes', in H. Alavi and J. Harriss (eds), *South Asia, Sociology of 'Developing Societies'*, pp. 268–75. Basingstoke: Macmillan.

Cain, M. 1978. 'The Household Life Cycle and Economic Mobility in Rural Bangladesh', *Population and Development Review* 4 (3): 421–38.

————. 1981. 'Risk and Insurance Perspectives on Fertility and Agrarian Change in India and Bangladesh', *Population and Development Review* 7(3): 435–74.

Caldwell, J.C., P. Caldwell, B.K. Caldwell, and I. Pieris. 1998. 'The Construction of Adolescence in a Changing World: Implications for

Sexuality, Reproduction and Marriage', *Studies in Family Planning* 29(2): 137–53.

Caplan, P. 1985. *Class and Gender in India: Women and their Organizations in a South Indian City*. London, New York: Tavistock Publications.

Carmines, E.G. and R.A. Zeller. 1979. *Reliability and Validity Assessment*. Newbury Park, California, London: Sage Publications.

Carswell, G. and G. De Neve. 2013. 'Women at the Crossroads: A Village Study of MGNREGA Implementation in Tamil Nadu.' *Economic and Political Weekly* 48(52): 82–93.

Chadha, G.K. 1999. 'Non-Farm Employment in Rural India', in T. S. Papola and A.N. Sharma (eds), *Gender and Employment in India*, pp. 139–80. Delhi: Vikas.

Chadha, G.K. and P.P. Sahu. 2002. 'Post Reform Setbacks in Rural Employment'. *Economic and Political Weekly* 37(21): 1998–2026

Chan, T.W and J.H. Goldthorpe. 2002. 'Is There a Status Order in Contemporary British Society? Evidence from the Occupational Structure of Friendship', *Oxford* Sociology Working Paper, 2002–3.

Chanana, K. 1996. 'Introduction', in A.M. Shah, B.S. Baviskar, E.A. Ramaswamy, and M.N. Srinivas (eds) *Women in Indian Society*, pp. 13–32. New Delhi, London: Sage.

Chandra, K. 2000a. 'Rising Scheduled Castes: Explaining the Success of the Bahujan Samaj Party', *Journal of Asian Studies* 59(1): 26–61.

―――. 2000b. 'The Transformation of Ethnic Politics in India: The Decline of Congress and the Rise of the Bahujan Samaj Party in Hoshiarpur', *Journal of Asian Studies* 59 (1): 26–61.

―――. 2004. *Why Ethnic Parties Succeed: Patronage and Ethnic Head Counts in India*. Cambridge: Cambridge University Press.

Charsley, S. 1998. '*Sanskritization*: The Career of an anthropological theory', *Contributions to Indian Sociology* 32: 528–48.

Chase, I.D. 1975. 'A Comparison of Men's and Women's Intergenerational Mobility in the United States', *American Sociological Review* 40(4): 483–505.

Chaudhuri, M. 1987. 'Class Analysis in a Village Society: A Cluster Theoretic Approach', *Economic and Political Weekly* 22(49): 2121–5.

Chaudhury, P. 2004. 'The "Creamy Layer": Political Economy of Reservations', *Economic and Political Weekly* 39(20): 1989–91.

Chekki, D. 1971. 'Social Stratification and Trends of Social Mobility in Modern India', *The Indian Journal of Social Work* 31(4): 367–80.

Chitnis. 1997. 'Definition of the Terms Scheduled Castes and Scheduled Tribes: A Crisis of Ambivalence', in V.A.P. Panandiker (ed.), *The*

Politics of Backwardness: Reservation Policies in India, pp. 88–107. New Delhi: Konark Publishers.

Ciotti, M. 2006. 'In the Past We Were a Bit "Chamar": Education as a Self and Community Engineering Process in Northern India', *Journal of the Royal Anthropological Institute* 12: 899–916.

Clark, J., C. Modgil, and S. Modgil (eds.). 1990. *John H. Goldthorpe: Consensus and Controversy*. London: Falmer.

Cohen, Y. 1986. 'Family Background and Economic Success Through Work and Marriage', *Research in Social Stratification and Mobility* 5: 173–97.

Convention on Elimination of All Forms of Discrimination Against Women. 2000. 'India's First Report'.

Crompton, R. and M. Mann (eds.). 1986. *Gender and Stratification*. Cambridge: Polity Press.

Damle, Y.B. 1968. 'Reference Group Theory With Regard to Mobility in Caste', in J. Silverberg (ed.), *Social Mobility in the Caste System in India: An Interdisciplinary Symposium*, pp. 95–102.The Hague, Paris: Mouton.

Das, B. 2000. 'Moments in a History of Reservations', *Economic and Political Weekly* 35 (43–44): 3831–4.

Davis, K. 1941. 'Intermarriage in Caste Societies', *American Anthropologist* 43(3): 376–95.

———. 1949. *Human society*. New York: Macmillan Co.

Deliege, R. 2002. 'Is There Still Untouchability in India', *Heidelberg Papers in South Asian and Comparative Politics* Working Paper No. 5, available at http://www.ub.uni-heidelberg.de/archiv/4010.

Desai, S. and V. Kulkarni. 2008. 'Changing Educational Inequalities in India in the Context of Affirmative Action', *Demography* 45(2): 245–70.

Deshpande, R. and S. Palshikar, 2008. 'Occupational Mobility: How Much Does Caste Matter?', *Economic and Political Weekly* 43(34): 61–70.

Deshpande, A. 2001. 'Caste at Birth? Redefining Disparity in India', *Review of Development Economics* 5(1): 130–44.

———. 2002. 'Assets Versus Autonomy? The Changing Face of the Gender-Caste Overlap in India', *Feminist Economics* 8(2): 19–35.

Deshpande, S. 2003. *Contemporary India: A Sociological View*. New Delhi: Penguin Books

———. 1999. 'Mapping a Distinctive Modernity: "Modernisation" as a Theme in Indian Sociology', *Institute of Economic Growth: Occasional Papers in Sociology* 1, November 1999: 1–45.

Deshpande, S. and L.K. Deshpande. 1999. 'Gender Discrimination in the Urban Labour Market', in T.S. Papola and A.N. Sharma (eds), *Gender and Employment in India*, pp. 223–48. Delhi: Vikas Publishing.

Dev, M.S. 2010. 'Agriculture Development,' in K. Basu and A. Maertens (eds) *The Concise Oxford Companion to Economics in India*, pp. 59–65. New Delhi: Oxford University Press.

Devi, D.R. 1993. 'Status of Women in India: A Comparison by State', *Asia-Pacific Population Journal* 8(4): 59–77.

Dickey, S. 2012. 'The Pleasures and Anxieties of Being in the Middle: Emerging Middle-Class Identities in Urban South India', *Modern Asian Studies* 46(3): 559–99.

DiPrete, T.A. 1990. 'Adding Covariates to Log Linear Models for the Study of Social Mobility', *American Sociological Review* 55(5): 757–73.

Dirks, N.B. 2001. *Castes of Mind: Colonialism and the Making of Modern India*. Princeton, N.J.: Princeton University Press.

Drèze, J. and H. Gazdar. 1997. 'Uttar Pradesh: The Burden of Inertia', in J. Drèze and A.K. Sen (eds), *Indian Development: Selected Regional Perspectives*, pp. 33–128. Oxford: Oxford University Press.

Drèze, J. and A.K. Sen. 2002. *India: Development and Participation*. New Delhi: Oxford University Press.

Driver, E.D. 1962. 'Caste and Occupational Structure in Central India', *Social Forces* 41(1): 26–31.

———. 1984. 'Social Class and Marital Homogamy in Urban South India', *Journal of Comparative Family Studies* 15(2): 195–210.

Driver, E.D. and A.E. Driver. 1987. *Social Class in Urban India: Essays on Cognitions and Structures*. Leiden: Brill.

D'Souza, V.S. and R.M. Sethi. 1972. 'Social Class and Occupational Prestige in India: A Case Study', *Sociological Bulletin* 21(1): 35–47.

Dube, L. 1996. 'Caste and Women', in M.N. Srinivas (ed.), *Caste: Its 20th Century Avatar*, pp. 1–27. New Delhi: Penguin.

Dube, S.C. 1955. *Indian Village*. London: Routledge and Kegan Paul.

Dumont, L. 1970. *Homo Hierarchicus: The Caste System and its Implications*. London: Weidenfeld and Nicolson.

Dushkin, L. 1979. 'Backward Class Benefits and Social Class in India, 1920–1950', *Economic and Political Weekly* 14(14): 661–7.

Dyson, T. 2006. 'Demographic and Related Change in India—Paper Presented at the British Academy Symposium on Politics and Society in Contemporary India: Change and Diversity; October 5', London.

Education Statistics at the Department of Education, Government of India website, available at http://www.education.nic.in/htmlweb/edusta.htm.

Erikson, R. 1984. 'Social Class of Men, Women and Families', *Sociology* 18(4): 500–14.

Erikson, R. and J.H. Goldthorpe. 1987. 'Commonality and Variation in Social Fluidity in Industrial Nations', *European Sociological Review* 3: 145–66.

———. 1992. *The Constant Flux: A Study of Class Mobility in Industrial Societies*. Oxford: Clarendon Press.

———. 2001. 'Trends in Class Mobility: The Post-War European Experience' in Grusky, D.B. (ed.) *Social Stratification: Class, Race and Gender in Sociological Perspective*, pp. 344–72, Colorado: Westview Press.

Evans, G. 1992. 'Testing the Validity of the Goldthorpe Class Schema', *European Sociological Review* 8(3): 211–32.

———. 1996. 'Putting Men and Women into Classes: An Assessment of the Cross-sex Validity of the Goldthorpe Class Schema', *Sociology* 30(2): 209–34.

———. 1998. 'On Tests of Validity and Social Class: Why Prandy and Blackburn are Wrong', *Sociology* 32(1): 189–202.

Evans, G. and C. Mills. 1998. 'Identifying Class Structure: A Latent Class Analysis of the Criterion-Related and Construct Validity of the Goldthorpe Class Schema', *European Sociological Review* 14(1): 87–106.

Featherman, D.L., F.L. Jones, and R.M. Hauser. 1975. 'Assumptions of Mobility Research in the United States: The Case of Occupational Status', *Social Science Research* 4: 329–60.

Fernandes, L. 2006. *India's New Middle Class: Democratic Politics in an Era of Economic Reform*. Minneapolis: University of Minnesota Press.

———. 2000. 'Restructuring The New Middle Class in Liberalizing India', *Comparative Studies of South Asia, Africa and the Middle East* 20 (1 and 2): 88–104.

Forbes, G.H. 1996. *Women in Modern India*. Cambridge: Cambridge University Press.

Froerer, P. 2011. 'Education, Inequality and Social Mobility in Central India', *European Journal of Development Research* 23: 695–711.

Fuller, C.J. (ed.). 1996. *Caste Today*. Delhi: Oxford University Press.

Fuller, C.J. and H. Narasimhan. 2014. *Tamil Brahmans: The. Making of a Middle-class Caste*. Chicago: The University of Chicago Press.

———. 2008. 'From Landlords to Software Engineers: Migration and Urbanization among Tamil Brahmans', *Comparative Studies in Society and History* 50 (1): 170–96

Gaiha, R. 1988. 'Income Mobility in Rural India', *Economic Development and Cultural Change* 36(2): 279–302.

Galanter, M. 1984. *Competing Equalities: Law and the Backward Classes in India*. Berkeley: University of California Press.

———. 1986. 'Pursuing Equality: An Assessment of India's Policy of Compensatory Discrimination for Disadvantaged Groups', in D.K. Basu and R. Sisson (eds), *Social and Economic Development in India: A Reassessment*, pp. 129–52. New Delhi: Sage Publications.

Gandhi, N. 1996. 'Purple and Red Banners: Joint Strategies for Working Women in the Informal Sector', in A. Chhachhi and R. Pittin (eds), *Confronting State, Capital and Patriarchy*, pp. 330–59. Basingstoke: Macmillan in association with the Institute of Social Studies.

Ganzeboom, H.B.G., P.M. De Graff and D.J. Treiman. 1992. 'A Standard International Socio-Economic Index of Occupational Status', *Social Science Research* 21: 1–56.

Ganzeboom, H.B.G., R. Luijkx, and D. Treiman. 1989. 'Intergenerational Class Mobility in Comparative Perspective', *Research in Social Stratification and Mobility* 8: 3–84.

Ganzeboom, H.B.G., D. Treiman, and W.C. Ultee. 1991. 'Comparative Intergenerational Stratification Research: Three Generations and Beyond', *Annual Review of Sociology* 17: 277–302.

Gatade, S. 2005. 'Phenomenon of False Caste Certificates', *Economic and Political Weekly* 40(43): 4587–88.

Ghurye, G.S. 1932. *Caste and Race in India*. London: Kegan Paul Trench Trubner.

Giddens, A. 1973. *The Class Structure of the Advanced Societies*. London: Hutchinson.

Giele, J.Z. and A.C. Smock. 1977. *Women: Roles and Status in Eight Countries*. New York: Wiley.

Gist, N.P. 1954. 'Caste Differentials in South India', *American Sociological Review* 19 (2): 126–37.

Glass, D.V. 1954. *Social Mobility in Britain*. London: Routledge and Kegan Paul.

Glenn, N.D., A.A. Ross, and J.C. Tully. 1974. 'Patterns of Intergenerational Mobility of Females Through Marriage', *American Sociological Review* 39(5): 683–99.

Glenn, N.D. 1977. Cohort Analysis. Volume 5 in the Series on Quantitative Applications in the Social Sciences. Beverly Hills, London: Sage Publications.

Goldthorpe, J.H. 1967. 'Social Stratification in Industrial Society', in S. Lipset and R. Bendix (eds), *Class, Status and Power: Social mobility in Industrial Society*, pp. 648–59. Berkeley: University of California Press.

Goldthorpe, J.H. 1980. *Social Mobility and Class Structure in Modern Britain* (with C. Llewellyn and C. Payne). Oxford: Clarendon Press.

————. 1983. 'Women and Class Analysis: In Defence of the Conventional View', *Sociology*, 17 (4): 465–88.

————. 1984. 'Women and Class Analysis: A Reply to the Replies', *Sociology* 18(4): 491–9.

————. 1987. *Social Mobility and Class Structure in Modern Britain* (with C. Llewellyn and C. Payne). Oxford: Clarendon Press.

————. 1992. 'Employment, Class, and Mobility: A Critique of Liberal and Marxist Theories of Long-term Change', in H. Haferkamp and N.J. Smelser (eds), *Social Change and Modernity*, pp. 122–46. Berkeley, Oxford: University of California Press.

————. 2000. *On Sociology: Numbers, Narratives, and the Integration of Research and Theory*. Oxford: Oxford University Press.

————. 2002. 'Occupational Sociology, Yes: Class Analysis, No: Comment on Grusky and Weeden's Research Agenda', *Acta Sociologica* 45: 211–17.

————. 2005. 'Progress in Sociology: The Case of Social Mobility Research', in S. Ed. Svallfors (ed.), *Analysing Inequality: Life Chances and Social Mobility in Comparative Perspective*, pp. 56–82. Stanford UP.

Goldthorpe, J.H. and K. Hope. 1974. *The Social Grading of Occupations: A New Approach and Scale*. Oxford: Clarendon Press.

Goldthorpe, J.H., D. Lockwood, F. Bechhofer and J. Platt. 1969. *The Affluent Worker in the Class Structure*. London: Cambridge University Press.

Goldthorpe, J.H. and A. McKnight. 2004. 'The Economic Basis of Social Class', *Centre for the Analysis of Social Exclusion* Paper 80.

Goldthorpe, J.H. and C. Mills. 2004. 'Trends in Intergenerational Class Mobility in Britain in the Late Twentieth Century', in R. Breen (ed.), *Social Mobility in Europe*, pp. 195–224. Oxford: Oxford University Press.

Goode, W.J. (ed.). 1970. *Changing Family Patterns in India*. New York: Free Press.

Grusky, D.B. (ed.). 2001. *Social Stratification: Class, Race, and Gender in Sociological Perspective*. Oxford: Westview.

Grusky, D.B. and M. Hauser. 1984. 'Comparative Social Mobility Revisited: Models of Convergence and Divergence in 16 Countries', *American Sociological Review* 49: 19–38.

Grusky, D.B. and K.A. Weeden. 2001. 'Decomposition Without Death: A Research Agenda for a New Class Analysis', *Acta Sociologica* 44: 203–18.

———. 2002. 'Class Analysis and the Heavy Weight of Convention', *Acta Sociologica* 45: 229–36.

Guha, P., M. Kara, S. Shyam, N. Dogra, V. Mahajan, L. Dube, S.A. Hasan, U.L. Sarkar and V Mazumdar. 1974. *Towards Equality: Report of the Committee on the Status of Women in India*. New Delhi: Government of India Ministry of Education and Social Welfare Department of Social Welfare.

Gupta, D. (ed.). 1991. *Social Stratification*. Delhi: Oxford University Press.

Gupta, M. 1988. 'Women in the Industries and Service Sector in India', *Equal Opportunities International* 7(4/5): 26–35.

Haberman, S.J. 1973. 'The Analysis of Residuals in Cross-classified Data', *Biometrics* 29(1): 205–20.

Halsey, A.H., A.F. Heath, and J.M. Ridge. 1980. *Origins and Destinations: Family, Class, and Education in Modern Britain*. Oxford: Oxford University Press.

Harriss-White, B. 2003. *India Working: Essays on Society and Economy*. Cambridge: Cambridge University Press.

Hayes, B.C. and R.L. Miller. 1993. 'The Silenced Voice: Female Social Mobility Patterns with Particular Reference to the British Isles', *British Journal of Sociology* 44 (4): 653–72.

Heath, A.F. 1981. *Social Mobility*. London: Fontana Paperbacks.

———. 2003. 'Social Mobility', *Oxford Encyclopedia of Economic History*, edited by J. Mokyr. Oxford: Oxford University Press.

Heath, A.F. and N. Britten. 1984. 'Women's Jobs Do Make a Difference', *Sociology* 18 (4): 473–90.

Heath, A.F. and J. Martin. 1997. 'Why Are There So Few Formal Measuring Instruments in Social and Political Research?', in L.E.A. Lyberg (ed.), *Survey Measurement and Process Quality*, pp. 71–86. New York: Wiley.

Heath, A.F. and C. Payne. 2000. 'Social Mobility', in A.H. Halsey and J. Webb (eds), *Twentieth-Century British Social Trends*, pp. 254–78. Basingstoke: Macmillan.

Heath, A.F. and Y. Yadav. 1999. 'The United Colours of Congress: Social Profile of Congress Voters, 1996 and 1998', *Economic and Political Weekly* 34 (34/35): 2518–28.

Hensman, R. 1996. 'Urban Working Class Women: The Need for Autonomy', in A. Chhachhi and R. Pittin (eds), *Confronting State Capital and Patriarchy*, pp. 183–204. Basingstoke: Macmillan in association with the Institute of Social Studies.

Heyer, J. 1992. 'The Role of Dowries and Daughters' Marriages in the Accumulation and Distribution of Capital in a South Indian Community', *Journal of International Development* 4(4): 419–36.

Hindustan Times. 2006. 'Mandal 2 Muddle', *Discussions available at* http://www.hindustantimes.com/news/.

Hirway, I., J. Unni. 1990. *Employment and Occupational Diversification of Women in India*. New Delhi: International Labour Organisation Asian Regional Team for Employment Promotion.

Hout, Michael. 1983. *Mobility Tables*. Beverly Hills: Sage Publications.

Jacob, P. 2001. 'Magnitude of the Women Workforce in India: An Appraisal of the NSS Estimates and Methods'. *Sarvekshana* 86th issue April-September 2001, 24(4): 1–8.

Jain, S.P. 1969. 'Social Mobility in a Town: An Intergenerational Analysis', *Economic and Political Weekly* 4(43): 1703–10.

Jaffrelot, C. 2000. 'The Rise of The Other Backward Classes in the Hindi Belt', *The Journal of Asian Studies* 59(1): 86–108.

Jayaram, N. 1996. 'Caste and Hinduism: Changing Protean Relationship', in M.N. Srinivas (ed.), *Caste: Its Twentieth Century Avatar*, pp. 69–86. New Delhi: Penguin.

Jeffrey, C. 2010. 'Timepass: Youth, Class and Time Among Unemployed Young Men in India', *American Ethnologist* 37(3): 465–41.

Jeffrey, C., R. Jeffery and P. Jeffery. 2010. 'Degrees without Freedom: The Impact of Formal Education on Dalit Young Men in North India', *Development and Change* 35(5): 963-86.

Jodhka S.S. 2012. *Caste*. Oxford India Short Introductions. Delhi: Oxford University Press.

———. 2014. *Caste in Contemporary India*. Delhi: Routledge India.

———. May 1997. 'From "Book View" to "Field View": Social Anthropological Constructions of the Indian Village', *QEH Working Paper*, 5.

Jodhka, S.S. and K. Newman. 2007. 'In the Name of Globalisation: Meritocracy, Productivity and the Hidden Language of Caste'. *Economic and Political Weekly* 42(41): 4125–32.

Jones, L. F. 1975. 'Measures of Father-to-Son Mobility: A Liberal or Radical Criterion of Evaluation?', *Quality and Quantity* 9: 361–9.

Jonsson, J.O. and C. Mills. 1993. 'Social Mobility in the 1970s and 1980s: A Study of Men and Women in England and Sweden', *European Sociological Review* 9(3): 229–48.

Jorapur, P.B. 1971. 'Intergenerational Occupational Mobility', *Indian Journal of Social Work* 31(4): 461–7.

Kaistha, K.C. 1987. 'Measuring Social Mobility through Occupational Prestige', *Sociological Bulletin* 3 (2): 82–98.

Kailash, K. K. 2012. 'The More Things Change, the More They Stay the Same in India: The *Bahujan* and the Paradox of the "Democratic Upsurge"', *Asian Survey* 52(2): 321–47.

Kapadia, K. 1991. *Discourses of Gender and Caste in Rural South India: An Analysis of the Ideology of Impurity.* Fantoft, Bergen, Norway: Chr. Michelsen Institute Dept. of Social Science and Development Research and Action Programme.

Karanth, G.K. 1996. 'Caste in Contemporary Rural India', in M. N. Srinivas (ed.), *Caste: Its Twentieth Century Avatar*, pp. 87–109. New Delhi: Penguin.

Kerr, C., J.T. Dunlop, F.H. Harbison and C.A. Myers. 1960. *Industrialism and Industrial Man.* Cambridge: Harvard University Press

Kishwar, M. 1996. 'Introduction', pp. 1–49 in *In Search of Answers* edited by M. Kishwar and R. Vanita. New Delhi: Manohar

Kishwar, M. and R. Vanita. (eds). 1996. *In Search of Answers: Indian Women's Voices from Manushi: A Selection from the First Five Years of Manushi.* New Delhi: Manohar.

Knoke, D. and P.J. Burke. 1980. *Log-linear Models.* Beverly Hills, California: Sage.

Kolenda, P. 1986. 'Caste in India Since Independence', in D.K. Basu and R. Sisson (eds), *Social and Economic Development in India: A Reassessment*, pp. 106–28. New Delhi: Sage Publications.

Kothari, R. 1970a. *Caste in Indian Politics.* Delhi: Orient Longman.

———. 1970b. *Politics in India.* Boston: Little Brown.

Krishna, A. 2014, 'Examining the Structure of Opportunity and Social Mobility in India: Who Becomes an Engineer?' *Development and Change* 45(1): 1–28.

———. 2013. 'Stuck in Place: Investigating Social Mobility in 14 Bangalore Slums', *Journal of Development Studies* 49(7): 1010–28.

Kulkarni, K. 1991. 'Distortion of Census Data on Scheduled Tribes', *Economic and Political Weekly*, 26(5): 205–8.

Kumar, S., A. Heath, and O. Heath. 2002a. 'Determinants of Social Mobility in India', *Economic and Political Weekly* 37(29): 2983–7.

———. 2002b. 'Changing Patterns of Social Mobility', *Economic and Political Weekly* 37(40): 4091–6.

Kumar, V. 2010. 'Teaching Caste and the Hindu Social Order: Dalits in Indian Sociology' in Maitrayee Chaudhuri (ed.) *Sociology in India*, pp. 360–80. Delhi: Rawat Publications.

Kundu, A. 1999. 'Trends and Patterns of Female Employment: A Case of Organised Informalisation', in T.S. Papola and A.N. Sharma (eds), *Gender and Employment in India*, pp. 52–70. Delhi: Vikas.

Kynch, J. and A.K. Sen. 1983. 'Indian Women: Well-Being and Survival', *Cambridge Journal of Economics* 7(3/4): 363–80.

Layte, R. and C.T. Whelan. 2004. 'Class Transformation and Trends in Social Fluidity in the Republic of Ireland 1973–94', in R. Breen (ed.),

Social Mobility in Europe, pp. 175–94. Oxford: Oxford University Press.

Liddle, J. 1988. 'Occupational Sex Segregation and Women's Work in India', *Equal Opportunities International* 7 (4/5): 7–25.

Liddle, J. and R. Joshi. 1986. *Daughters of Independence: Gender, Caste, and Class in India*. New Delhi: Kali for Women.

Lipset, S.M. and R. Bendix. 1959. *Social Mobility in Industrial Society*. Berkeley: University of California Press.

Lockwood, D. 1958. *The Blackcoated Worker: A Study in Class Consciousness*. London: Allen and Unwin.

———. 1989. *The Blackcoated Worker: A Study in Class Consciousness*. Oxford: Clarendon Press.

Mach, B.W. 2004. 'Intergenerational Mobility in Poland: 1972–88–94', in R. Breen (ed.), *Social Mobility in Europe*, pp. 269–86. Oxford, New York: Oxford University Press.

Mandelbaum, D.G. 1970. *Society in India*. Berkeley: University of California Press.

Marnane, P.J.H. 1967. 'Individual Social Mobility in India', *Sociological Bulletin* 16 (2): 60–6.

Marriott. 1968. 'Multiple Reference in Indian Caste Systems', in J. Silverberg (ed.), *Social Mobility in the Caste System in India: An Interdisciplinary Symposium*, pp. 103–14. The Hague, Paris: Mouton.

Marshall, Gordon. 1997. *Repositioning Class: Social Inequality in Industrial Societies*. London/New Delhi: Sage Publications.

———. 1998. *A Dictionary of Sociology*. Oxford: Oxford University Press.

Marshall, G., H. Newby, D. Rose, and C. Volger. 1988. *Social Class in Modern Britain*, London: Hutchinson.

Marshall, G., S. Roberts, C. Burgoyne, A. Swift, and D. Routh. 1995. 'Class, Gender and the Asymmetry Hypothesis', *European Sociological Review* 11: 1–15.

Mary, J. and K. Lalita. 1995. 'Background Report on Gender Issues in India: Key Findings and Recommendations', *BRIDGE Report (Development—Gender): Institute of Development Studies*, 32.

Mathur, A. 1994. 'Work Participation, Gender and Economic Development: A Quantitative Anatomy of the Indian Scenario', *Journal of Development Studies* 30 (2): 466–504.

Mayer, A. 1996. 'Caste in an Indian Village: Change and Continuity 1954-1992', in C.J. Fuller (ed.) *Caste Today*, pp. 32–64. Delhi: Oxford University Press.

McMillan, A. 2005. *Standing at the Margins: Representation and Electoral Reservation in India*. Oxford: Oxford University Press.

McNay, K., T. Unni, and R. Cassen. 2004. 'Employment', in T. Dyson, Cassen, R. and L. Visaria (eds), *Twenty-First Century India-Population, Economy, Human Development, and the Environment*, vol. 158–77. Oxford: Oxford University Press.

McRae, S. 1990. 'Women and Class Analysis', in J. Clark, C. Modgil, and S. Modgil (eds), *John H. Goldthorpe: Consensus and Controversy, Consensus and Controversy. Falmer Sociology Series; 3*, pp. 117–33. London: Falmer Press.

Mehra, S., M.L. Sharma and T.M. Dak. 1985. 'Social Mobility Trends in Rural Haryana in the Context of Regional Advancement'. *The Indian Journal of Social Work* 46(1): 85–93.

Merton, R.K. 1957. *Social Theory and Social Structure*. [Glencoe, Ill]: Free Press.

Metzger, M. 2015, January. 'The Indian Dream? World Bank says Social Mobility in India comparable to U.S. http://www.newsweek.com/indian-dream-world-bank-says-social-mobility-india-comparable-us-301088 (last accessed on 01 October 2017)

Mies, M. 1980. *Indian Women and Patriarchy: Conflicts and Dilemmas of Students and Working Women*, Translated by S.K. Sarkar. New Delhi: Concept.

Miles, A. 1999. *Social Mobility in Nineteenth—and Early Twentieth-Century England*. Basingstoke: Macmillan.

Miller, B.D. 1981. *The Endangered Sex: Neglect of Female Children in Rural North India*. Delhi: Oxford University Press.

Miller, R.L. and B. C. Hayes. 1990. 'Gender and Intergenerational Mobility', in G. Payne and P. Abbott (eds), *The Social Mobility of Women: Beyond Male Mobility Models*, pp. 61–71. London: The Falmer Press.

Mills, C. 1994. 'Rational Choice Marxism and Social Class Boundaries', *Rationality and Society* 6(2): 218–42.

Ministry of Labour and Employment, Government of India. 2005–6. 'Women and Work', pp. 75–9, available at http://www.labour.nic.in.

Misra, S. and T. Niranjana. 2005. 'Thinking Through "Region"', *Economic and Political Weekly* 40(44–5): 4674–8.

Mitra, S.K. and V.B. Singh. 1999. *Democracy and Social Change in India: A Cross-Sectional Analysis of the National Electorate*. Thousand Oaks, CA; London: Sage.

Momsen, J.H. 1991. *Women and Development in the Third World*. London: Routledge.

Mukherji, P.N. 2012. Social Mobility and Social Structure: Towards a Conceptual-Methodological Reorientation, *Sociological Bulletin* 61(1): 26–52.

Mukhopadhyay, S. 1981. 'Women Workers of India: A Case of Market Segmentation', in ARTEP (ed.), *Women in the Indian Labour Force*. Geneva: ILO.

Munshi, K. and M. Rosenzweig. 2006. 'Traditional Institutions Meet the Modern World: Caste, Gender, and Schooling Choice in a Globalizing Economy', *American Economic Review* 96(4): 1225–52.

Naudet, J. 2008. '"Paying back to Society": Upward Social Mobility among Dalits', *Contributions to Indian Sociology* 42(3): 413–41.

Nayyar, D. 2006. 'Economic Growth in Independent India: Lumbering Elephant or Running Tiger?', *Economic and Political Weekly* 41(15): 1451–8.

Nichols, D.P. 1997. 'What Kind of Contrasts Are There?' *From SPSS Keywords*, 63, available at http://www.ats.ucla.edu/stat/SPSS/library/contrast.htm.

Nijhawan, N.K. 1969. '"Inter-generational Occupational Mobility', *Economic and Political Weekly* 4(39): 1553–7.

Osella, F. and C. Osella. 2000. *Social Mobility in Kerala: Modernity and Identity in Conflict*. London: Pluto Press.

Pande, G. 2006. 'The Time of the Dalit Conversion', *Economic and Political Weekly* 41 (18): 1779–88.

Pankaj, A. and R. Tankha. 2010. 'Empowerment Effects of the NREGS on Women Workers: A Study in Four States.' *Economic and Political Weekly* 45(30): 45–55

Panini, M.N. 1996. 'The Political Economy of Caste', in M. N. Srinivas (ed.), *Caste: Its Twentieth Century Avatar*, pp. 28–68. New Delhi: Penguin.

———. 2001. 'Caste, Race and Human Rights', *Economic and Political Weekly* 36(35): 3344–6.

Papola, T.S. 2010. 'Employment Trends', in Kaushik Basu and Annemie Maertens (eds) *The Concise Oxford Companion to Economics in India*, pp. 421–28, New Delhi: Oxford University Press.

Papola, T.S. and A.N. Sharma. 1999. *Gender and Employment in India*. New Delhi: Indian Society of Labour Economics and Institute of Economic Growth Delhi in association with Vikas Publishing House.

Parkin, F. 1979. *Marxism and Class Theory: A Bourgeois Critique*. New York: Columbia University Press.

Parry, J. 1980. 'Ghosts, greed and sin: the occupational identity of the Benares Funeral Priests', *Man* 15(1): 88–111.

———. 1999. 'Two Cheers for Reservations: The Satnamis and the Steel Plant', in Ramachandran Guha and Jonathan P. Parry (eds)

Institutions and Inequalities: Essays in Honour of Andre Béteille, pp. 128–69. Delhi: Oxford University Press.

Parsons, T. 1960. *Structure and Process in Modern Societies*. Glencoe: Free Press.

Parthasarathy, G. and K.A. Nirmala. 1999. 'Marginalisation Hypothesis and Post Green Revolution Period', in T.S. Papola and A.N. Sharma (eds), *Gender and Employment in India*, pp. 122–38. Delhi: Vikas.

Patnaik, U. 1976. 'Class Differentiation within the Peasantry: An Approach to Analysis of Indian Agriculture', *Economic and Political Weekly Review of Agriculture*: A82–A101.

Payne, G. 1989. 'Social Mobility', *British Journal of Sociology* 40(3): 471–92.

Payne, G. and P. Abbott (eds). 1990. *The Social Mobility of Women: Beyond Male Mobility Models*. London: Falmer.

Phillips, W.S.K. 1978. 'The Emerging Patterns of Urban Social Stratification in India', *Sociological Bulletin* 27(2): 173–89.

Pocock, D.F. 1993. 'The Hypergamy of the Patidars', in P. Uberoi (ed.), *Family, Kinship and Marriage in India*, Oxford in India Readings in Sociology and Social Anthropology, pp. 330–40. Delhi: Oxford University Press.

Prandy, K. 1990. 'The Revised Cambridge Scale of Occupations', *Sociology* 24(4): 629–55.

———. 1998a. 'Deconstructing Classes; Critical Comments on the Revised Social Classification', *Work Employment and Society* 12(4): 743–53.

———. 1998b. 'Class and Continuity in Social Reproduction: An Empirical Investigation', *The Sociological Review*: 340–65.

Radhakrishnan, P. 1990. 'Two Steps Backward', *Frontline* 7(18): 19–24.

———. 1996. 'Mandal Commission Report: A Sociological Critique', in M.N. Srinivas (ed.), *Caste: Its Twentieth Century Avatar*, pp. 203–20. New Delhi: Penguin.

Raheja, G.G. 1988. *The Poison in the Gift: Ritual, Prestation, and the Dominant Caste in a North Indian Village*. Chicago: University of Chicago Press.

Raju, S. 1991. 'Gender and Deprivation. A Theme Revisited with a Geographical Perspective', *Economic and Political Weekly* 26(49): 2827–39.

Ram, Nandu. 1988. *Mobile Scheduled Castes—Rise of a New Middle Class*. Delhi: South Asia Books.

Ramu, G.N. 1988. 'Wife's Economic Status and Marital Power: A Case of Single and Dual-earner Couples', *Sociological Bulletin* 37(1 and 2): 49–69.

Ramu, G.N. and P.D. Wiebe. 1973. 'Occupational and Educational Mobility in Relation to Caste in Urban India', *Sociology and Social Work* 58(1): 84–94.

Reddy, K.M.M. 1998. *Marriage, Population and Society: Demographic Perspectives of a Social Institution*. Delhi: Kanishka Publishers.

Reid, I. 1998. *Class in Britain*. Cambridge: Polity Press.

Rose, D. 1998. 'Commentary Once More unto the Breach: In Defence of Class Analysis Yet Again', *Work, Employment and Society* 12(4): 755–67.

Rose, D. and G. Marshall. 1986. 'Constructing the (W)right Classes', *Sociology* 20: 440–55.

Rose, D. and D. J. Pevalin. 2003. *A Researcher's Guide to the National Statistics Socio-Economic Classification*. London: Sage.

Rosenfeld, R.A. 1978. 'Women's Intergenerational Occupational Mobility', *American Sociological Review* 4 (1): 36–46.

Saha, D. 2017. 'Rising Income Levels, Stability Linked To Declining Female Workforce Participation In India', *IndiaSpend*, 4 May 2017. Available at: http://www.indiaspend.com/cover-story/rising-income-levels-stability-linked-to-declining-female-workforce-par-ticipation-in-india-84594 [accessed 10 June 2017].

Sarvekshana. October 2001–March 2002. 'An Integrated Summary of Employment and Unemployment Survey Results 55th Round', 25 (2/3 87th Issue).

Saunders, P. 1990. *Social Class and Stratification*. London: Routledge.

Seal, K.C. 1981. 'Women in the Labour Force in India: A Macro Level Statistical Profile', in ARTEP (ed.), *Women in the Indian Labour Force*. Geneva: ILO.

Shah, A.M. 1996. 'Job Reservation and Efficiency' in M.N. Srinivas (ed.) *Caste: Its Twentieth Century Avatar*. Delhi: Penguin.

Shah, A.M. and Desai, I.P. 1988. *Division and Hierarchy: An Overview of Caste in Gujarat*. Delhi: Hindustan Publishing Corporation.

Sharda, B.D. 1977. *Status Attainment in Rural India*. Delhi: Ajanta Publications (India).

Sharma, K. 1996. 'Women and Development: Research and Policy Perspectives', in D.C. Vir and K. Mahajan (eds), *Contemporary Indian Women*, vol. 1 Delhi: New Academic Publishers.

Sharma, K.L. 1984. 'Caste and Class in India: Some Conceptual Problems', *Sociological Bulletin* 33(1 and 2): 1–28.

Shavit, Y. and Blossfeld H.P. 1993. *Persistent Inequality: Changing Educational Attainment in Thirteen Countries*. Boulder, CO: Westview Press.

Sheth, D.L. 1991. 'The Future of Caste in India. A Dialogue', *Contributions to Indian Sociology* 25(2): 331–3421.

———. 1997. 'Reservations Policy Revisited,' in V.A.P. Panandiker (ed.), *The Politics of Backwardness*, pp. 221–39. New Delhi: Konark Publishers.

———. 1999. 'Secularisation of Caste and Making of New Middle Class'. *Economic and Political Weekly* 34(34/35): 2502–10.

Silverberg, J. (ed.). 1968. *Social Mobility in the Caste System in India: An Interdisciplinary Symposium*. The Hague: Mouton.

Singh, Y. 1994. *Modernisation of Indian Tradition*. Jaipur: Rawat.

Sivaram, P. 1990. *Social Mobility: A Sociological Study*. New Delhi: Discovery Pub. House.

Sivaramayya, B. 1996. 'The Mandal Judgement: A Brief Description and Critique', in M.N. Srinivas (ed.), *Caste: Its Twentieth Century Avatar*, pp. 221–43. New Delhi: Penguin.

Sorokin, P.A. 1928. *Contemporary Sociological Theories*. New York; London: Harper and Brothers.

Sovani, N.V. and K. Pradhan. 1955. 'Occupational Mobility in Poona City Between Three Generations', *Indian Economic Review* 2(4): 23–36.

Srinivas, M.N. 1962. *Caste in Modern India and Other Essays*. London: Asia Publishing House.

———. 1966. *Social Change in Modern India*. Berkeley: University of California Press.

———. 1987. *The Dominant Caste and Other Essays*. Delhi: Oxford University Press.

———. 1989. 'Some Reflections on Dowry', in M.N. Srinivas (ed.), *The Cohesive Role of Sanskritisation and Other Essays*. Delhi: Oxford University Press.

———. 1996a. *Village, Caste, Gender, and Method: Essays in Indian Social Anthropology*. Delhi, Oxford: Oxford University Press.

———. 1996b. *Caste: its Twentieth Century Avatar*. New Delhi: Penguin.

———. 2003. 'An Obituary on Caste as a System', *Economic and Political Weekly* Special Article, 1 February 2003, available from www.epw.org.in.

Srivastava, N. 1999. 'Striving for a Toe-Hold: Women in the Organised Sector', in T.S. Papola and A.N. Sharma (eds), *Gender and Employment in India*, pp. 181–205. Delhi: Vikas Publishing.

———. 2003. '... And Promises to Keep: The Challenge of Gender Disparities in India's Economic Development', *Indian Journal of Economics* 84(332): 123–46.

Stewart, A, K. Prandy, and R.M. Blackburn. 1980. *Social Stratifications and Occupations*. London: The Macmillan Press Ltd.

Swaminathan, M. 1989. *Inequality and Economic Mobility: An Analysis of Panel Data from a South Indian Village*. Dphil Thesis, University of Oxford.

Szelenyi, S. 2001. 'The "Woman Problem" in Stratification Theory and Research', in David B. Grusky (ed.) *Social Stratification: Class, Race and Gender in Sociological Perspective*, pp. 681–88. Colorado: Westview Press.

Tharamangalam, J. 1996. 'Caste among Christians in India', in M.N. Srinivas (ed.), *Caste: Its 20th Century Avatar*, pp. 263–91. New Delhi: Penguin.

———. 2006. 'Caste Cauldron Mandal II', available at *http://timesofindia. indiatimes.com/specialcoverage/1482489.cms*.

Treiman, D.J. 1970. 'Industrialisation and Social Stratification', in E.O. Laumann (ed.), *Social Stratification—Research and Theory for the 1970s*, pp. 207–34. Indianapolis: Bobbs-Merril.

Tyree, A. and J. Treas. 1974. 'The Occupational and Marital Mobility of Women', *American Sociological Review* 39(3): 293–302.

Uberoi, P. (ed.) 1993. *Family, Kinship and Marriage in India*. Delhi: Oxford University Press.

Vaid, D. 2004. 'Gendered Inequality in Educational Transitions', *Economic and Political Weekly* 39(35): 3927–38.

———. 2007. 'Class Mobility of Women and Men in India', DPhil thesis, Oxford, U.K: Department of Sociology, University of Oxford.

———. 2012. 'The Caste-Class Association: An Empirical Analysis', *Asian Survey* 52 (2): 395–422.

———. 2014a. 'Class and Social Mobility', *Seminar* 663: 51–7 (November).

———. 2014b. 'Caste in Contemporary India: Flexibility and Persistence', *Annual Review of Sociology* 40: 391–410 (July/August).

———. 2016. 'Patterns of Social Mobility and the Role of Education in India', *Contemporary South Asia*, 24 (3): 285–312.

———. 2017. 'The City, Education and Social Mobility: Women's Narratives from Delhi', in William T. Pink and George W. Noblit (eds), *The Second International Handbook of Urban Education*, pp. 347–68. Springer International Publishing: Switzerland.

Vaid, D. and A.F. Heath. 2010. 'Unequal Opportunities: Class, Caste and Social Mobility', in Anthony F. Heath and Roger Jeffery (eds.) *Diversity and Change in Modern India: Economic, Social and Political Approaches*, pp. 129–164. Oxford: Oxford University Press.

Vallet, L.A. . 2004. 'Change in Intergenerational Class Mobility in France from the 1970s to the 1990s and its Explanation: An Analysis Following the CASMIN Approach', in R. Breen (ed.), *Social Mobility in Europe*, pp. 115–48. Oxford; New York: Oxford University Press.

Varshney, A. 2000. 'Is India Becoming More Democratic?', *The Journal of Asian Studies* 59(1): 3–25.

Visaria, P.M. 1967. 'The Sex Ratio of the Population of India and Pakistan and Regional Variations during 1901–1961', in A. Bose (ed.), *Pattern of Population Change in India 1951–1961*, pp. 334–371. Bombay: Allied Publishers.

———. 1971. *The Sex Ratio of the Population of India*. New Delhi: Ministry of Home Affairs, Office of the Registrar General.

———. 1999. 'Level and Pattern of Female Employment, 1911–1994', in T.S. Papola and A.N. Sharma (eds), *Gender and Employment in India*, pp. 23–51. Delhi: Vikas.

———. 1997. 'Urbanization in India: An Overview', in G.W. Jones and P.M. Visaria (eds), *Urbanization in Large Developing Countries: China, Indonesia, Brazil, and India*, pp. 266–88. Oxford: Clarendon Press.

Weber, M. 1953. 'Class, Status and Party', in R. Bendix and S. Lipset (eds) *Class, Status and Power: Social Stratification in Comparative Perspective*, pp. 21–8. London: Routledge and Kegan Paul Ltd.

———. 1958. *The Religion of India: The Sociology of Hinduism and Buddhism*. Glencoe, Ill.: Free Press.

———. 1978. *Economy and Society: An Outline of Interpretive Sociology* [with G. Roth and C. Wittich]. Berkeley: University of California Press.

———. 2001 [1958]. 'Class, Status, Party', in D.B. Grusky (ed.), *Social Stratification*, pp. 132–42. Oxford: Westview.

Weiner, M. 1989. *The Indian Paradox: Essays in Indian Politics*. New Delhi/Newbury Park/London: Sage Publications.

Weiner, M., M.F. Katzenstein, and K.V.N. Rao. 1981. 'India's Preferential Policies: Migrants, the Middle Classes, and Ethnic Equality', Chicago: University of Chicago Press.

Weisskopf, T.E. 2004. 'Impact of Reservation on Admissions to Higher Education In India', *Economic and Political Weekly* 39(39): 4339–49.

———. 2006. 'Is Positive Discrimination a Good Way to Aid Disadvantaged Ethnic Communities?' *Economic and Political Weekly* 41(8): 717–726.

Westergaard, J. 1990. 'Social Mobility in Britain', in J. Clark, C. Modgil, and S. Modgil (eds), *John H. Goldthorpe: Consensus and Controversy, Falmer sociology series*, 3, pp. 277–86. London: The Falmer Press.

Wright, E.O. 1985. *Classes*. London: Verso.

———. 1997. *Class Counts: Comparative Studies in Class Analysis*: Cambridge University Press.

———. 1998 [1989]. *The Debate on Classes*. London: Verso.

———. 2001a. 'Variations of Marxist Conceptions of Class Structure', in D.B. Grusky (ed.) *Social Stratification*, pp. 112–15. Oxford: Westview.

———. 2001b. 'A General Framework for the Analysis of Class Structure', in D.B. Grusky (ed.), *Social Stratification*, pp. 116–28. Oxford: Westview Press.

———. 2005a. 'Social Class', in G. Ritzer (ed.) *Encuclopaedia of Social Theory*, pp. 717–24. Thousand Oaks, CA: Thousand Oaks.

———. (ed.). 2005b. *Approaches to Class Analysis*. Cambridge: Cambridge University Press.

Xie, Y. 1992. 'The Log-Multiplicative Layer Effect Model for Comparing Mobility Tables', *American Sociological Review* 57: 3: 380–95.

Xaxa, V. 2003. 'Tribes in India', in V. Das (ed.) *Oxford India Companion to Sociology and Social Anthropology*, pp. 373–408. Delhi: Oxford University Press.

Yadav, S., C.P. Mishra, and P. Srivastava. 2003. 'Caste: A Major Determinant of Socio-Economic Status of Rural Households', *Demography India* 32 (1): 123–36.

Yagnik, A. 1981. 'Spectre of Caste War', *Economic and Political Weekly* 16(13): 553–5.

Zwart, F. 2000. 'The Logic of Affirmative Action: Caste, Class and Quotas in India', *Acta Sociologica* 43(3): 235–49.

Index

About the Author

Divya Vaid teaches sociology at the Centre for the Study of Social Systems, Jawaharlal Nehru University (JNU), New Delhi. She has a DPhil in sociology from the University of Oxford, UK. Prior to joining JNU, Divya was a postdoctoral associate at the Centre for Research on Inequalities and the Life Course (CIQLE) at the Department of Sociology, Yale University, USA. She was also a visiting associate fellow at the Centre for the Study of Developing Societies (CSDS) and an associate fellow at Lokniti, CSDS, Delhi. She specializes in the study of social mobility and inequality, with a keen interest in class and education and gender and urban life. She teaches courses on social stratification, social mobility, and statistics. In addition to chapters in edited volumes, Divya's work has appeared in various journals, including, the *Annual Review of Sociology*, *Contemporary South Asia*, *Asian Survey*, and the *Economic and Political Weekly*.